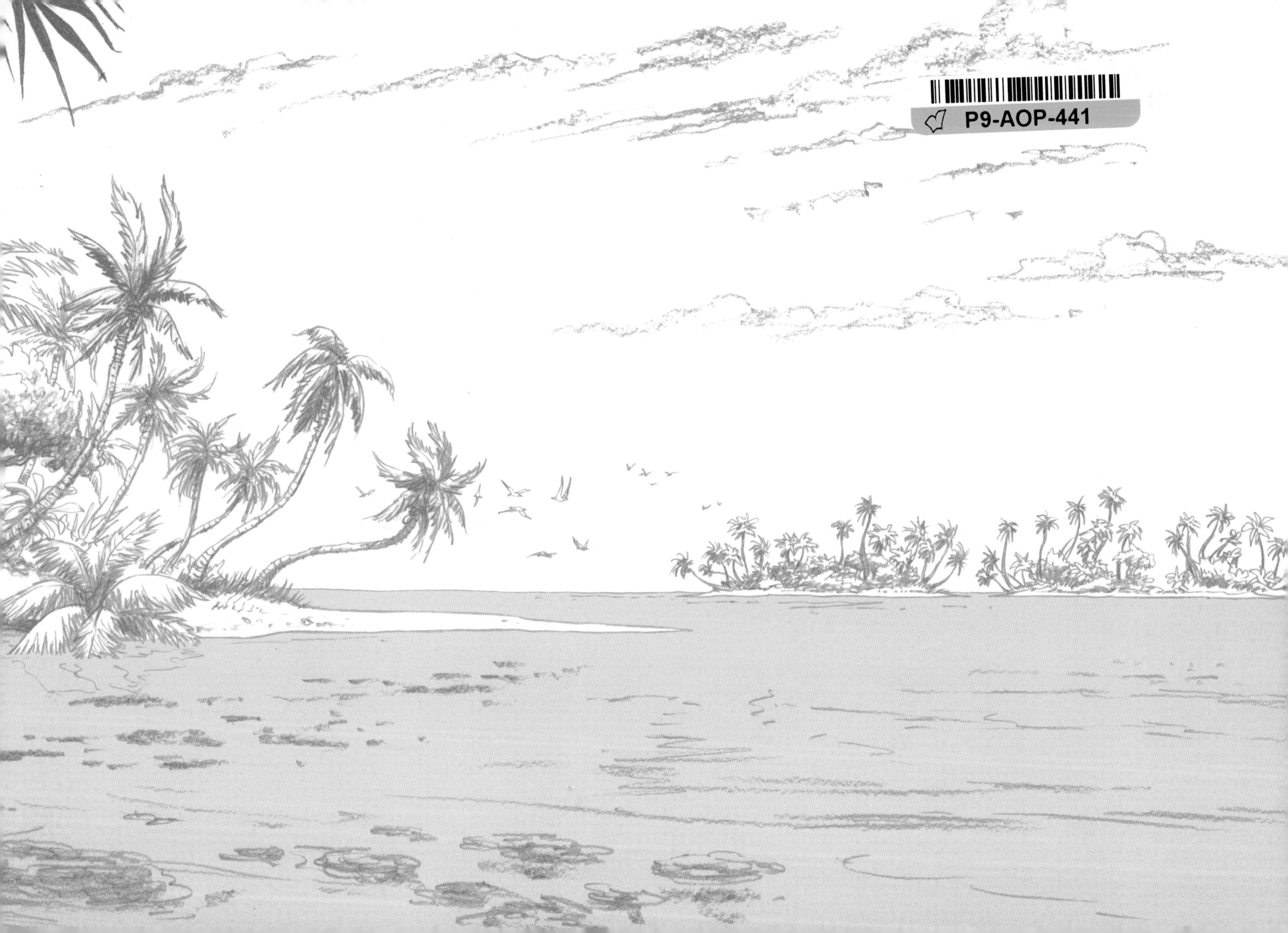

Pacific

Art:
Martin Trystram & Romain Baudy

Story:
Martin Trystram & Romain Baudy

Colors:
Kyung-Eun Park & Martin Trystram

Translation:
Jessica Burton

Editor
Lizzie Kaye

Collection Designer
Dan Bura

Senior Editor
Andrew James

Titan Comics Editorial
Tom Williams, Jessica Burton, Amoona Soahin

Production Manager
Obi Onuora

Production Supervisors
Jackie Flook,
Maria Pearson

Production Assistant
Peter James

Art Director
Oz Browne

Senior Sales Manager
Steve Tothill

Direct Sales & Marketing Manager
Ricky Claydon

Senior Marketing & Press Executive
Owen Johnson

Publishing Manager
Darryl Tothill

Publishing Director
Chris Teather

Operations Director
Leigh Baulch

Executive Director
Vivian Cheung

Publisher
Nick Landau

Pacfic ISBN: 9781785856877

Published by Titan Comics. A division of Titan Publishing Group Ltd. 144 Southwark St. London, SE1 0UP

 A CIP catalogue record for this title is available from the British Library. First edition: September 2016

10 9 8 7 6 5 4 3 2 1

Printed in China. Titan Comics. TC1927

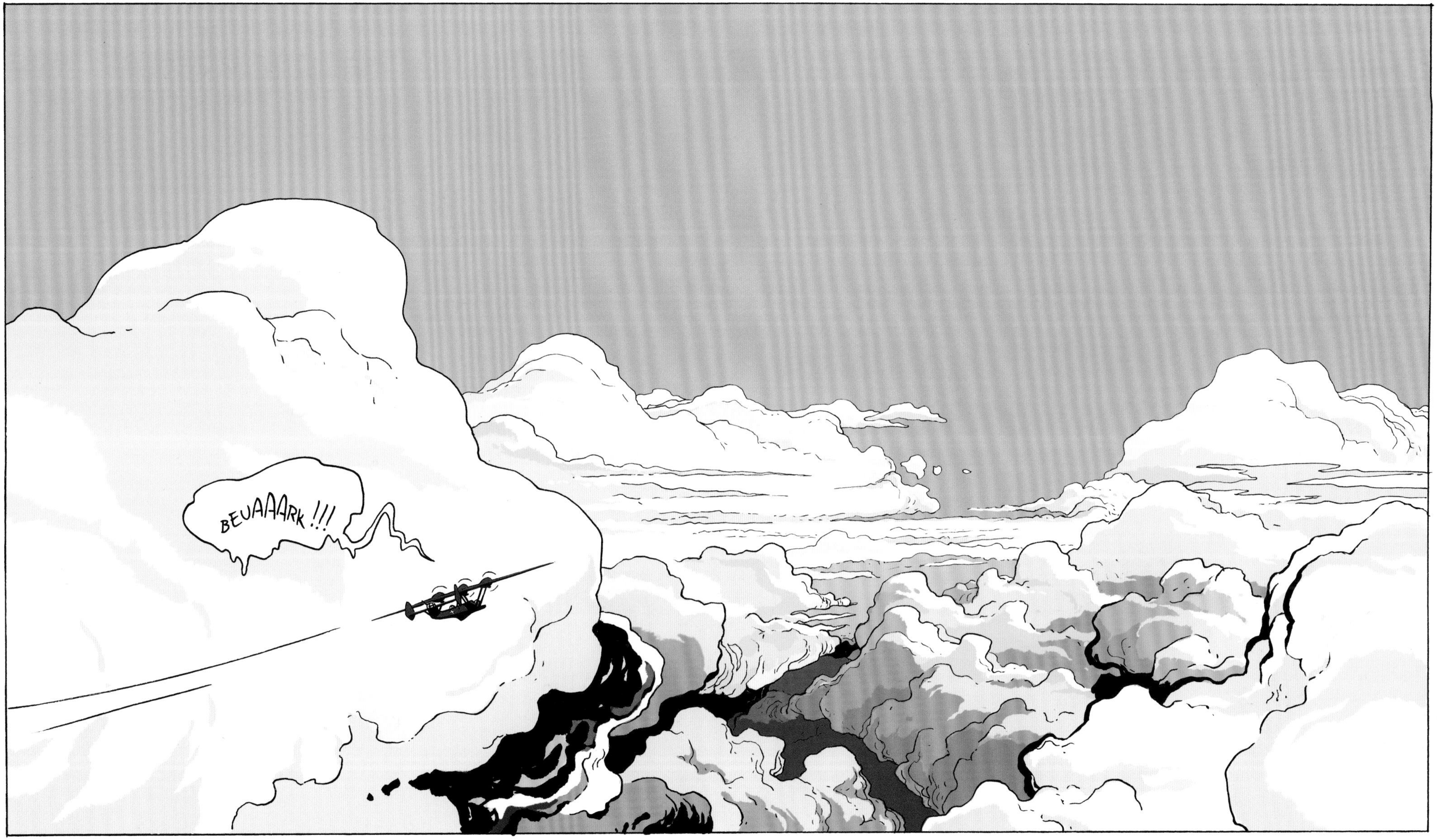
BEUAAARk !!!

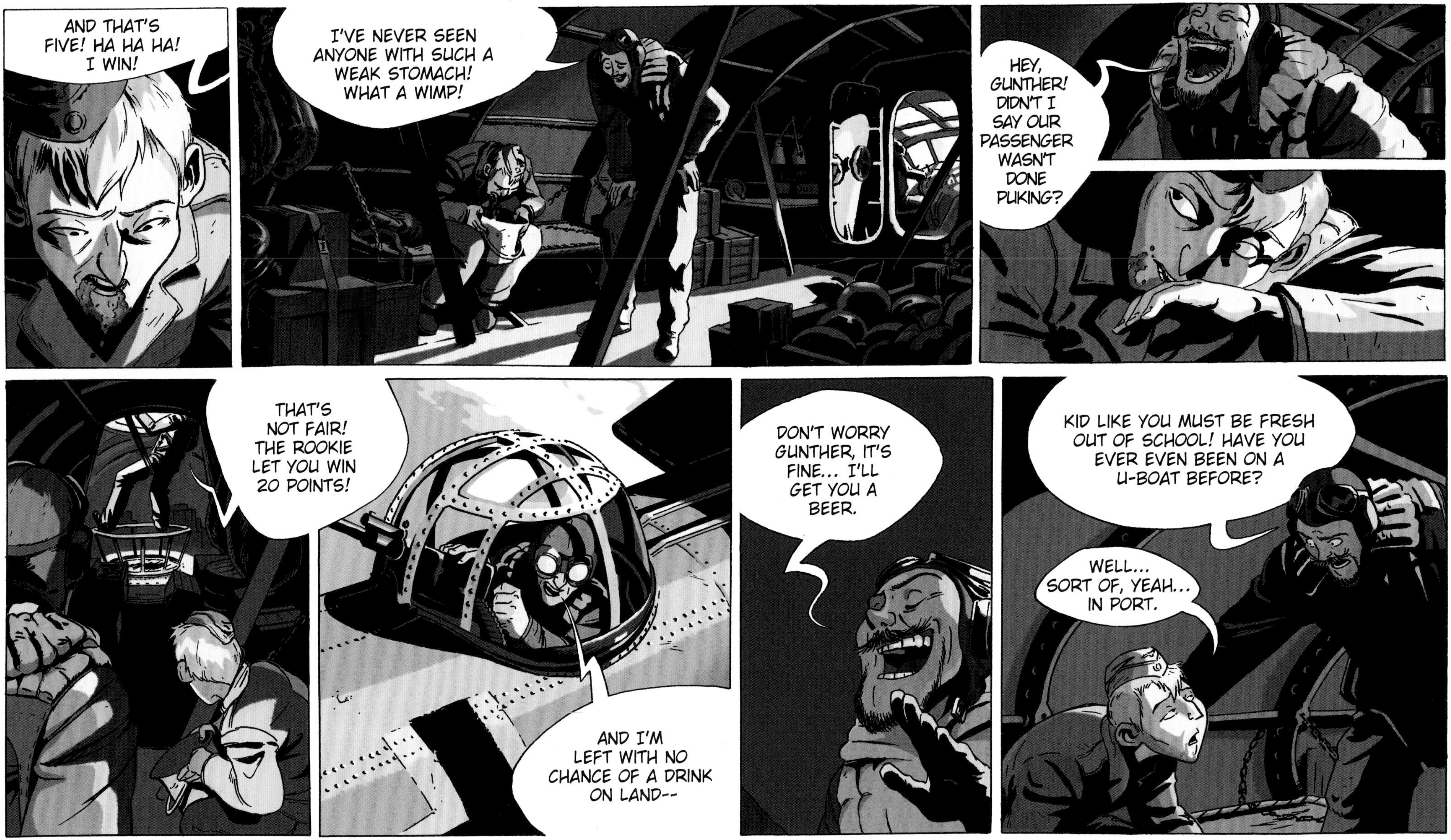
AND THAT'S FIVE! HA HA HA! I WIN!
I'VE NEVER SEEN ANYONE WITH SUCH A WEAK STOMACH! WHAT A WIMP!
HEY, GUNTHER! DIDN'T I SAY OUR PASSENGER WASN'T DONE PUKING?
THAT'S NOT FAIR! THE ROOKIE LET YOU WIN 20 POINTS!
AND I'M LEFT WITH NO CHANCE OF A DRINK ON LAND--
DON'T WORRY GUNTHER, IT'S FINE... I'LL GET YOU A BEER.
KID LIKE YOU MUST BE FRESH OUT OF SCHOOL! HAVE YOU EVER EVEN BEEN ON A U-BOAT BEFORE?
WELL... SORT OF, YEAH... IN PORT.

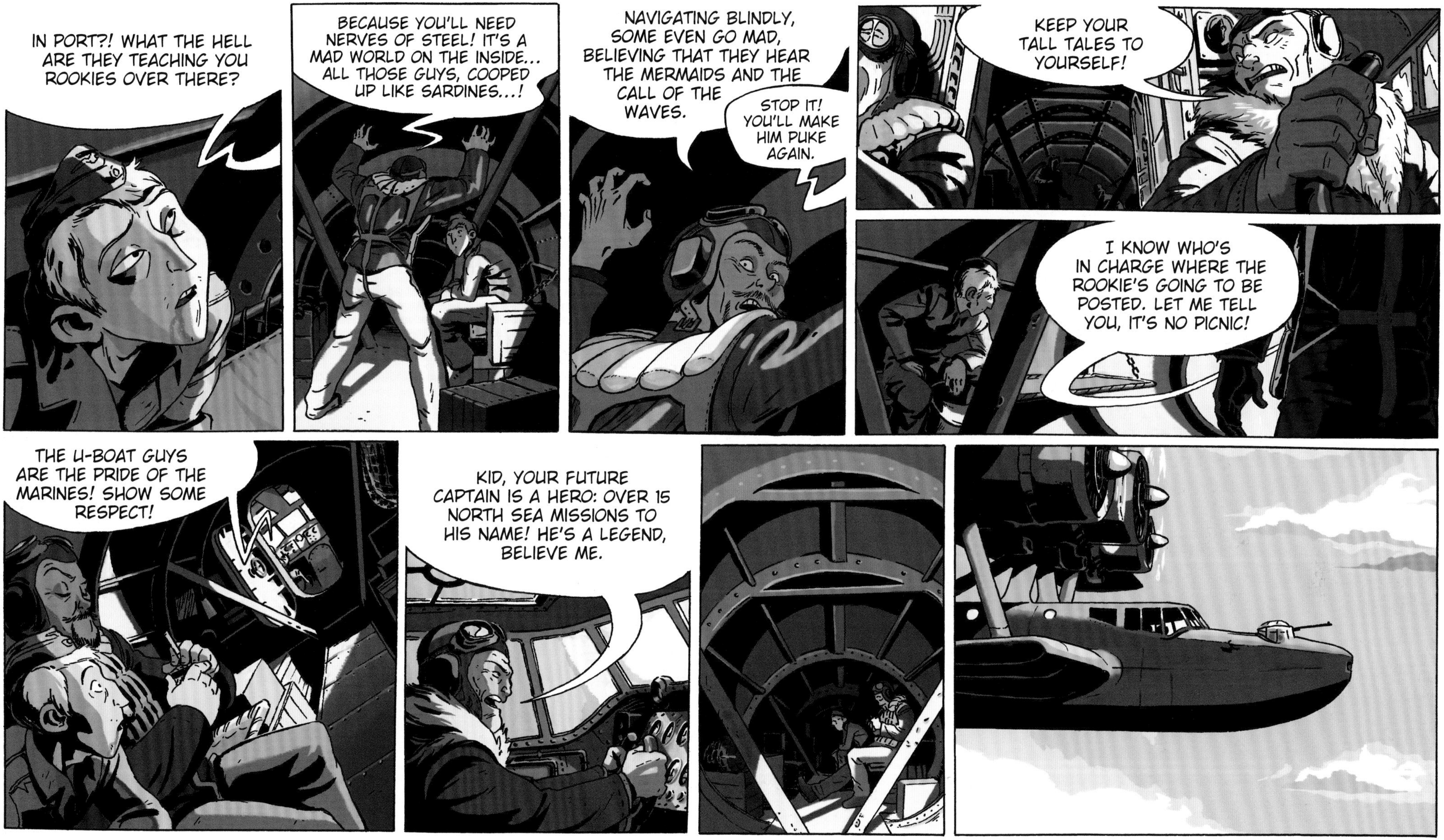
IN PORT?! WHAT THE HELL ARE THEY TEACHING YOU ROOKIES OVER THERE?
BECAUSE YOU'LL NEED NERVES OF STEEL! IT'S A MAD WORLD ON THE INSIDE... ALL THOSE GUYS, COOPED UP LIKE SARDINES...!
NAVIGATING BLINDLY, SOME EVEN GO MAD, BELIEVING THAT THEY HEAR THE MERMAIDS AND THE CALL OF THE WAVES.
STOP IT! YOU'LL MAKE HIM PUKE AGAIN.
KEEP YOUR TALL TALES TO YOURSELF!
I KNOW WHO'S IN CHARGE WHERE THE ROOKIE'S GOING TO BE POSTED. LET ME TELL YOU, IT'S NO PICNIC!
THE U-BOAT GUYS ARE THE PRIDE OF THE MARINES! SHOW SOME RESPECT!
KID, YOUR FUTURE CAPTAIN IS A HERO: OVER 15 NORTH SEA MISSIONS TO HIS NAME! HE'S A LEGEND, BELIEVE ME.

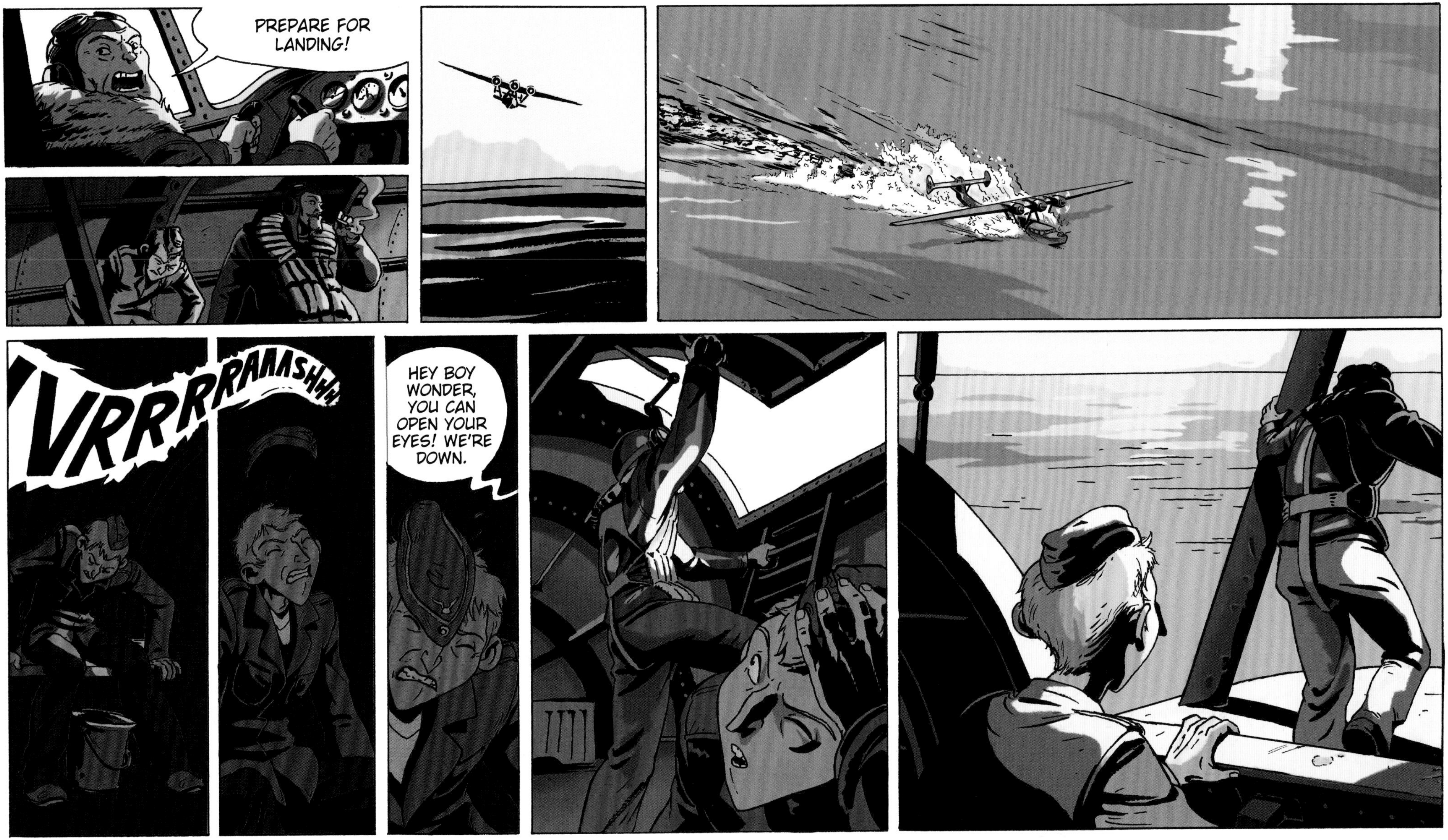
PREPARE FOR LANDING!
VRRRRAAASHWW
HEY BOY WONDER, YOU CAN OPEN YOUR EYES! WE'RE DOWN.

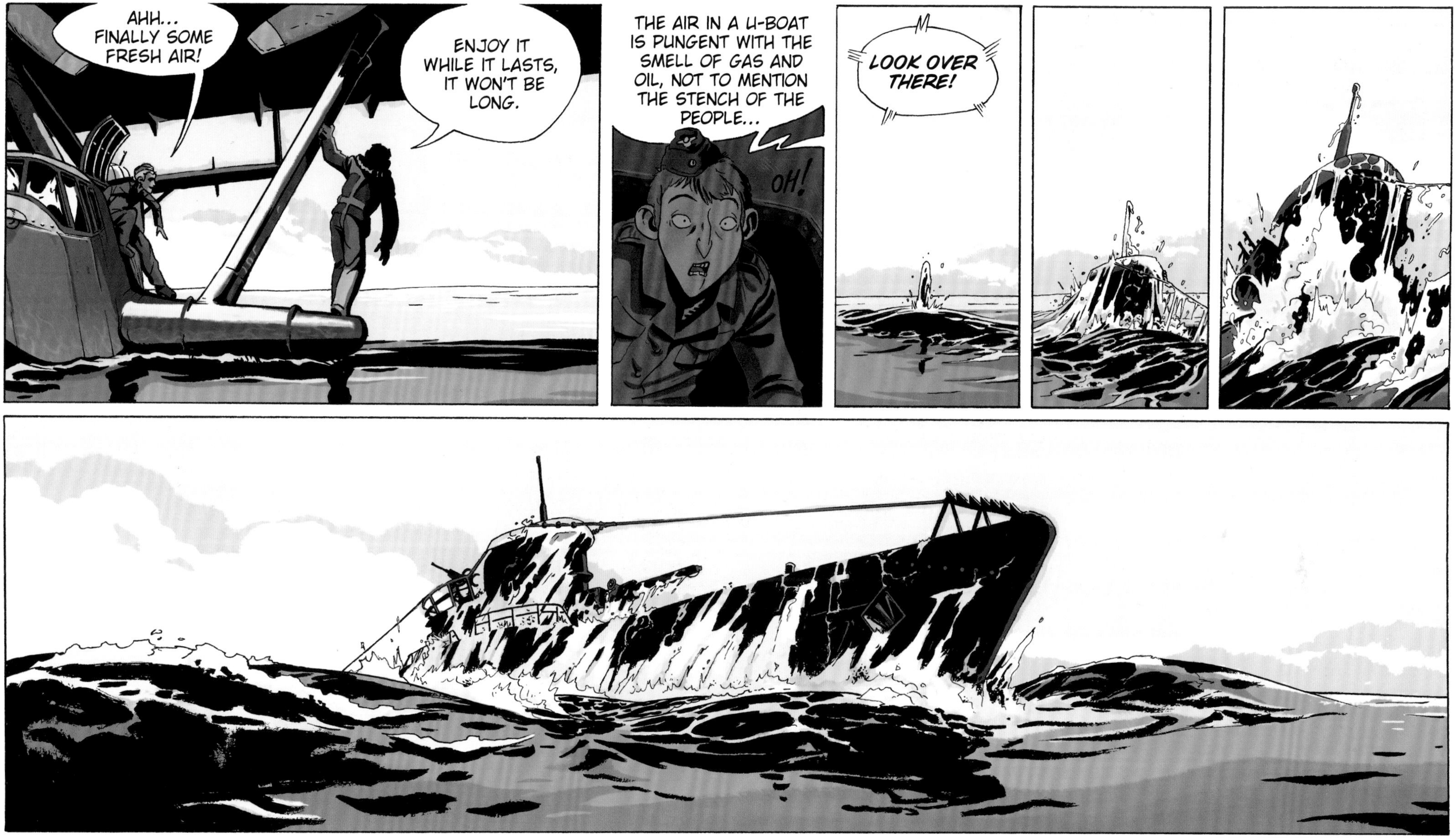
AHH... FINALLY SOME FRESH AIR!
ENJOY IT WHILE IT LASTS, IT WON'T BE LONG.
THE AIR IN A U-BOAT IS PUNGENT WITH THE SMELL OF GAS AND OIL, NOT TO MENTION THE STENCH OF THE PEOPLE...
OH!
LOOK OVER THERE!

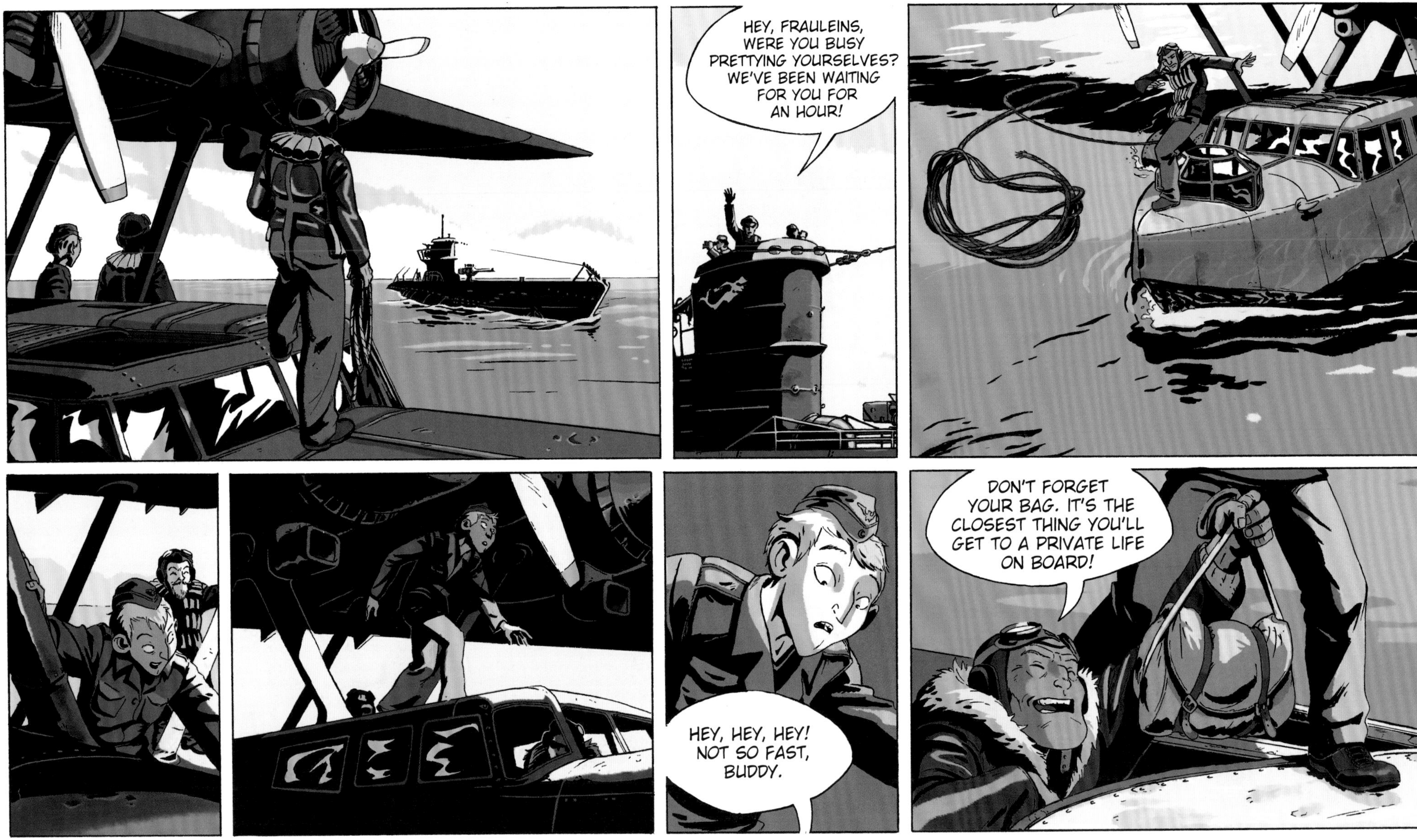
HEY, FRAULEINS, WERE YOU BUSY PRETTYING YOURSELVES? WE'VE BEEN WAITING FOR YOU FOR AN HOUR!
HEY, HEY, HEY! NOT SO FAST, BUDDY.
DON'T FORGET YOUR BAG. IT'S THE CLOSEST THING YOU'LL GET TO A PRIVATE LIFE ON BOARD!

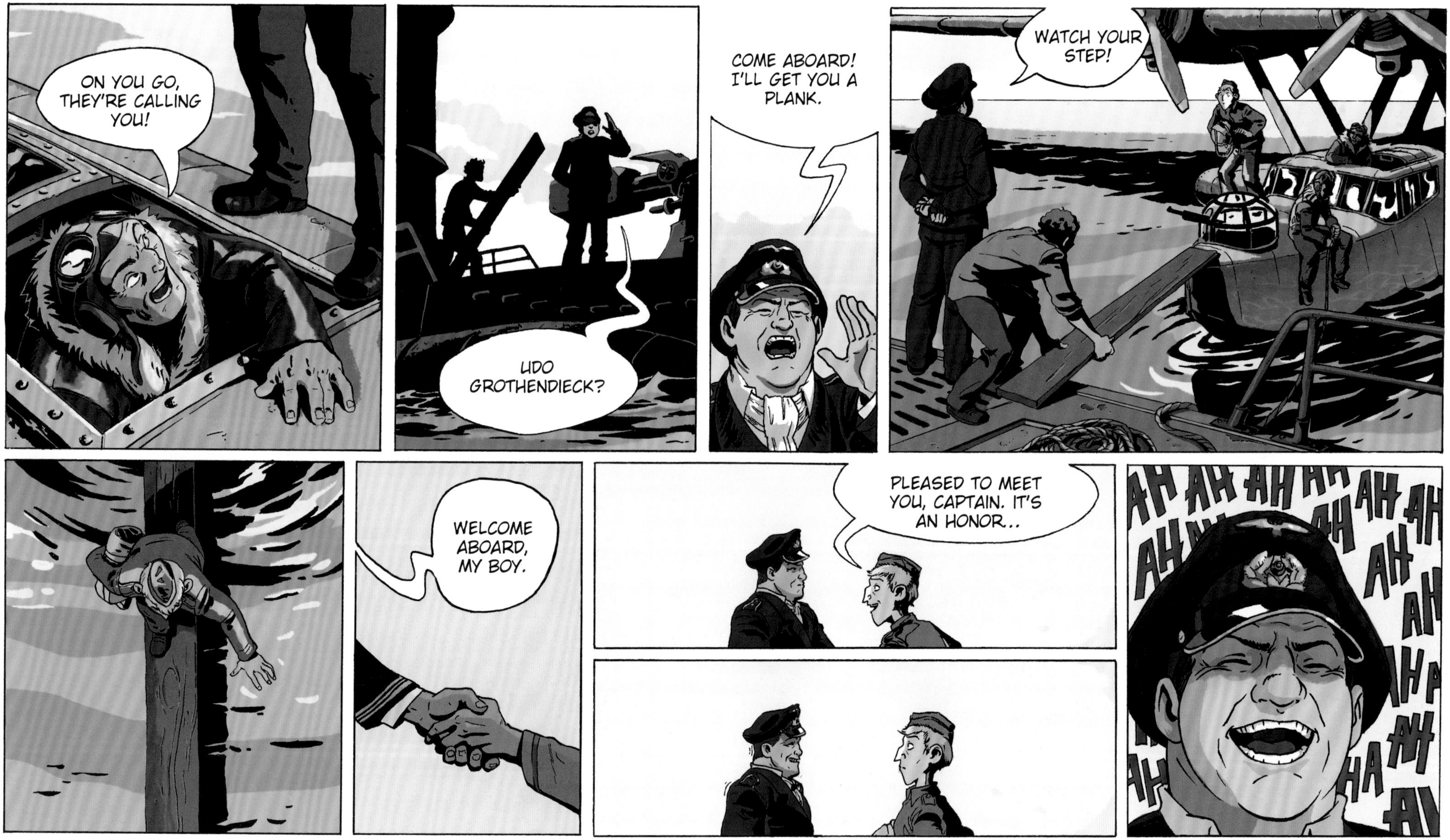
ON YOU GO, THEY'RE CALLING YOU!
UDO GROTHENDIECK?
COME ABOARD! I'LL GET YOU A PLANK.
WATCH YOUR STEP!
WELCOME ABOARD, MY BOY.
PLEASED TO MEET YOU, CAPTAIN. IT'S AN HONOR...
AH AH AH AH AH AH AH AH AH AH AH AH AH AH AH AH AH AH

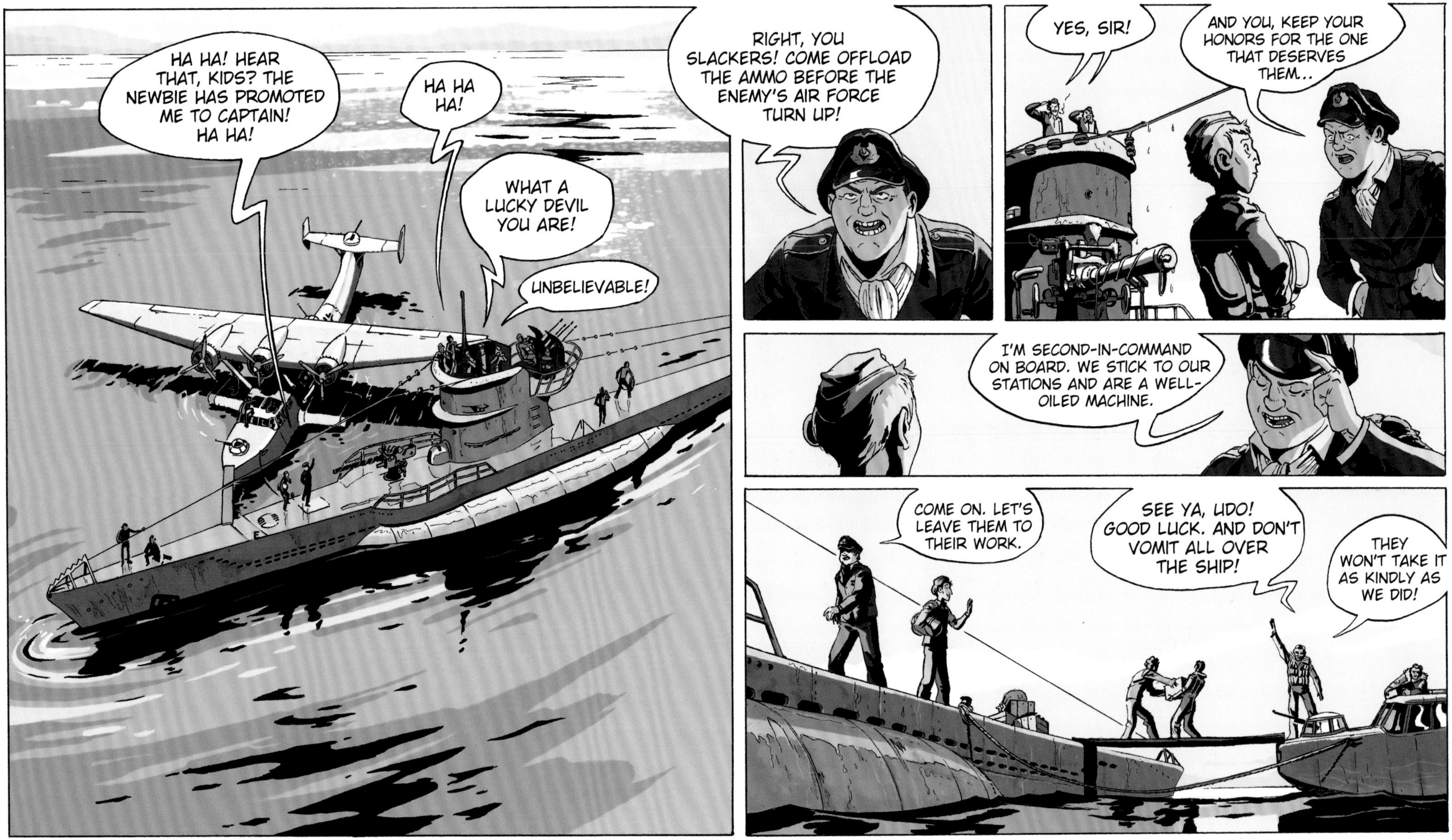
HA HA! HEAR THAT, KIDS? THE NEWBIE HAS PROMOTED ME TO CAPTAIN! HA HA!
HA HA HA!
WHAT A LUCKY DEVIL YOU ARE!
UNBELIEVABLE!
RIGHT, YOU SLACKERS! COME OFFLOAD THE AMMO BEFORE THE ENEMY'S AIR FORCE TURN UP!
YES, SIR!
AND YOU, KEEP YOUR HONORS FOR THE ONE THAT DESERVES THEM..
I'M SECOND-IN-COMMAND ON BOARD. WE STICK TO OUR STATIONS AND ARE A WELL-OILED MACHINE.
COME ON. LET'S LEAVE THEM TO THEIR WORK.
SEE YA, UDO! GOOD LUCK. AND DON'T VOMIT ALL OVER THE SHIP!
THEY WON'T TAKE IT AS KINDLY AS WE DID!

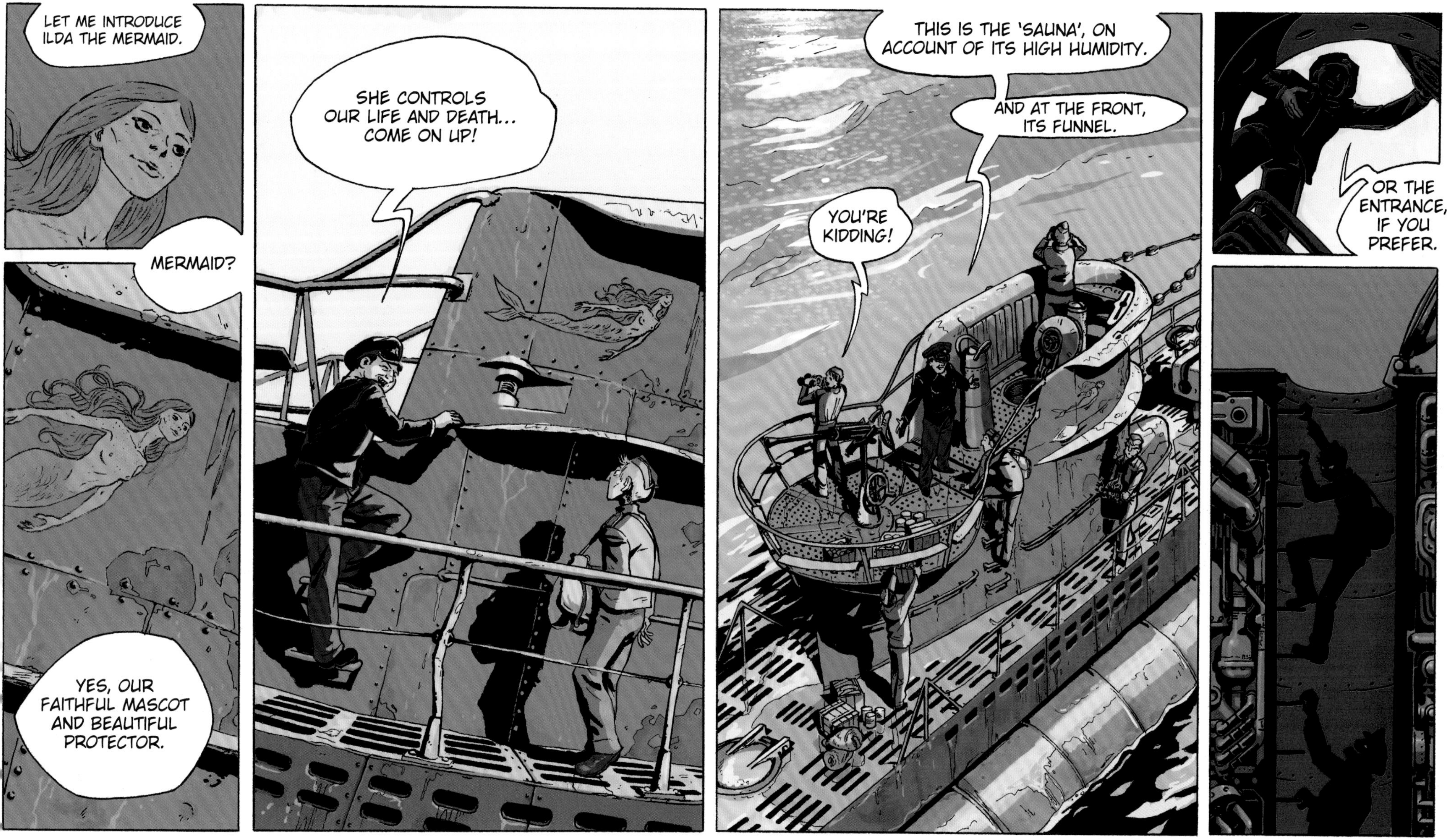
LET ME INTRODUCE ILDA THE MERMAID.
MERMAID?
YES, OUR FAITHFUL MASCOT AND BEAUTIFUL PROTECTOR.
SHE CONTROLS OUR LIFE AND DEATH... COME ON UP!
THIS IS THE 'SAUNA', ON ACCOUNT OF ITS HIGH HUMIDITY.
AND AT THE FRONT, ITS FUNNEL.
YOU'RE KIDDING!
OR THE ENTRANCE, IF YOU PREFER.

GENTS, THIS IS UDO, OUR NEW RADIO CONTROLLER. YOU'LL HAVE TO EXCUSE HIM, HE GOT WOBBLY ON THE PLANE RIDE OVER.

GUTEN TAG!

HEY!

I HOPE YOU LAST LONGER THAN YOUR PREDECESSOR.

OH? AND, UM, WHY IS THAT?

OH, NEVER MIND... HERE IS OUR BEST TEAM MEMBER.

THE PERISCOPE!

THE EYE OF THE SHIP. THE UNDERWATER CYCLOPS. IF ANYTHING WERE TO HAPPEN TO IT, WE'D BE COMPLETELY BLIND.

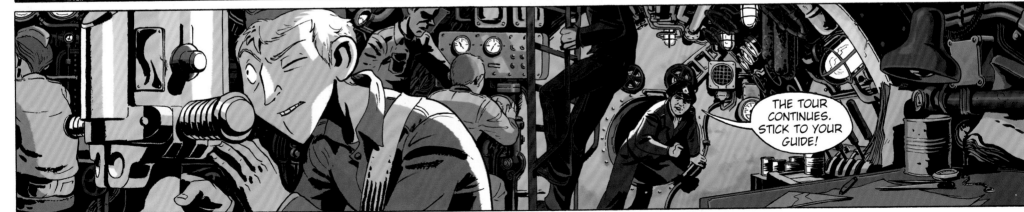

THE TOUR CONTINUES. STICK TO YOUR GUIDE!

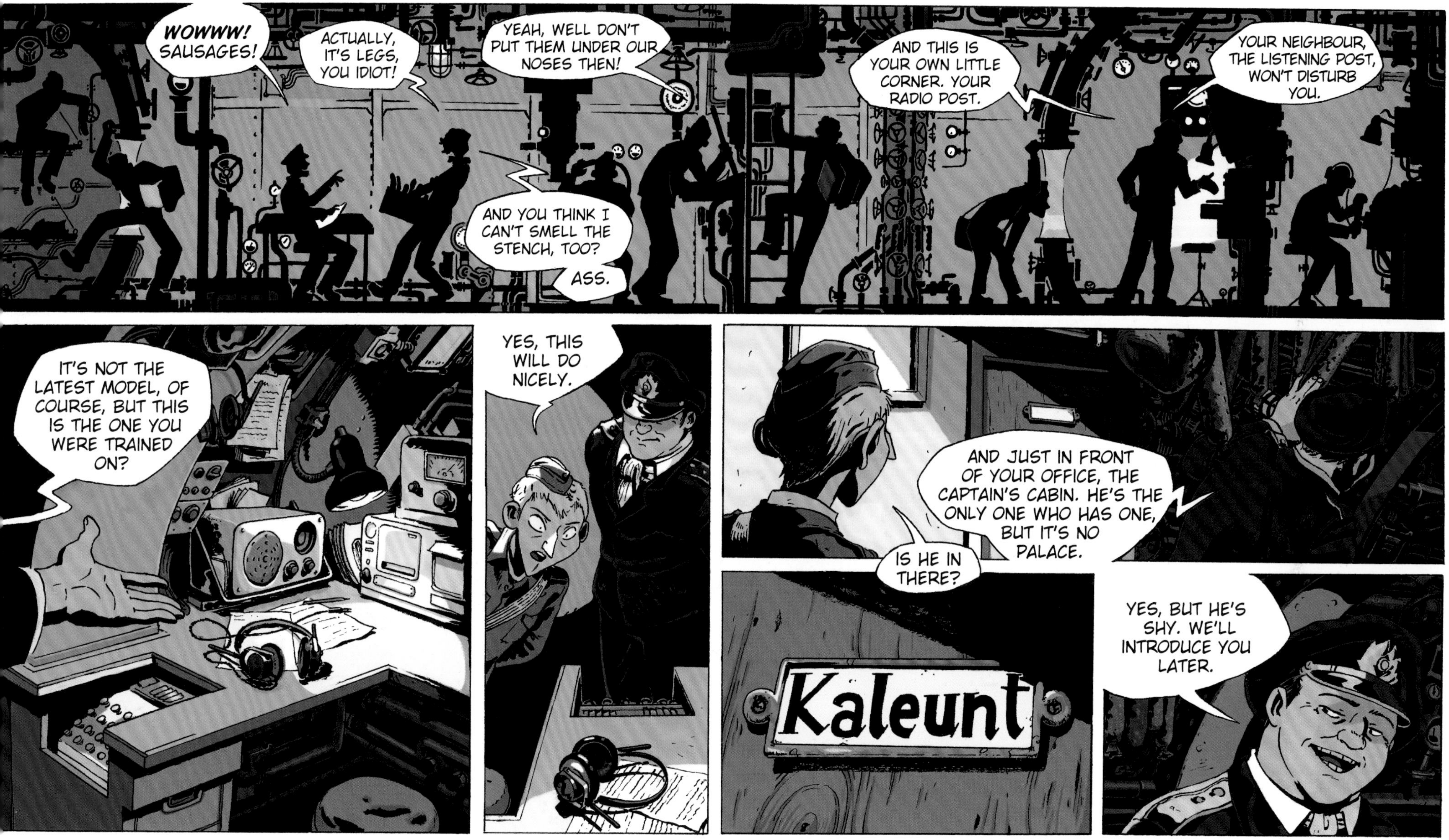
WOWWW! SAUSAGES!
ACTUALLY, IT'S LEGS, YOU IDIOT!
YEAH, WELL DON'T PUT THEM UNDER OUR NOSES THEN!
AND YOU THINK I CAN'T SMELL THE STENCH, TOO?
ASS.
AND THIS IS YOUR OWN LITTLE CORNER. YOUR RADIO POST.
YOUR NEIGHBOUR, THE LISTENING POST, WON'T DISTURB YOU.
IT'S NOT THE LATEST MODEL, OF COURSE, BUT THIS IS THE ONE YOU WERE TRAINED ON?
YES, THIS WILL DO NICELY.
AND JUST IN FRONT OF YOUR OFFICE, THE CAPTAIN'S CABIN. HE'S THE ONLY ONE WHO HAS ONE, BUT IT'S NO PALACE.
IS HE IN THERE?
Kaleunt
YES, BUT HE'S SHY. WE'LL INTRODUCE YOU LATER.

AND NOW, THE MOST IMPORTANT PLACE ON BOARD... DESPITE ITS SIZE!

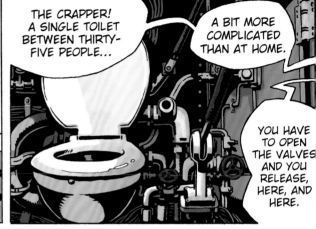

THE CRAPPER! A SINGLE TOILET BETWEEN THIRTY-FIVE PEOPLE...

A BIT MORE COMPLICATED THAN AT HOME.

YOU HAVE TO OPEN THE VALVES AND YOU RELEASE, HERE, AND HERE.

THEN YOU HAVE TO PUMP HARD. WHEN SUBMERGED THE PRESSURE IS INCREDIBLE!

AND MAKE SURE YOU CLOSE THE VALVES, I'M NOT KIDDING!

WE DON'T MESS AROUND WITH THIS... THERE WAS A U-BOAT THAT SUNK BECAUSE OF ONE SUCH SHITTY STORY.

AND FINALLY, AT THE BOW OF THE SHIP, WE HAVE THE TORPEDO ROOM WHICH ALSO SERVES AS THE SLEEPING QUARTERS.

I'LL LEAVE YOU TO GET ACQUAINTED WITH YOUR COMRADES.

UM... NICE TO... MEET YOU. I'M THE NEW RADIO OPERATOR... AND I...

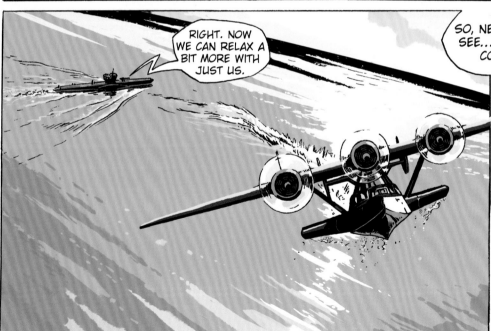

RIGHT. NOW WE CAN RELAX A BIT MORE WITH JUST US.

SO, NEW RADIO, LET'S SEE... WHERE D'YOU COME FROM?

YOU SEE HOW HE'S ANSWERING YOU?

WHAT A COWARD!

I WOULDN'T TAKE NONE OF THAT!

BUT LOOK HERE, YOU'RE HIDING A LITTLE TREASURE...

GIVE IT HERE!!!

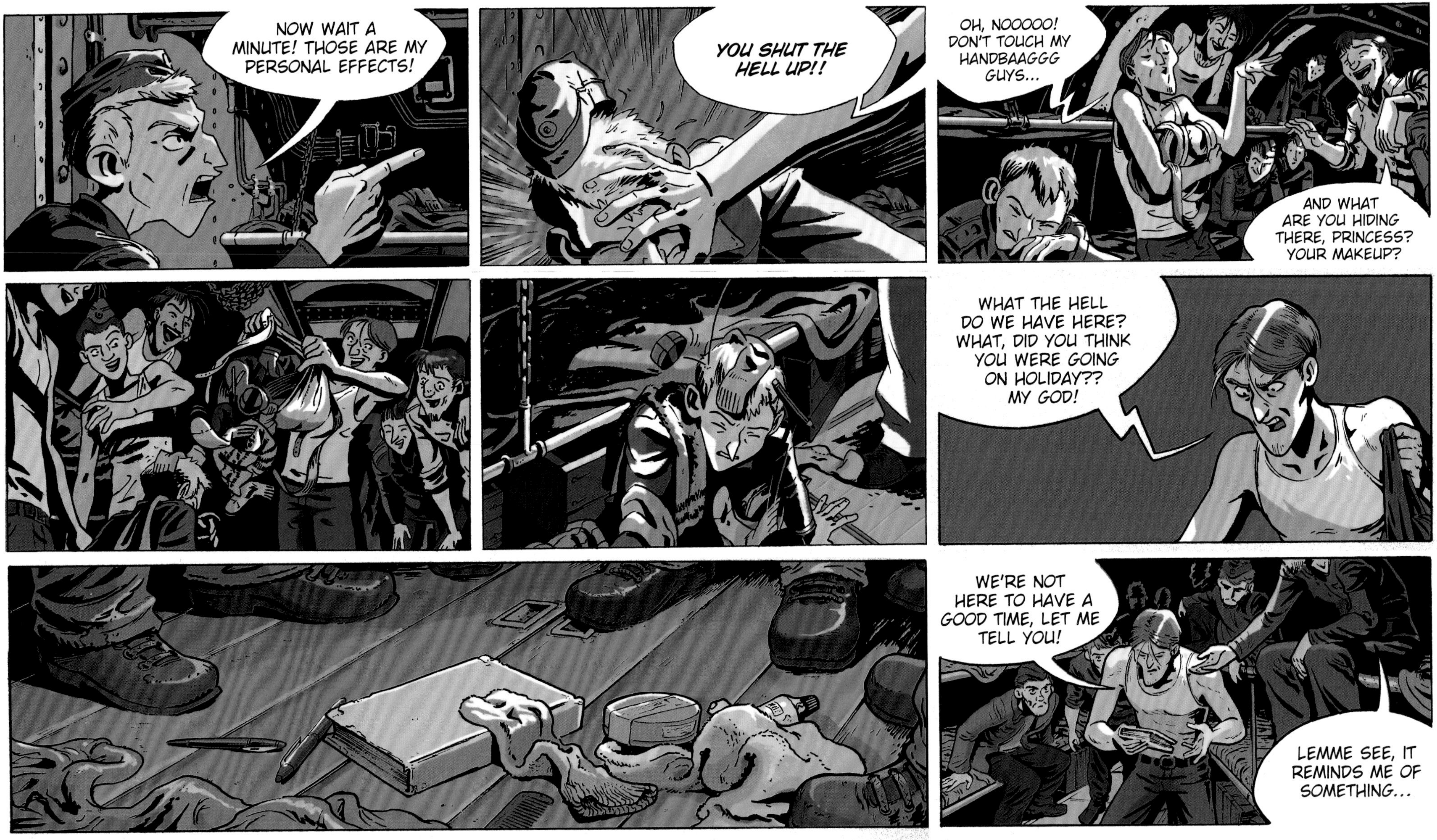
NOW WAIT A MINUTE! THOSE ARE MY PERSONAL EFFECTS!
YOU SHUT THE HELL UP!!
OH, NOOOOO! DON'T TOUCH MY HANDBAAGGG GUYS...
AND WHAT ARE YOU HIDING THERE, PRINCESS? YOUR MAKEUP?
WHAT THE HELL DO WE HAVE HERE? WHAT, DID YOU THINK YOU WERE GOING ON HOLIDAY?? MY GOD!
WE'RE NOT HERE TO HAVE A GOOD TIME, LET ME TELL YOU!
LEMME SEE, IT REMINDS ME OF SOMETHING...

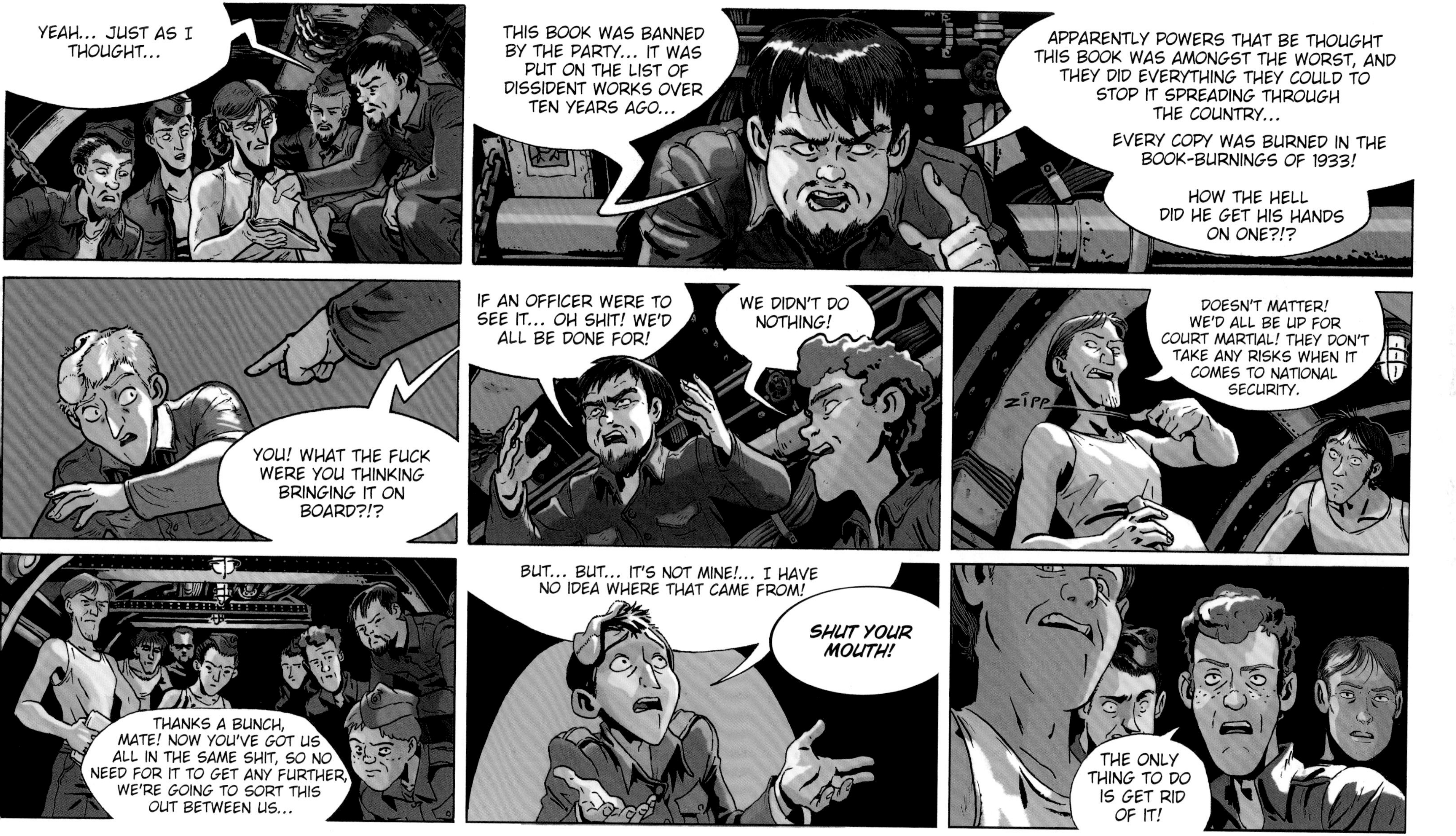
YEAH... JUST AS I THOUGHT...
THIS BOOK WAS BANNED BY THE PARTY... IT WAS PUT ON THE LIST OF DISSIDENT WORKS OVER TEN YEARS AGO...
APPARENTLY POWERS THAT BE THOUGHT THIS BOOK WAS AMONGST THE WORST, AND THEY DID EVERYTHING THEY COULD TO STOP IT SPREADING THROUGH THE COUNTRY...
EVERY COPY WAS BURNED IN THE BOOK-BURNINGS OF 1933!
HOW THE HELL DID HE GET HIS HANDS ON ONE?!?
YOU! WHAT THE FUCK WERE YOU THINKING BRINGING IT ON BOARD?!?
IF AN OFFICER WERE TO SEE IT... OH SHIT! WE'D ALL BE DONE FOR!
WE DIDN'T DO NOTHING!
DOESN'T MATTER! WE'D ALL BE UP FOR COURT MARTIAL! THEY DON'T TAKE ANY RISKS WHEN IT COMES TO NATIONAL SECURITY.
ZIPP
THANKS A BUNCH, MATE! NOW YOU'VE GOT US ALL IN THE SAME SHIT, SO NO NEED FOR IT TO GET ANY FURTHER, WE'RE GOING TO SORT THIS OUT BETWEEN US...
BUT... BUT... IT'S NOT MINE!... I HAVE NO IDEA WHERE THAT CAME FROM!
SHUT YOUR MOUTH!
THE ONLY THING TO DO IS GET RID OF IT!

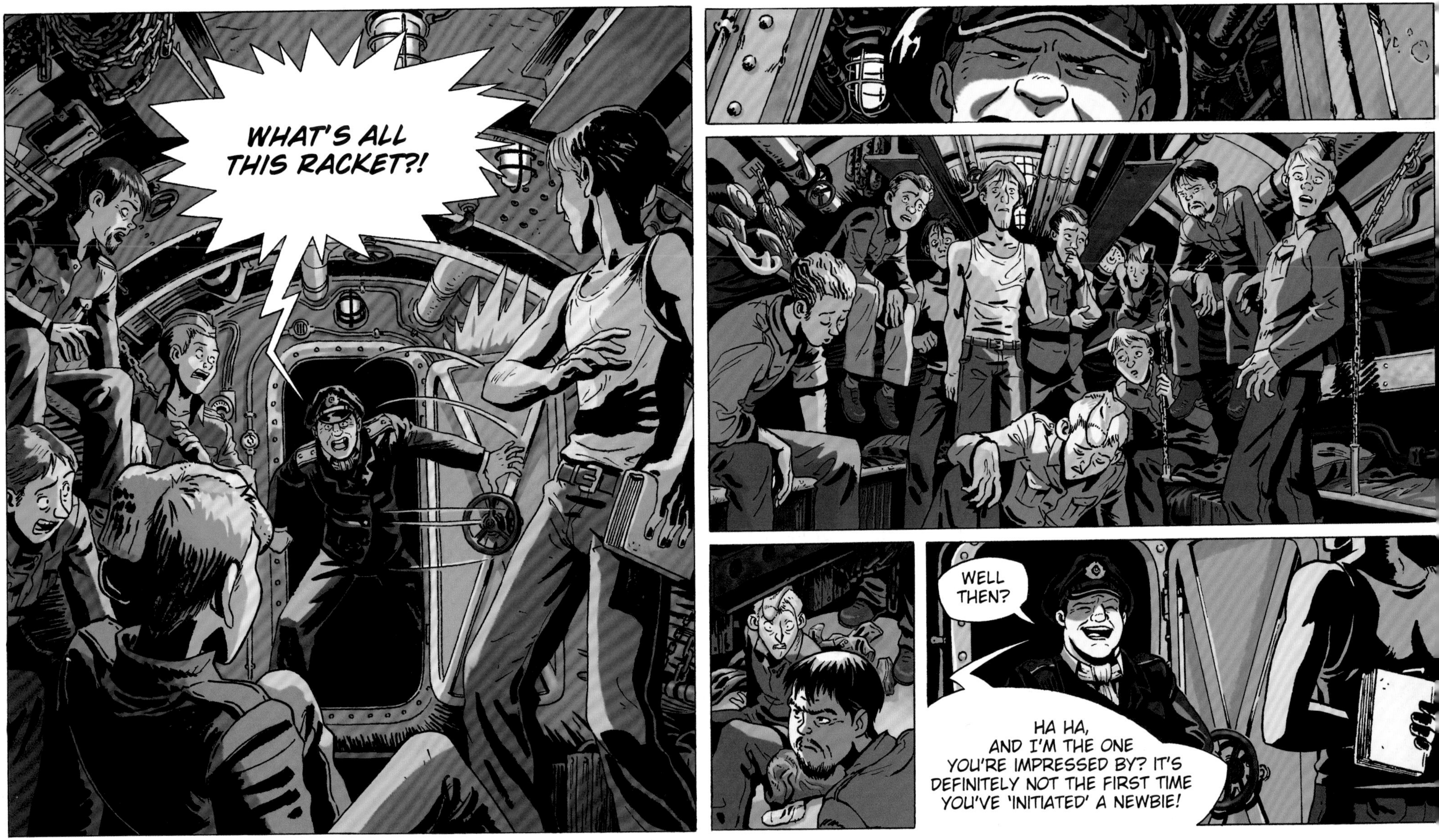
WHAT'S ALL THIS RACKET?!
WELL THEN?
HA HA, AND I'M THE ONE YOU'RE IMPRESSED BY? IT'S DEFINITELY NOT THE FIRST TIME YOU'VE 'INITIATED' A NEWBIE!

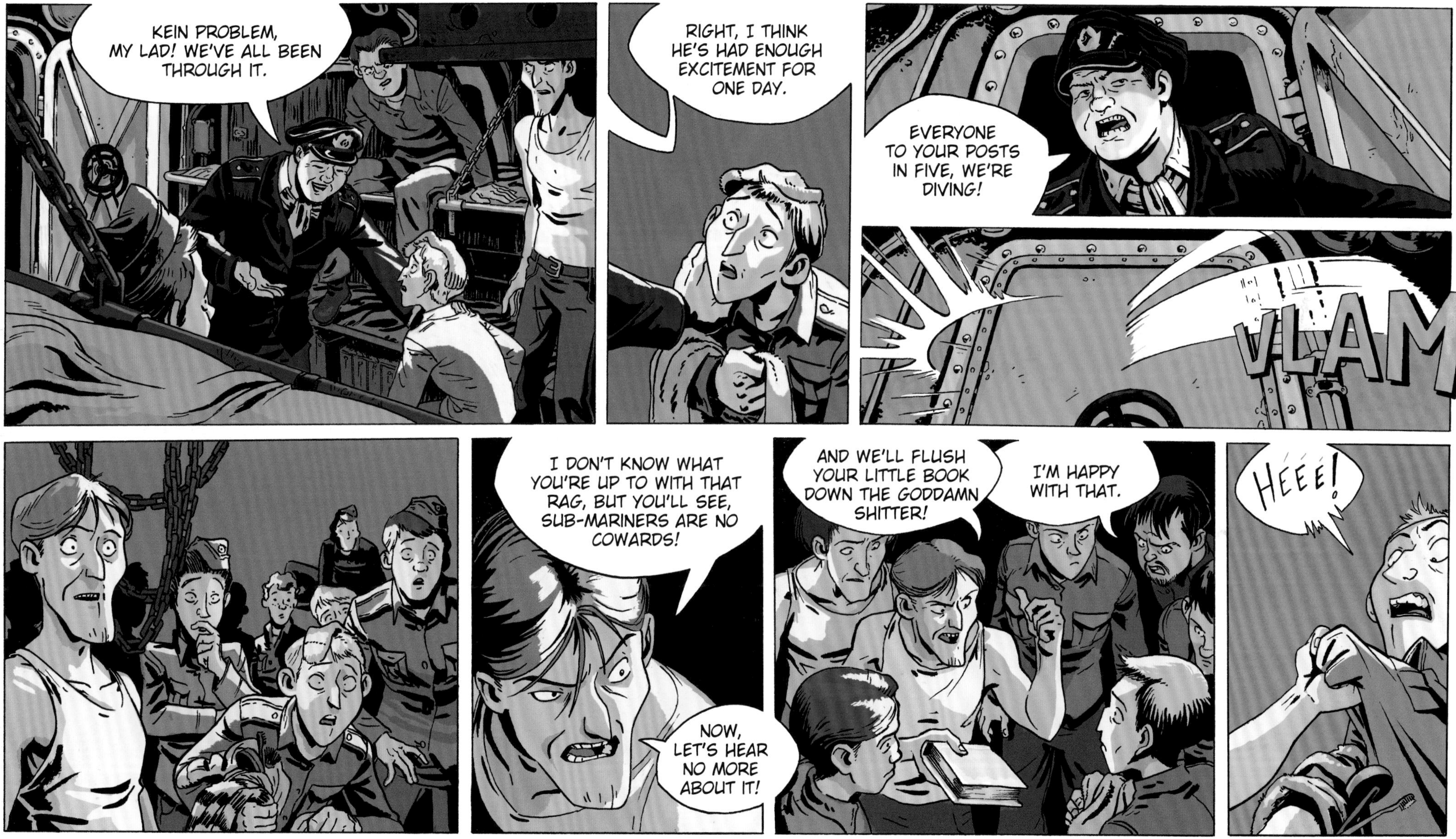
KEIN PROBLEM, MY LAD! WE'VE ALL BEEN THROUGH IT.
RIGHT, I THINK HE'S HAD ENOUGH EXCITEMENT FOR ONE DAY.
EVERYONE TO YOUR POSTS IN FIVE, WE'RE DIVING!
VLAM
I DON'T KNOW WHAT YOU'RE UP TO WITH THAT RAG, BUT YOU'LL SEE, SUB-MARINERS ARE NO COWARDS!
NOW, LET'S HEAR NO MORE ABOUT IT!
AND WE'LL FLUSH YOUR LITTLE BOOK DOWN THE GODDAMN SHITTER!
I'M HAPPY WITH THAT.
HEEE!

ALL CLEAR!
BRING THE BOOK, HANS.
GIMME THAT TRASH SO ONLY THE FISH CAN READ IT.
TCHOMP TCHOMP TCHOMP
A WORD OF ADVICE: IN FUTURE, YOU KEEP YOURSELF IN LINE.
CHAPTER OVER, LET'S GO!

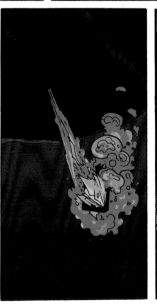

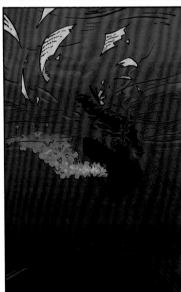

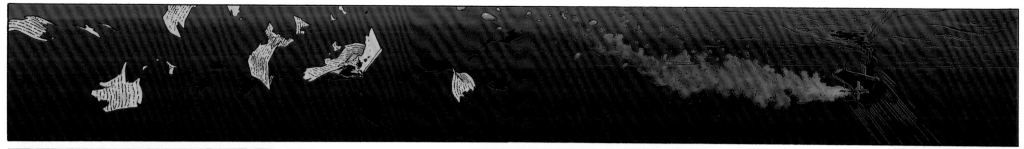

PLIC
PLIC
FIRST DIVE, MY COCO?
PLIC
PLIC
PLIC
PLIC
YOU GET USED TO THE HUMIDITY FAST ENOUGH... I CALL EVERYONE HERE 'COCO,' IS THAT ALRIGHT WITH YOU?
YEAH, UH, YOU...
MAINTAIN PERISCOPE DEPTH... SPEED AT EIGHT KNOTS.
OH, FORGIVE ME! I'M ROSENBART. I'M IN MECHANICS.
HEADING NORTH-NORTH-EAST.
NOTHING TO REPORT, WE'VE GOT PLAIN SAILING AHEAD OF US.

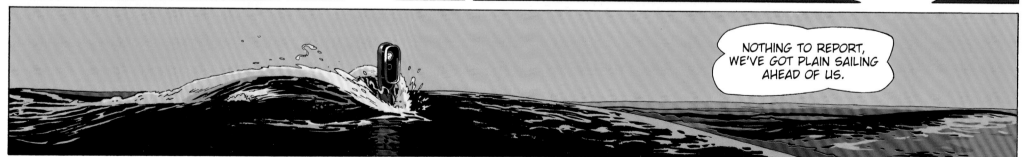

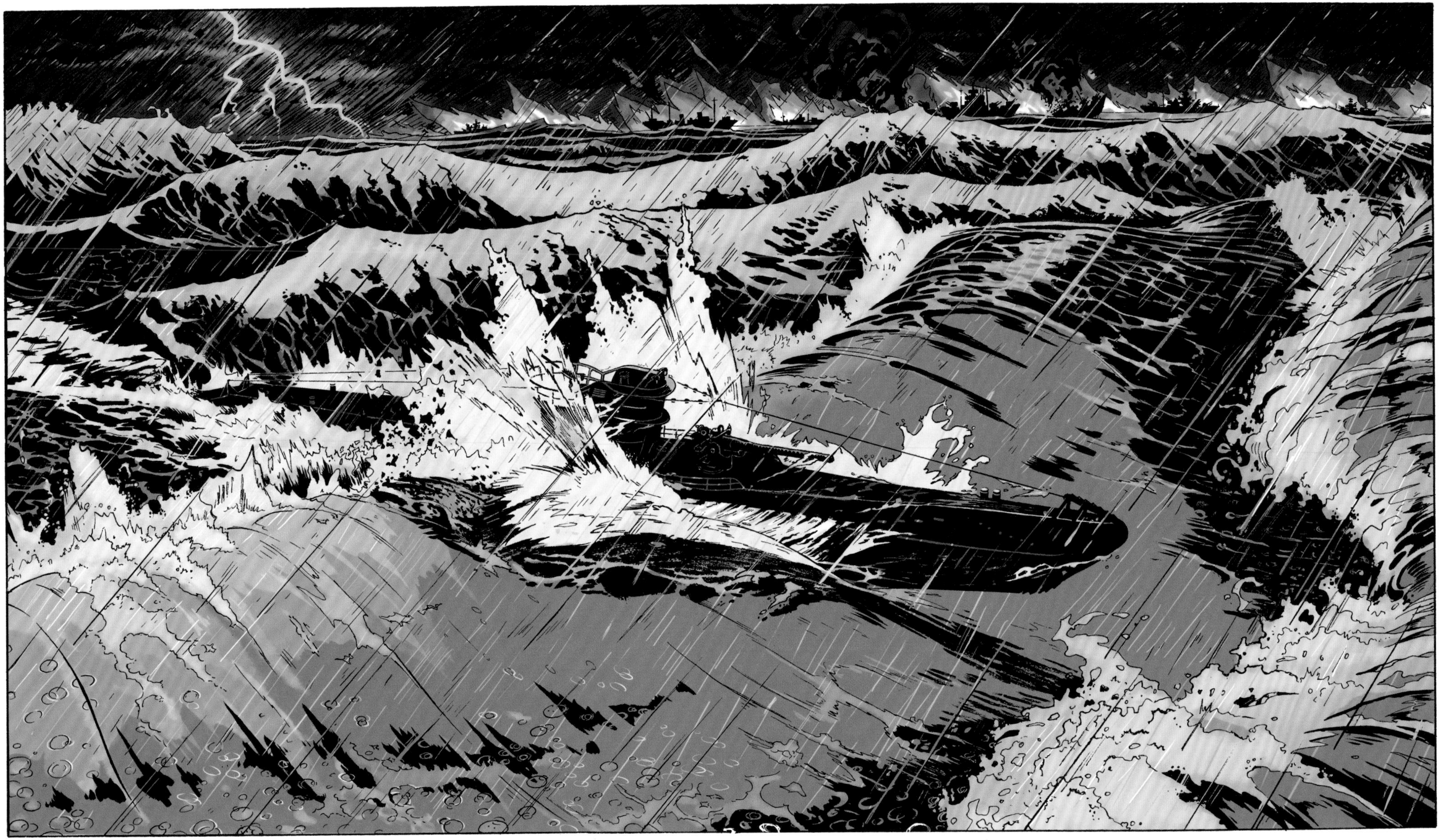

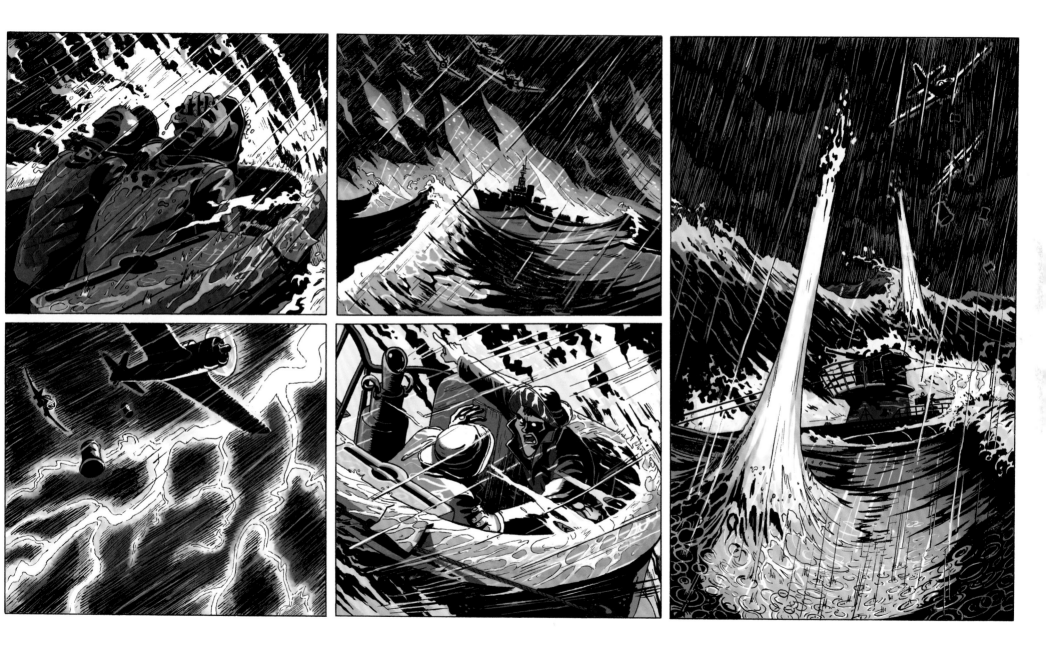

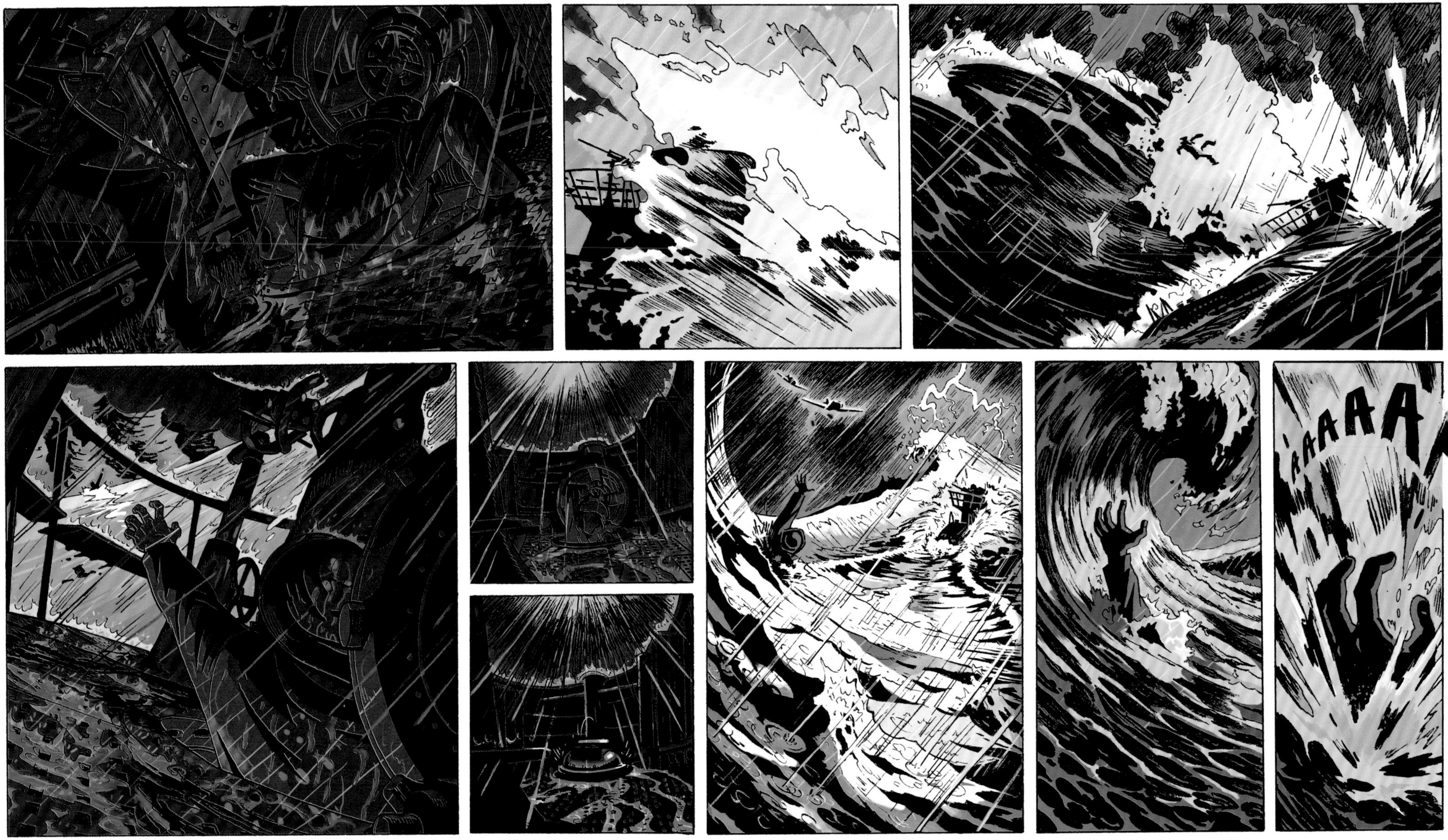
AAAAA

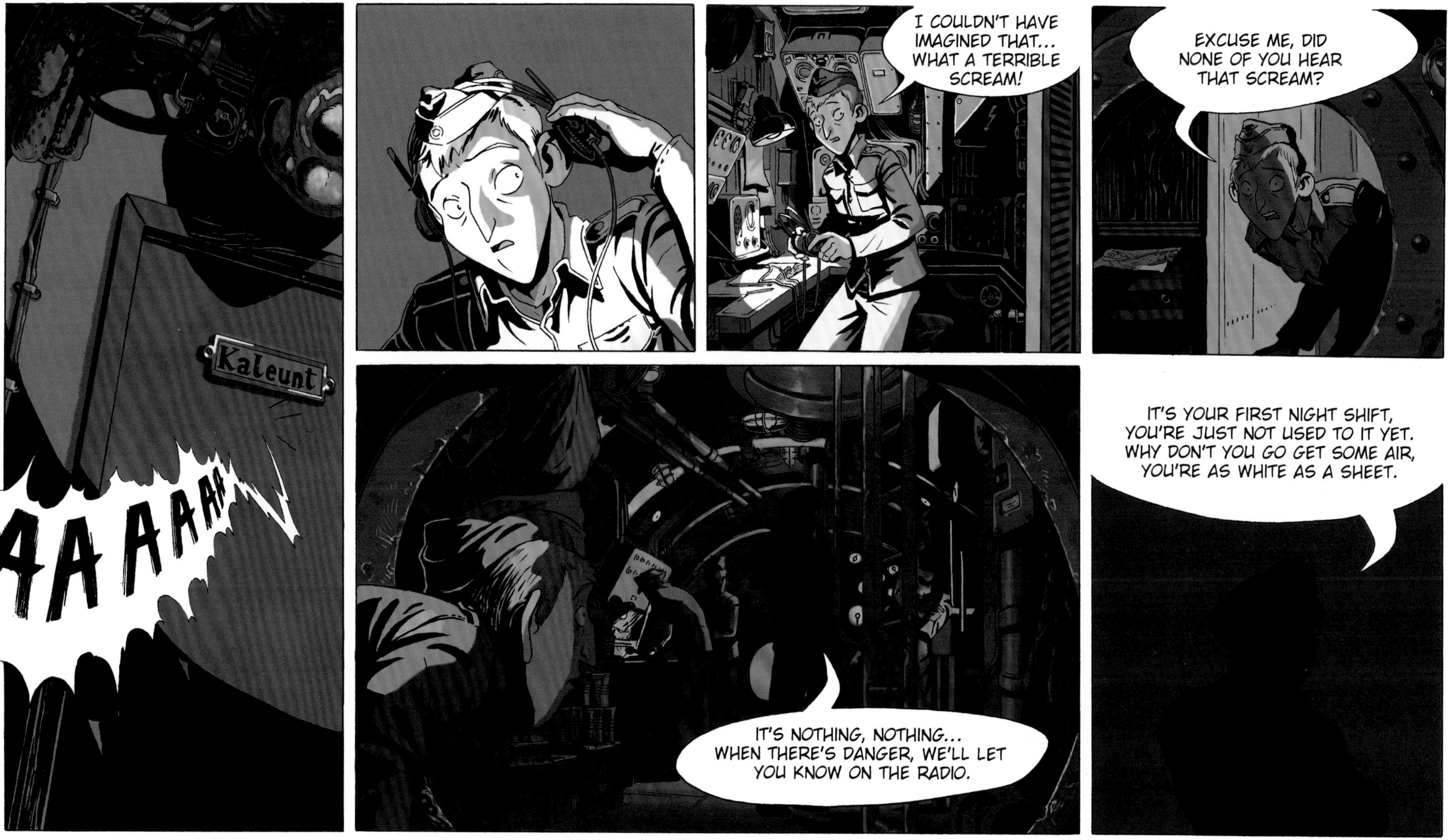
Kaleunt
AAAAAAA
I COULDN'T HAVE IMAGINED THAT... WHAT A TERRIBLE SCREAM!
EXCUSE ME, DID NONE OF YOU HEAR THAT SCREAM?
IT'S NOTHING, NOTHING... WHEN THERE'S DANGER, WE'LL LET YOU KNOW ON THE RADIO.
IT'S YOUR FIRST NIGHT SHIFT, YOU'RE JUST NOT USED TO IT YET. WHY DON'T YOU GO GET SOME AIR, YOU'RE AS WHITE AS A SHEET.

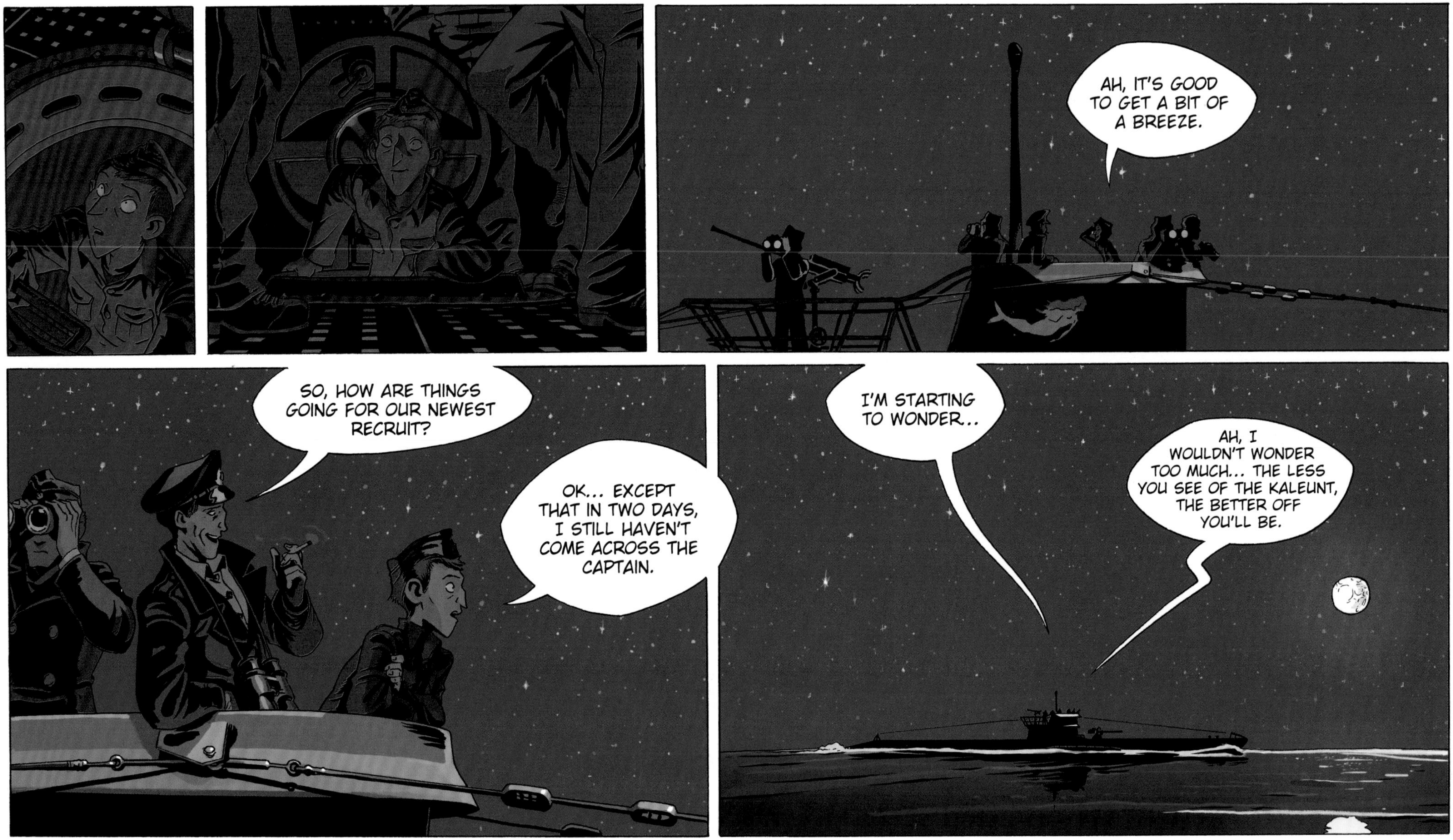
AH, IT'S GOOD TO GET A BIT OF A BREEZE.
SO, HOW ARE THINGS GOING FOR OUR NEWEST RECRUIT?
OK... EXCEPT THAT IN TWO DAYS, I STILL HAVEN'T COME ACROSS THE CAPTAIN.
I'M STARTING TO WONDER...
AH, I WOULDN'T WONDER TOO MUCH... THE LESS YOU SEE OF THE KALEUNT, THE BETTER OFF YOU'LL BE.

WHALE AND HER LITTLE'UN UP AHEAD!

LOOK, THEY'RE DIVING!

...IT'S FUNNY, THEY CAME TO THE SURFACE FOR A BIT OF FRESH AIR, JUST LIKE US!

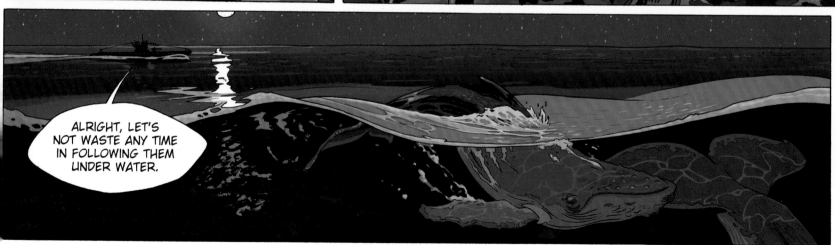

ALRIGHT, LET'S NOT WASTE ANY TIME IN FOLLOWING THEM UNDER WATER.

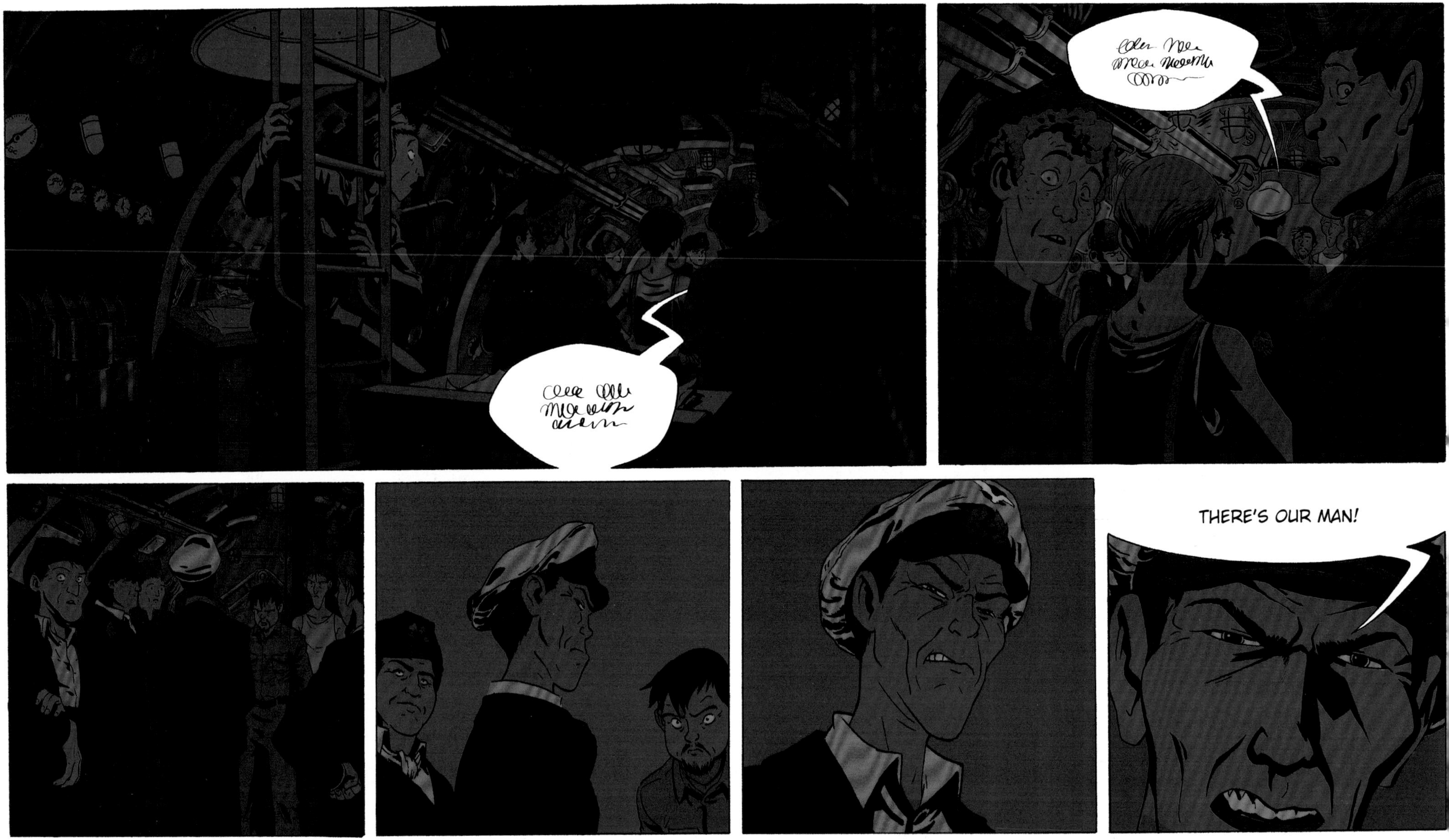
THERE'S OUR MAN!

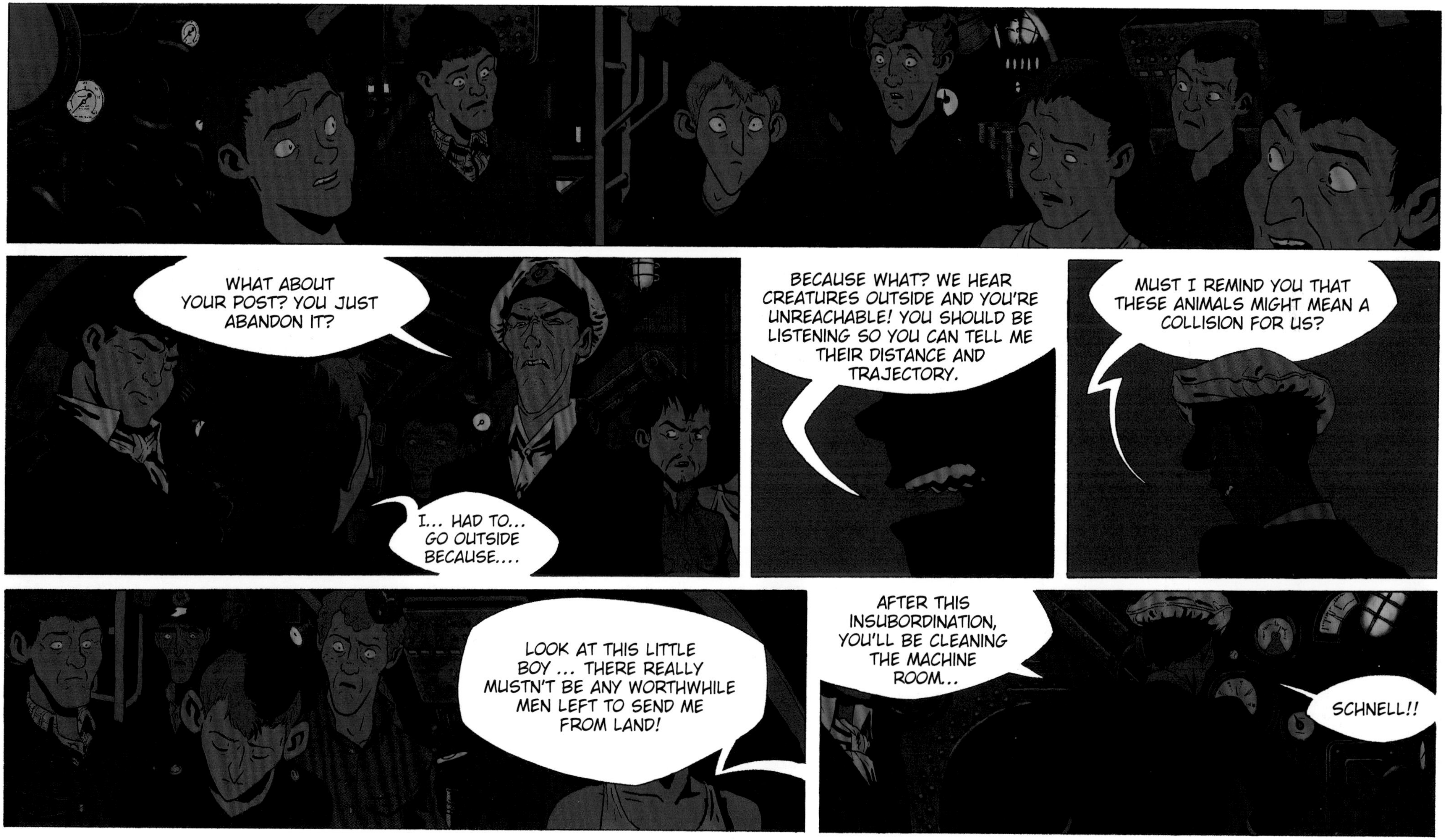
WHAT ABOUT YOUR POST? YOU JUST ABANDON IT?
I... HAD TO... GO OUTSIDE BECAUSE....
BECAUSE WHAT? WE HEAR CREATURES OUTSIDE AND YOU'RE UNREACHABLE! YOU SHOULD BE LISTENING SO YOU CAN TELL ME THEIR DISTANCE AND TRAJECTORY.
MUST I REMIND YOU THAT THESE ANIMALS MIGHT MEAN A COLLISION FOR US?
LOOK AT THIS LITTLE BOY ... THERE REALLY MUSTN'T BE ANY WORTHWHILE MEN LEFT TO SEND ME FROM LAND!
AFTER THIS INSUBORDINATION, YOU'LL BE CLEANING THE MACHINE ROOM...
SCHNELL!!

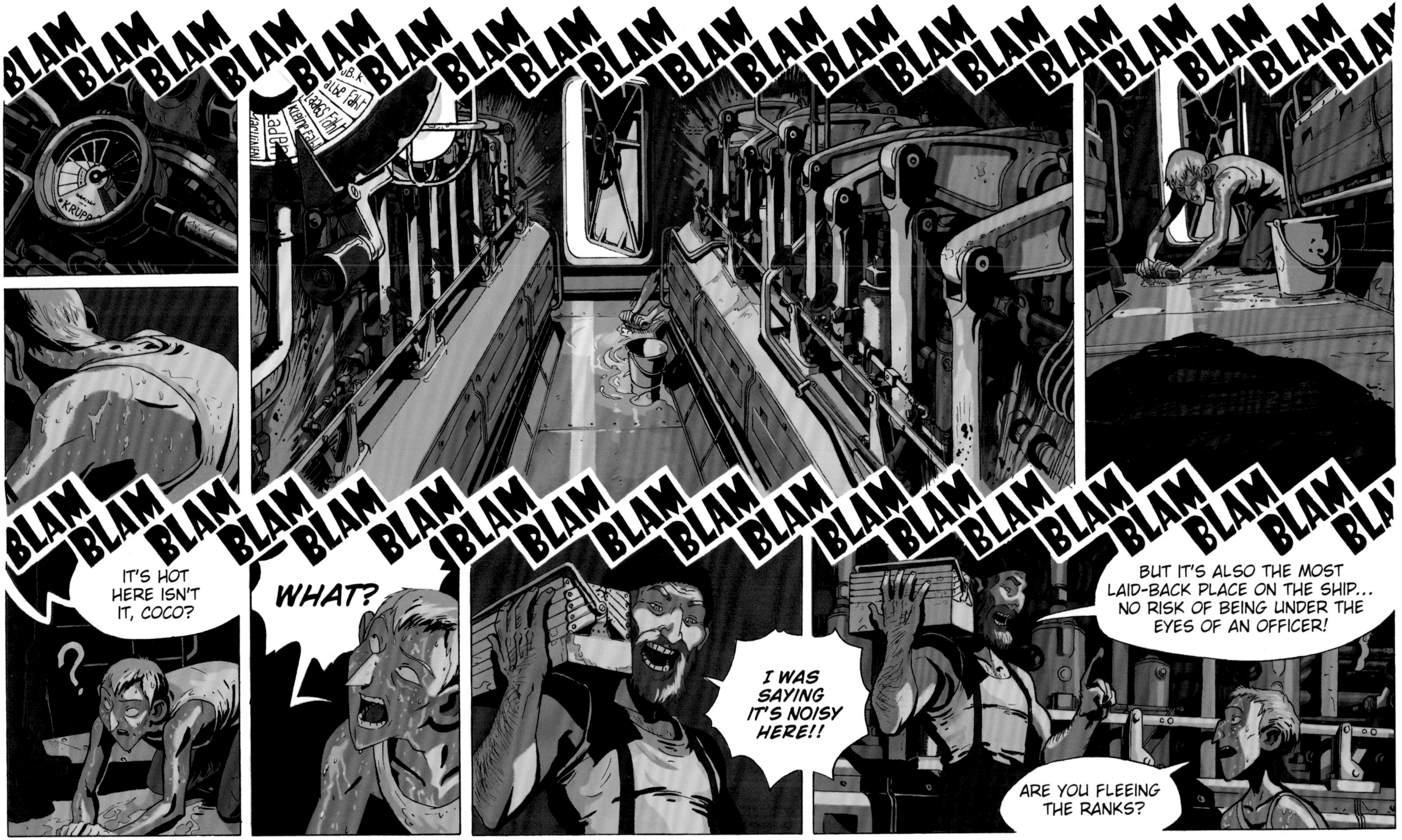
BLAM BLAM BLAM BLAM BLAM BLAM BLAM BLAM BLAM BLAM BLAM BLAM BLAM BLAM BLAM BLAM BLAM BLAM
KRUPP
BLAM BLAM BLAM BLAM BLAM BLAM BLAM BLAM BLAM BLAM BLAM BLAM BLAM BLAM BLAM BLAM BLAM BLAM
IT'S HOT HERE ISN'T IT, COCO?
?
WHAT?
I WAS SAYING IT'S NOISY HERE!!
BUT IT'S ALSO THE MOST LAID-BACK PLACE ON THE SHIP... NO RISK OF BEING UNDER THE EYES OF AN OFFICER!
ARE YOU FLEEING THE RANKS?

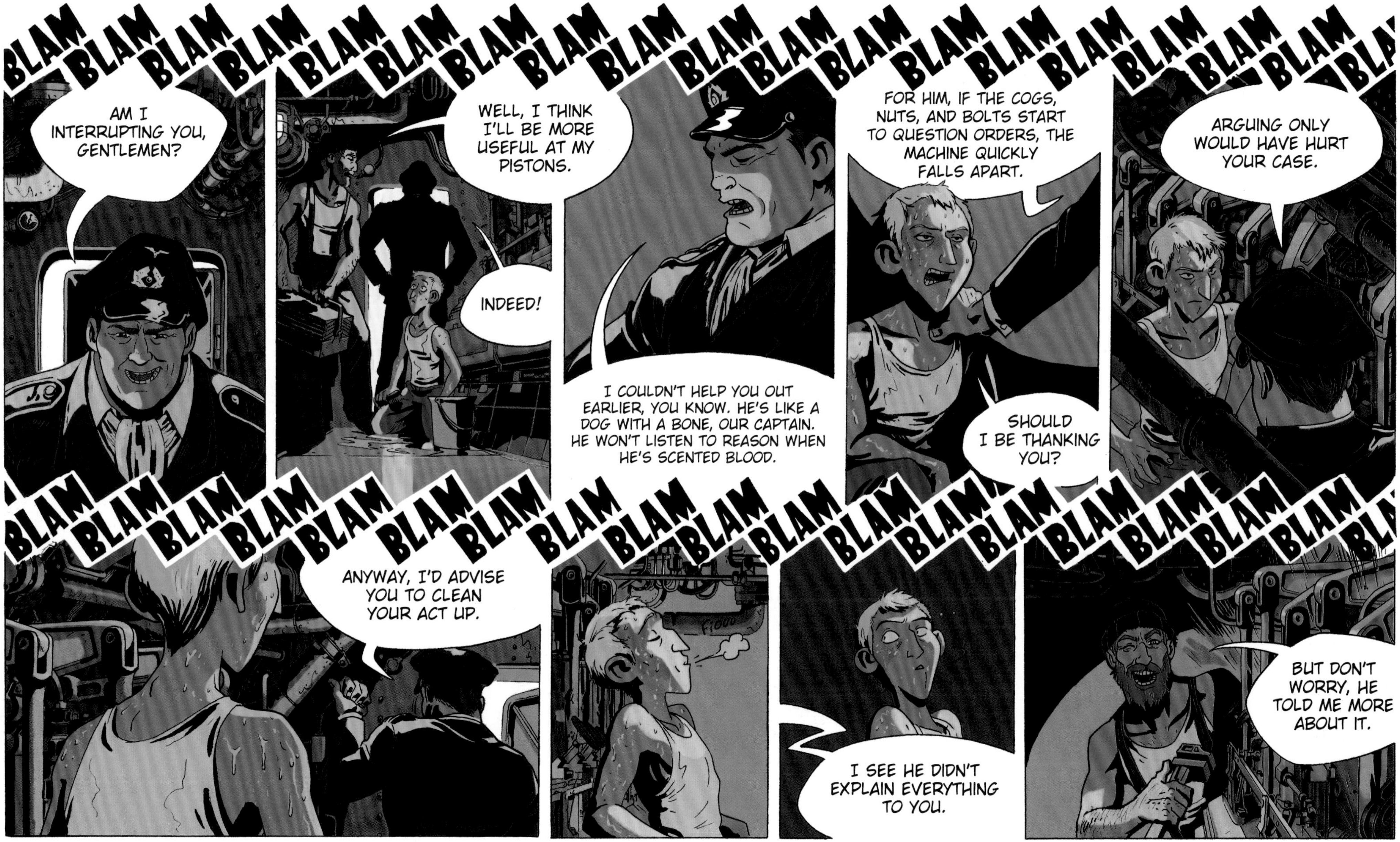
BLAM BLAM BLAM BLAM BLAM BLAM BLAM BLAM BLAM BLAM BLAM BLAM BLAM BLAM BLAM BLAM BLAM BLAM
AM I INTERRUPTING YOU, GENTLEMEN?
WELL, I THINK I'LL BE MORE USEFUL AT MY PISTONS.
INDEED!
I COULDN'T HELP YOU OUT EARLIER, YOU KNOW. HE'S LIKE A DOG WITH A BONE, OUR CAPTAIN. HE WON'T LISTEN TO REASON WHEN HE'S SCENTED BLOOD.
FOR HIM, IF THE COGS, NUTS, AND BOLTS START TO QUESTION ORDERS, THE MACHINE QUICKLY FALLS APART.
SHOULD I BE THANKING YOU?
ARGUING ONLY WOULD HAVE HURT YOUR CASE.
BLAM BLAM BLAM BLAM BLAM BLAM BLAM BLAM BLAM BLAM BLAM BLAM BLAM BLAM BLAM BLAM BLAM BLAM BLAM
ANYWAY, I'D ADVISE YOU TO CLEAN YOUR ACT UP.
FIOUU
I SEE HE DIDN'T EXPLAIN EVERYTHING TO YOU.
BUT DON'T WORRY, HE TOLD ME MORE ABOUT IT.

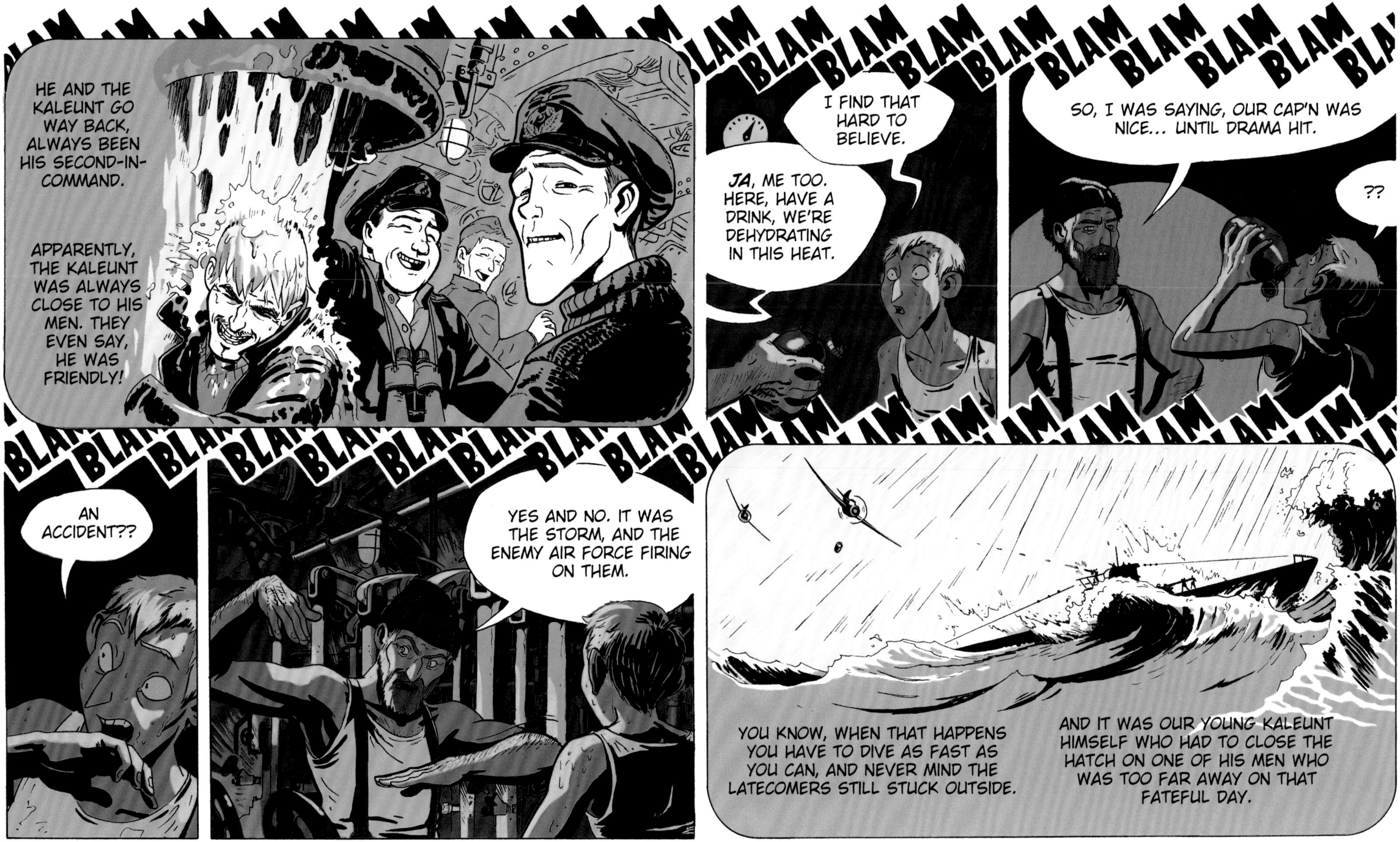

BLAM BLAM BLAM BLAM BLAM BLAM BLAM BLAM BLAM
HE AND THE KALEUNT GO WAY BACK, ALWAYS BEEN HIS SECOND-IN-COMMAND.
APPARENTLY, THE KALEUNT WAS ALWAYS CLOSE TO HIS MEN. THEY EVEN SAY, HE WAS FRIENDLY!
BLAM BLAM BLAM BLAM BLAM BLAM BLAM BLAM BLAM
I FIND THAT HARD TO BELIEVE.
JA, ME TOO. HERE, HAVE A DRINK, WE'RE DEHYDRATING IN THIS HEAT.
SO, I WAS SAYING, OUR CAP'N WAS NICE... UNTIL DRAMA HIT.
??
BLAM BLAM BLAM BLAM BLAM BLAM BLAM BLAM BLAM
AN ACCIDENT??
YES AND NO. IT WAS THE STORM, AND THE ENEMY AIR FORCE FIRING ON THEM.
YOU KNOW, WHEN THAT HAPPENS YOU HAVE TO DIVE AS FAST AS YOU CAN, AND NEVER MIND THE LATECOMERS STILL STUCK OUTSIDE.
AND IT WAS OUR YOUNG KALEUNT HIMSELF WHO HAD TO CLOSE THE HATCH ON ONE OF HIS MEN WHO WAS TOO FAR AWAY ON THAT FATEFUL DAY.

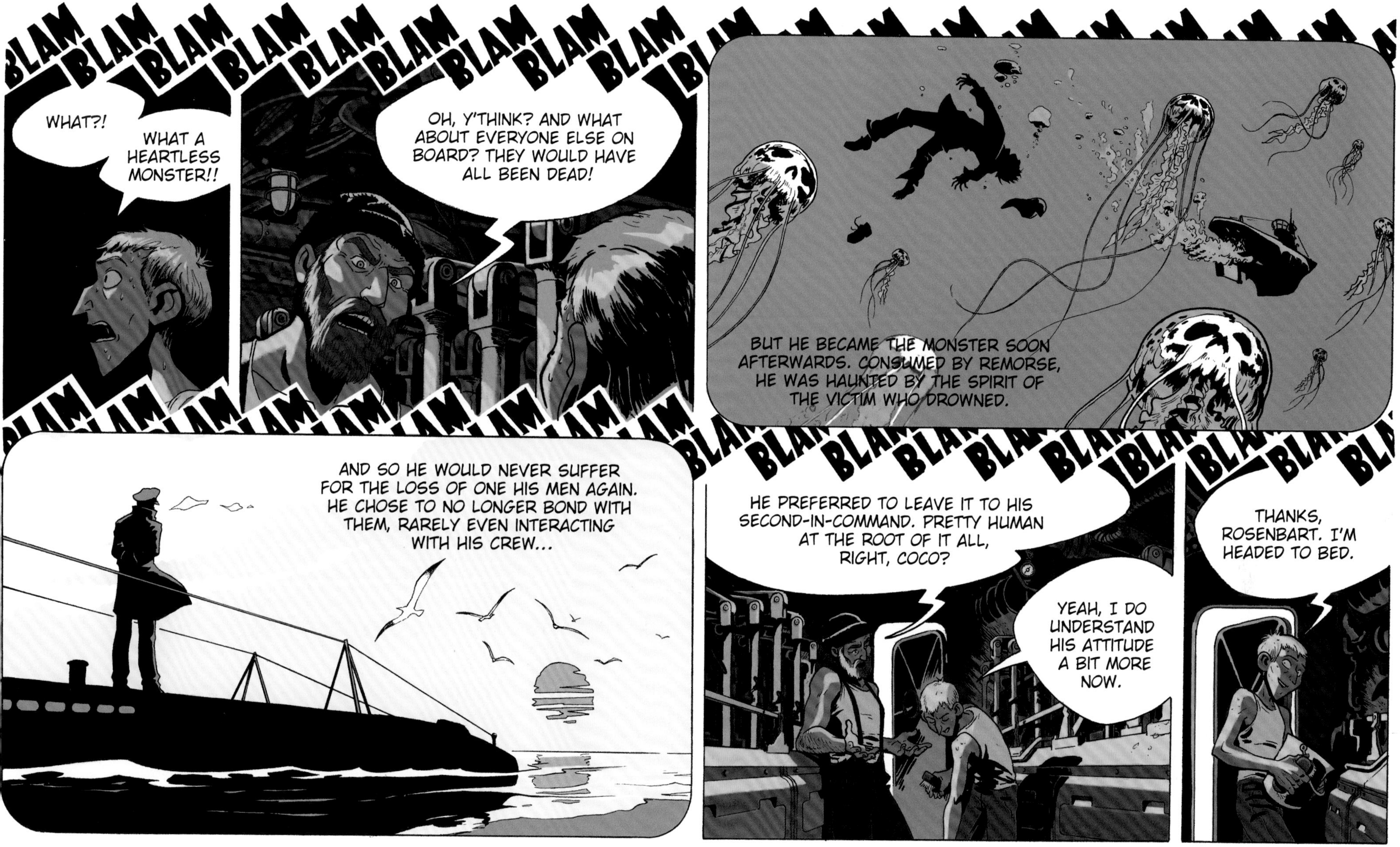
BLAM BLAM BLAM BLAM BLAM BLAM BLAM BLAM BLAM
WHAT?!
WHAT A HEARTLESS MONSTER!!
OH, Y'THINK? AND WHAT ABOUT EVERYONE ELSE ON BOARD? THEY WOULD HAVE ALL BEEN DEAD!
BUT HE BECAME THE MONSTER SOON AFTERWARDS. CONSUMED BY REMORSE, HE WAS HAUNTED BY THE SPIRIT OF THE VICTIM WHO DROWNED.
AND SO HE WOULD NEVER SUFFER FOR THE LOSS OF ONE HIS MEN AGAIN. HE CHOSE TO NO LONGER BOND WITH THEM, RARELY EVEN INTERACTING WITH HIS CREW...
BLAM BLAM BLAM BLAM BLAM BLAM BLAM
HE PREFERRED TO LEAVE IT TO HIS SECOND-IN-COMMAND. PRETTY HUMAN AT THE ROOT OF IT ALL, RIGHT, COCO?
YEAH, I DO UNDERSTAND HIS ATTITUDE A BIT MORE NOW.
THANKS, ROSENBART. I'M HEADED TO BED.

34

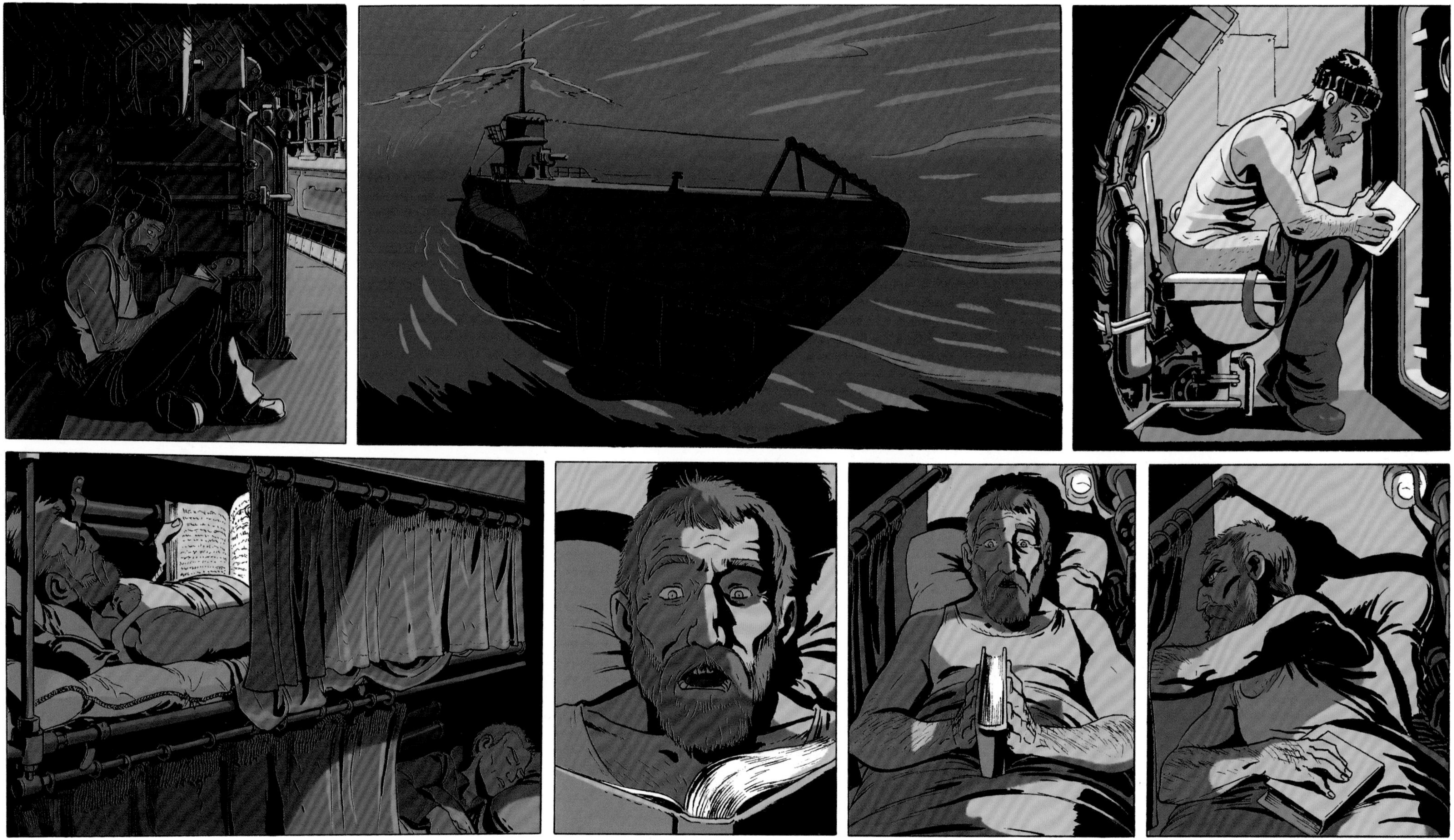

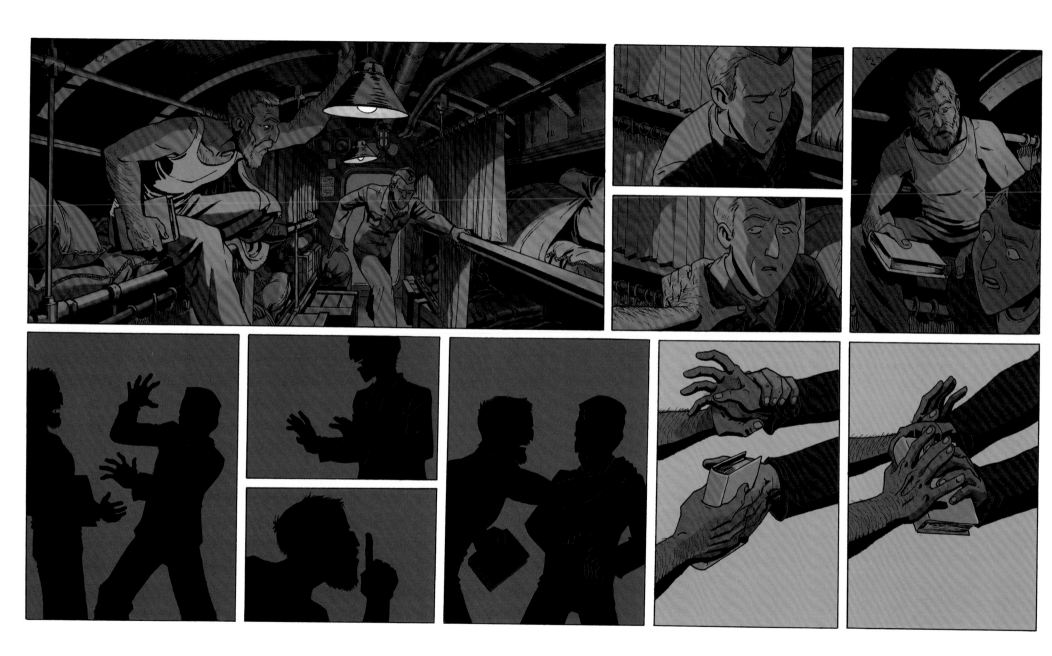

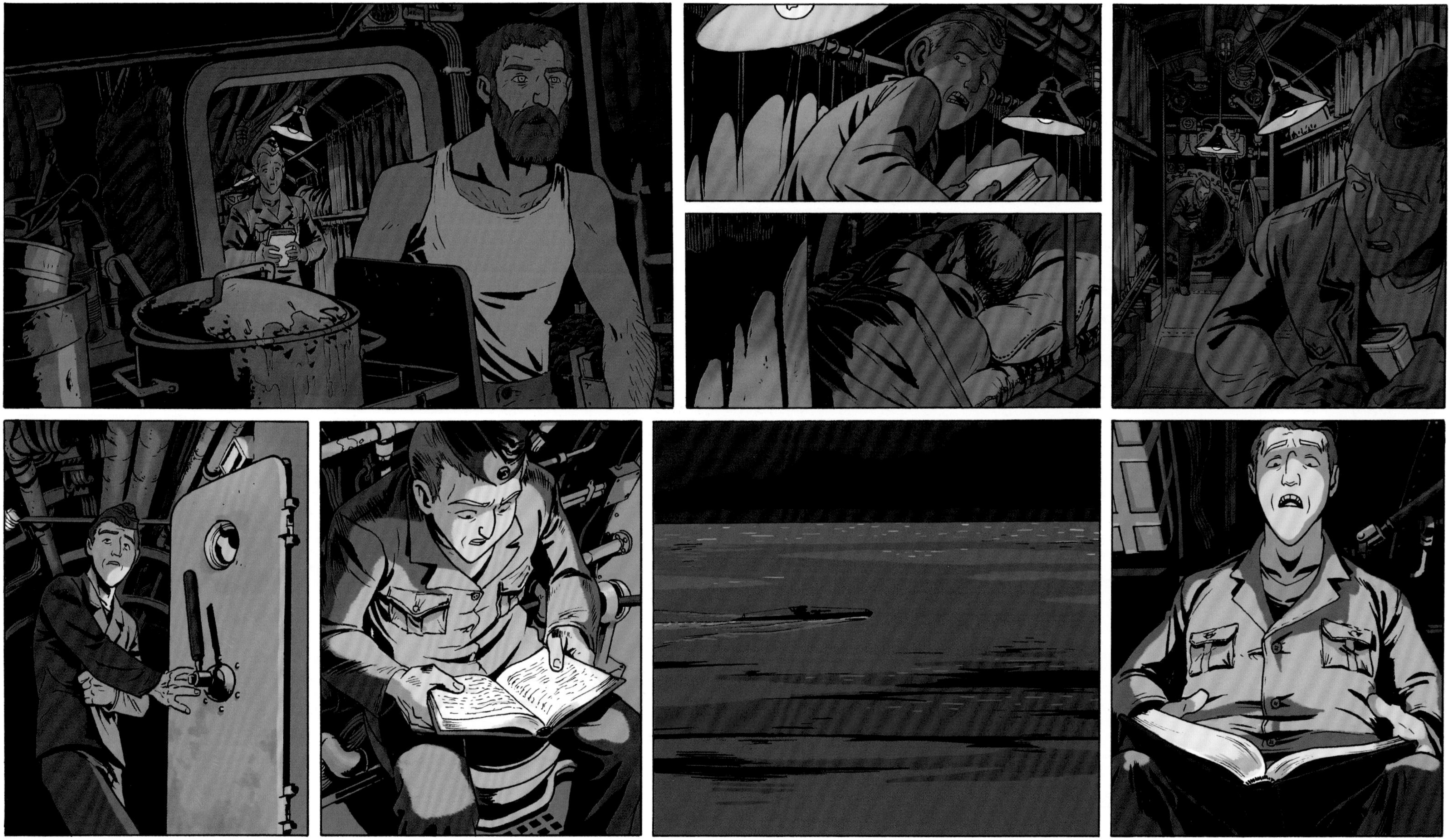

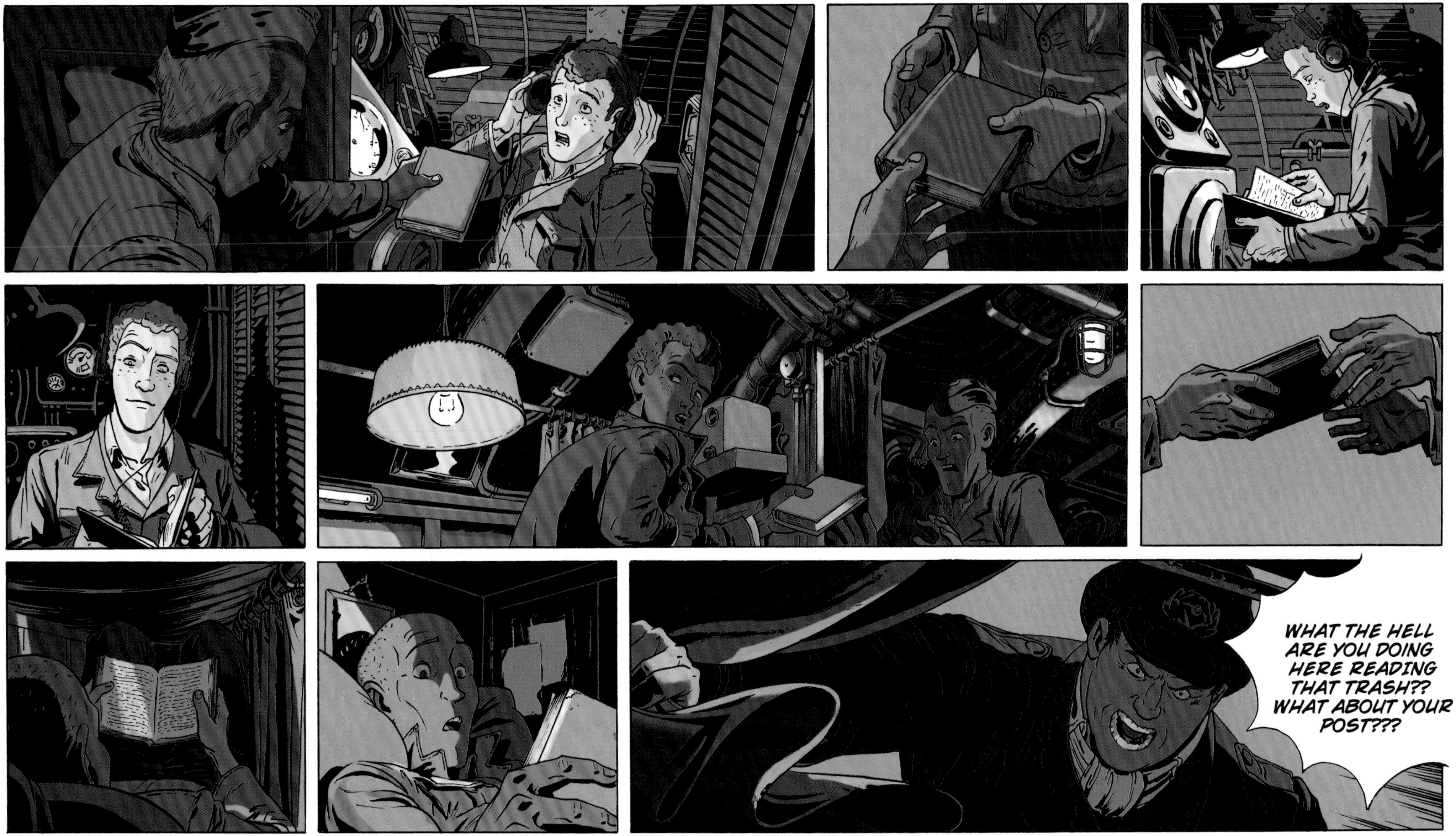
WHAT THE HELL ARE YOU DOING HERE READING THAT TRASH?? WHAT ABOUT YOUR POST???

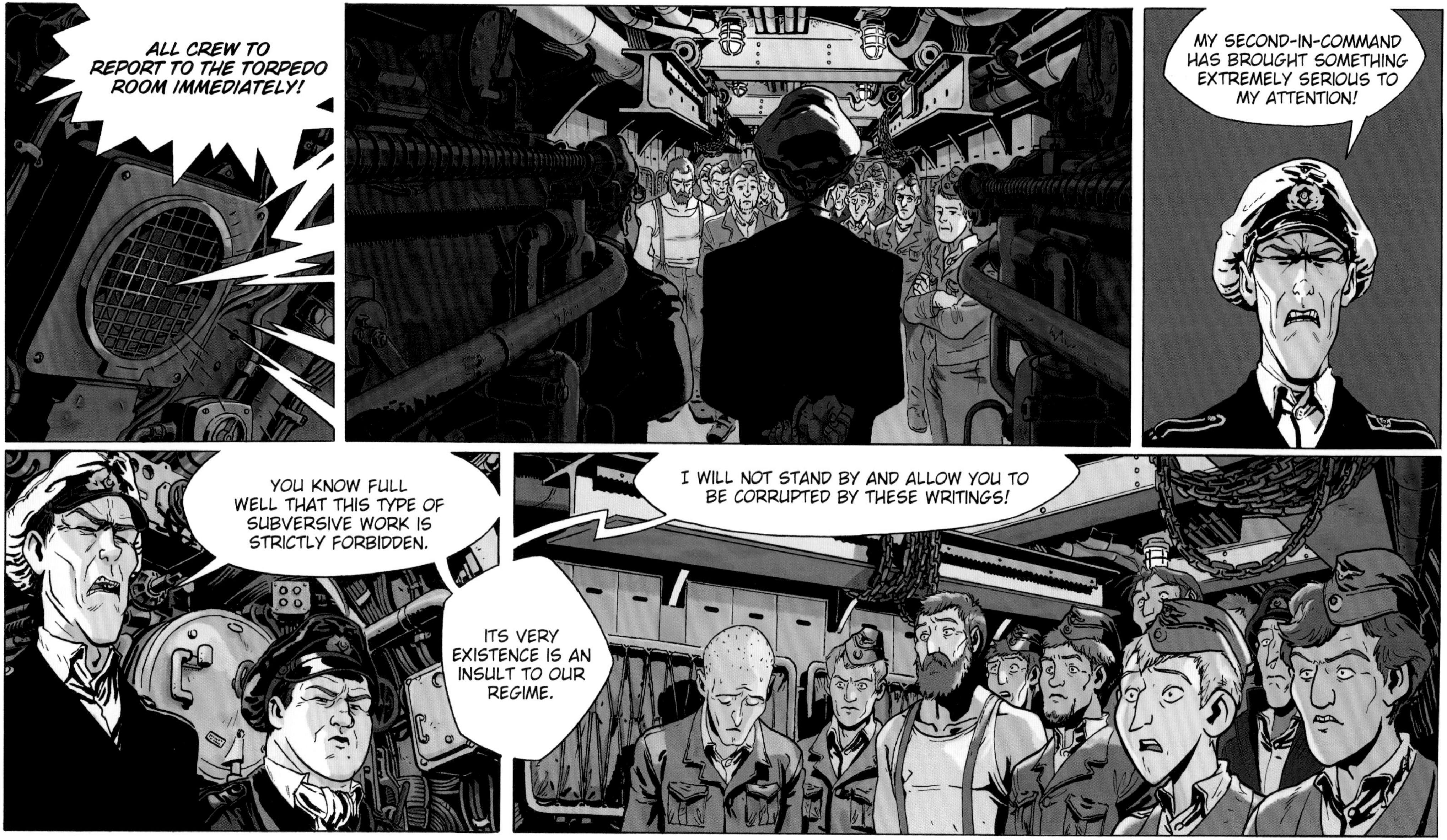
ALL CREW TO REPORT TO THE TORPEDO ROOM IMMEDIATELY!
MY SECOND-IN-COMMAND HAS BROUGHT SOMETHING EXTREMELY SERIOUS TO MY ATTENTION!
YOU KNOW FULL WELL THAT THIS TYPE OF SUBVERSIVE WORK IS STRICTLY FORBIDDEN.
ITS VERY EXISTENCE IS AN INSULT TO OUR REGIME.
I WILL NOT STAND BY AND ALLOW YOU TO BE CORRUPTED BY THESE WRITINGS!

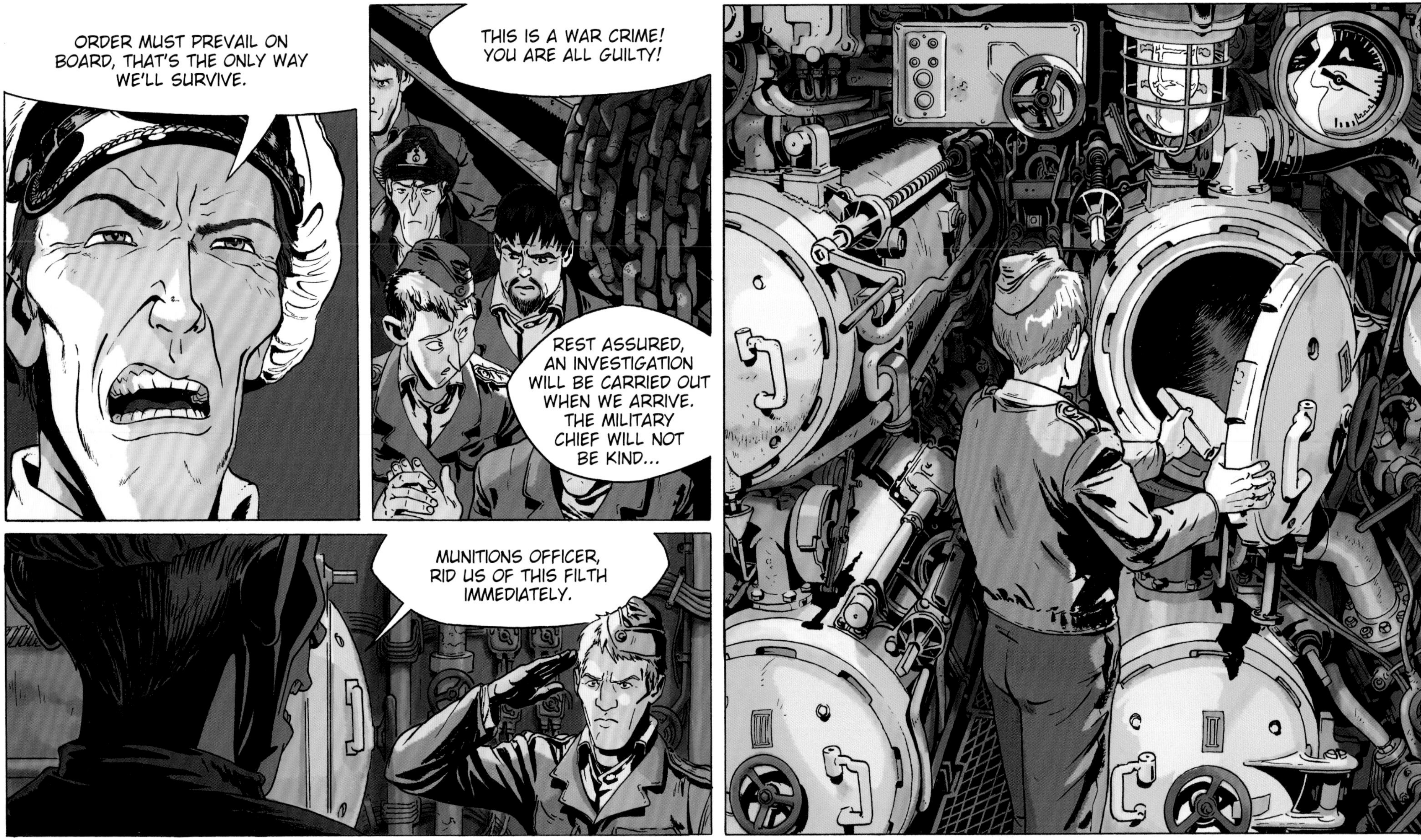
ORDER MUST PREVAIL ON BOARD, THAT'S THE ONLY WAY WE'LL SURVIVE.
THIS IS A WAR CRIME! YOU ARE ALL GUILTY!
REST ASSURED, AN INVESTIGATION WILL BE CARRIED OUT WHEN WE ARRIVE. THE MILITARY CHIEF WILL NOT BE KIND...
MUNITIONS OFFICER, RID US OF THIS FILTH IMMEDIATELY.

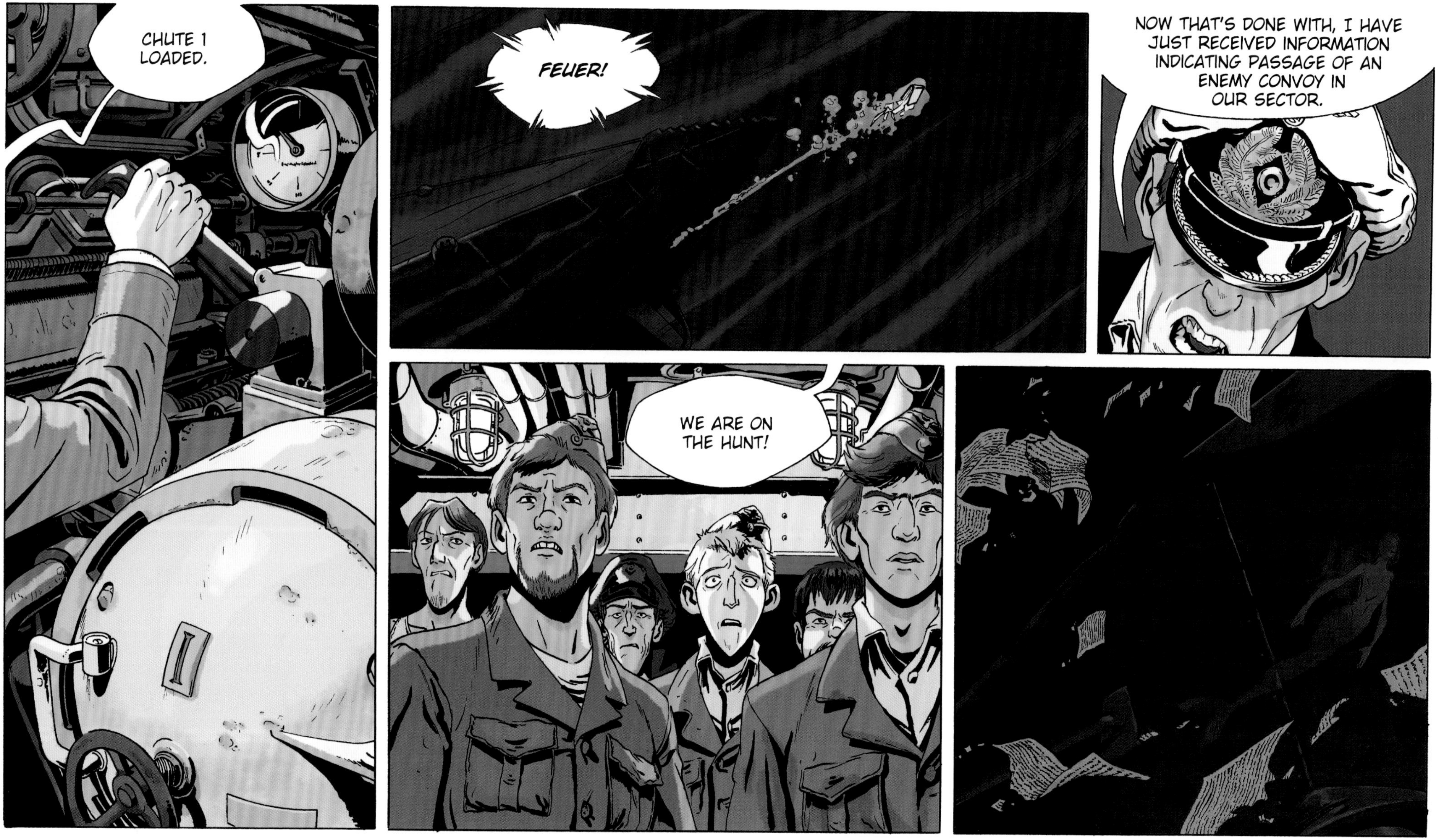
CHUTE 1 LOADED.
FEUER!
NOW THAT'S DONE WITH, I HAVE JUST RECEIVED INFORMATION INDICATING PASSAGE OF AN ENEMY CONVOY IN OUR SECTOR.
WE ARE ON THE HUNT!

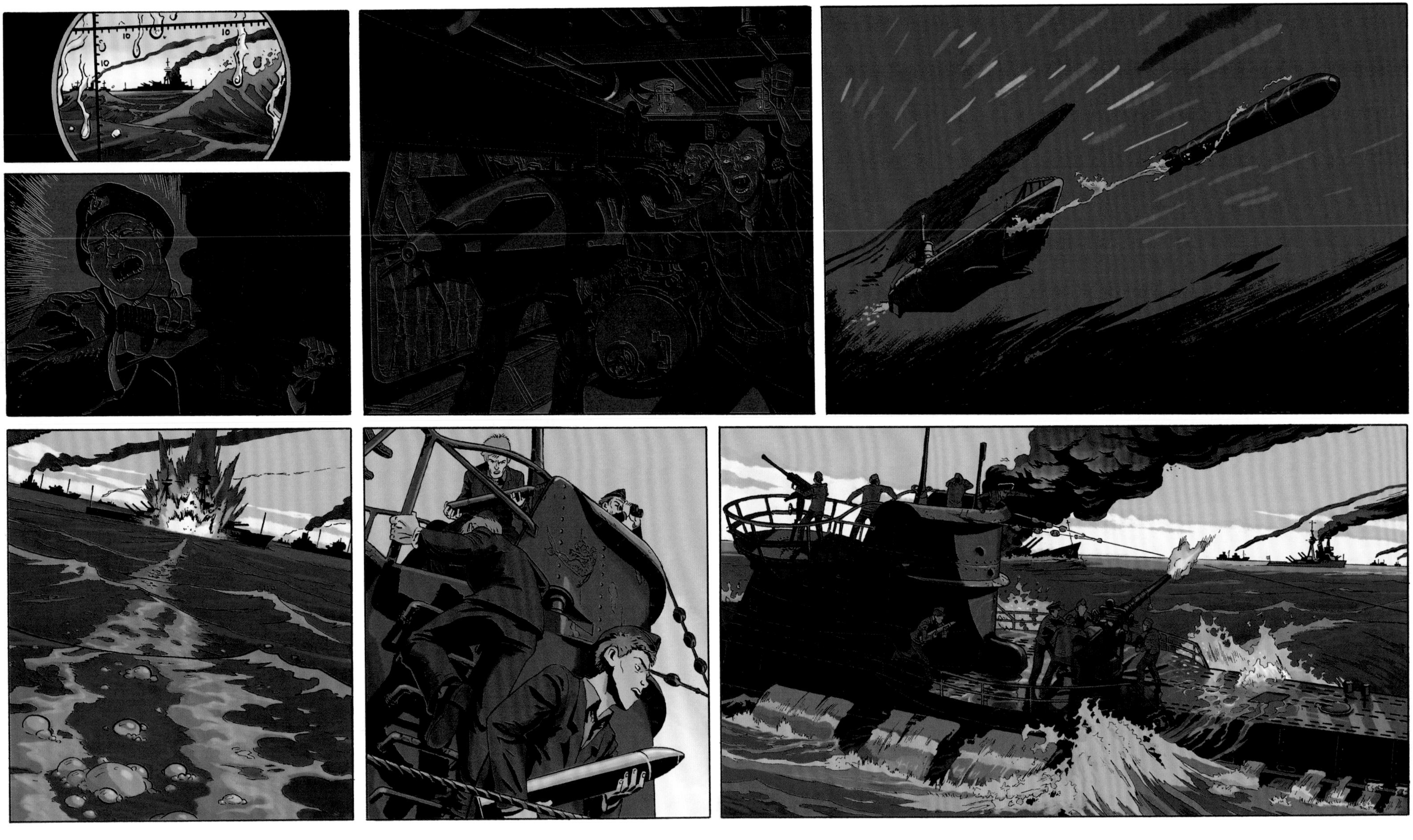

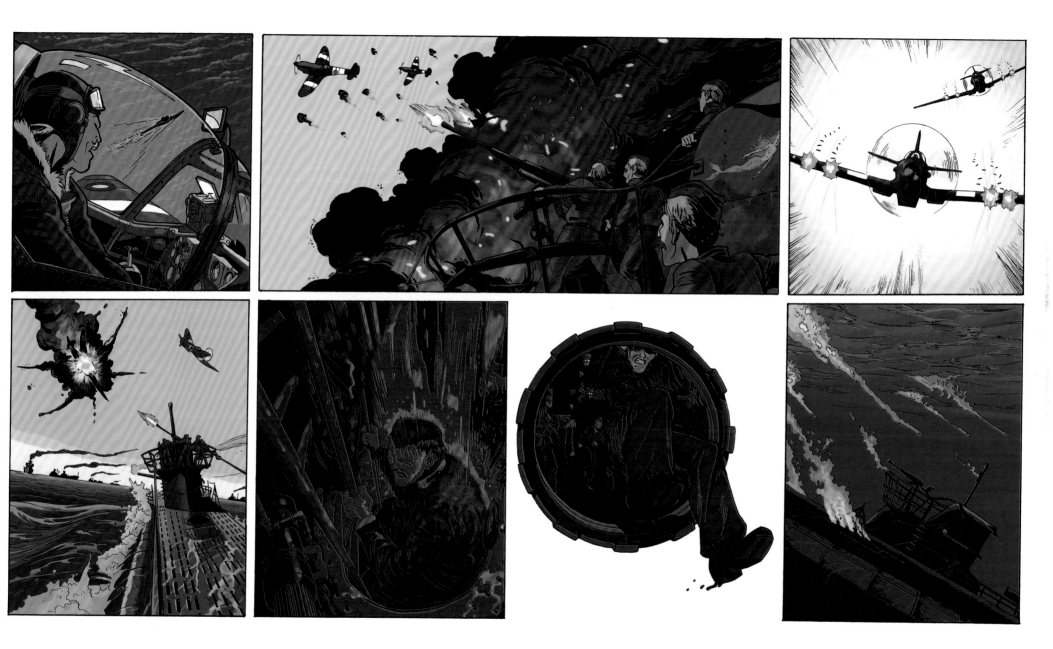

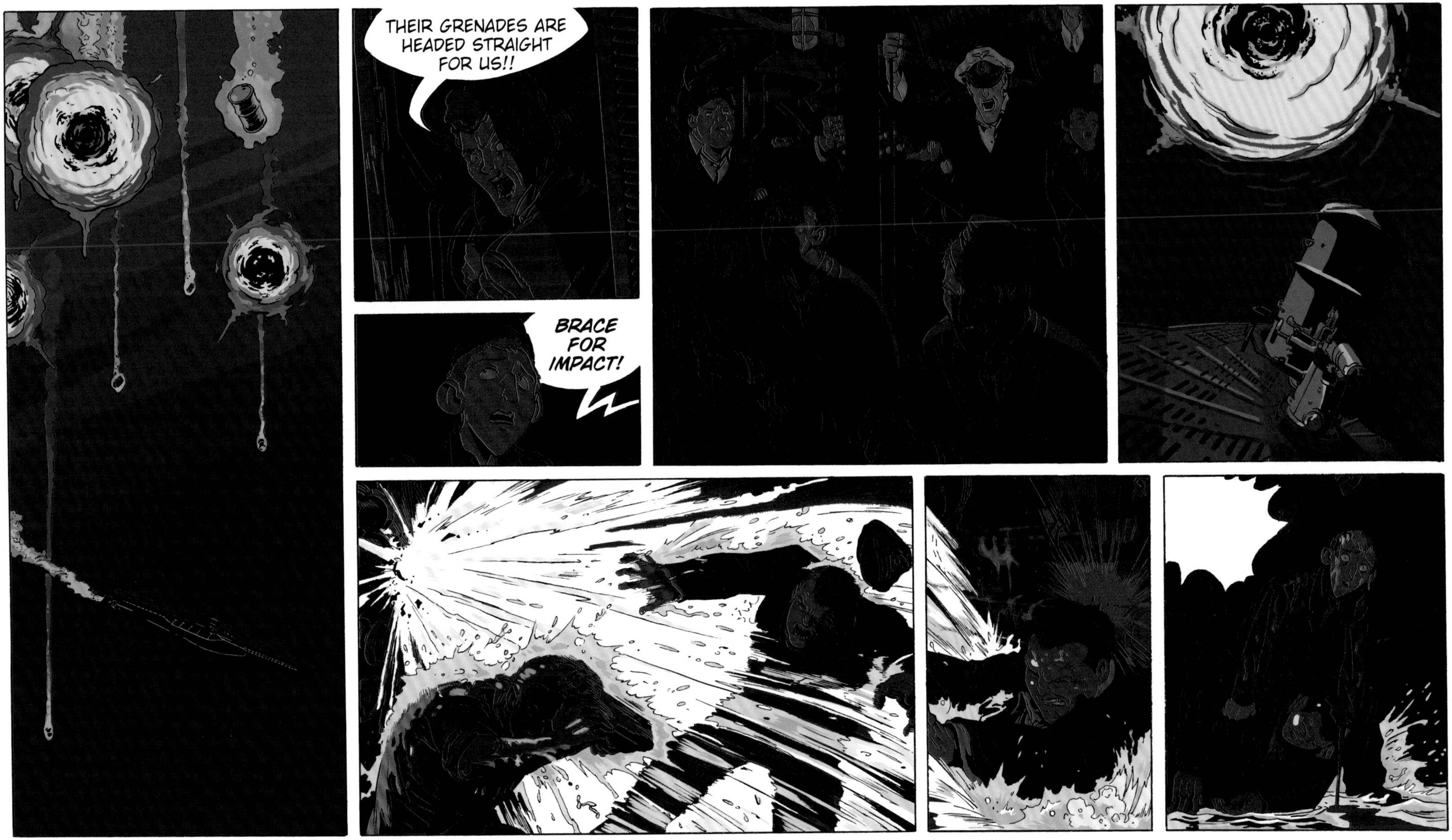
THEIR GRENADES ARE HEADED STRAIGHT FOR US!!
BRACE FOR IMPACT!

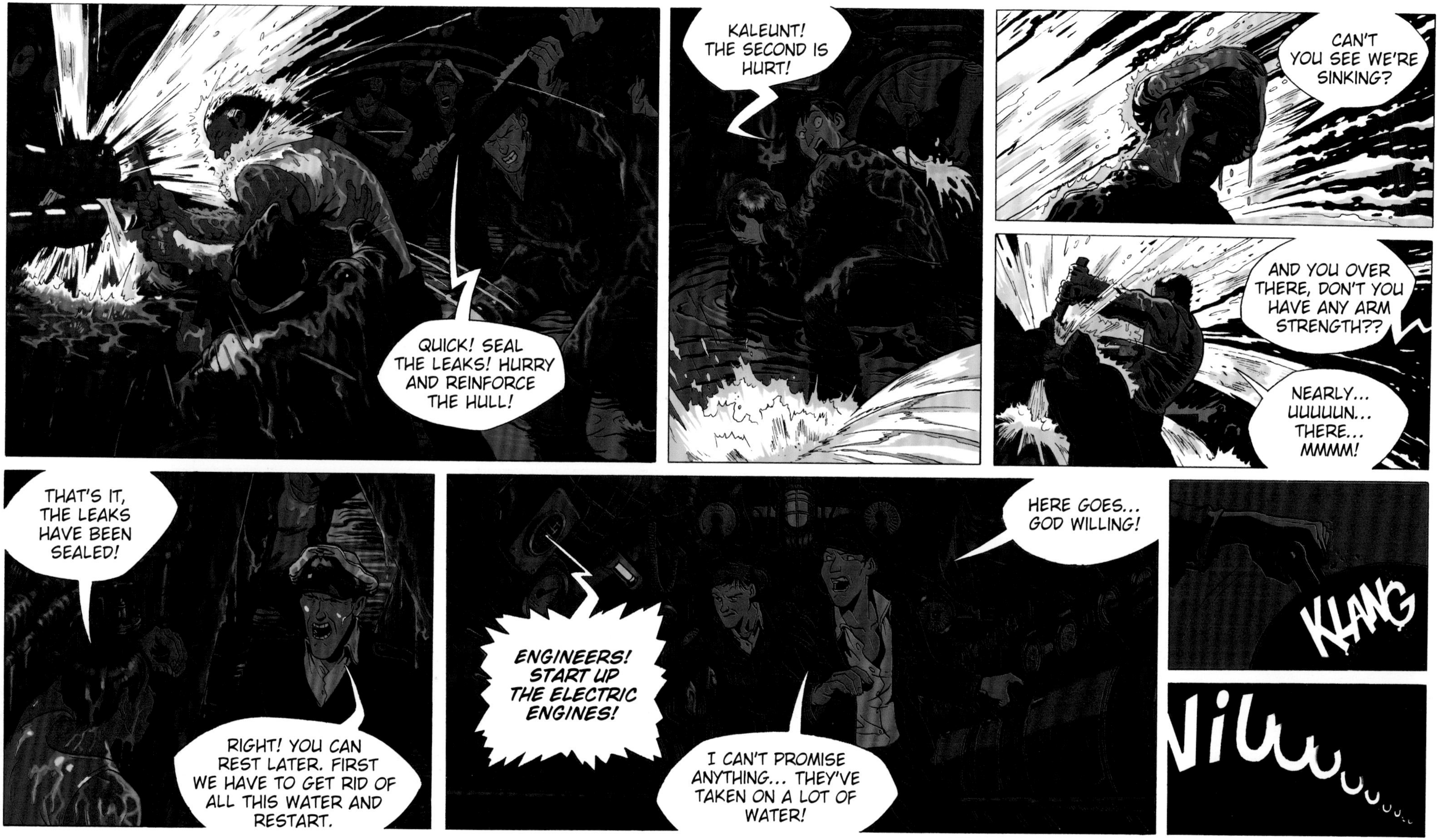
QUICK! SEAL THE LEAKS! HURRY AND REINFORCE THE HULL!
KALEUNT! THE SECOND IS HURT!
CAN'T YOU SEE WE'RE SINKING?
AND YOU OVER THERE, DON'T YOU HAVE ANY ARM STRENGTH??
NEARLY... UUUUUN... THERE... MMMM!
THAT'S IT, THE LEAKS HAVE BEEN SEALED!
RIGHT! YOU CAN REST LATER. FIRST WE HAVE TO GET RID OF ALL THIS WATER AND RESTART.
ENGINEERS! START UP THE ELECTRIC ENGINES!
HERE GOES... GOD WILLING!
I CAN'T PROMISE ANYTHING... THEY'VE TAKEN ON A LOT OF WATER!
KLANG
NIUUUUUU...

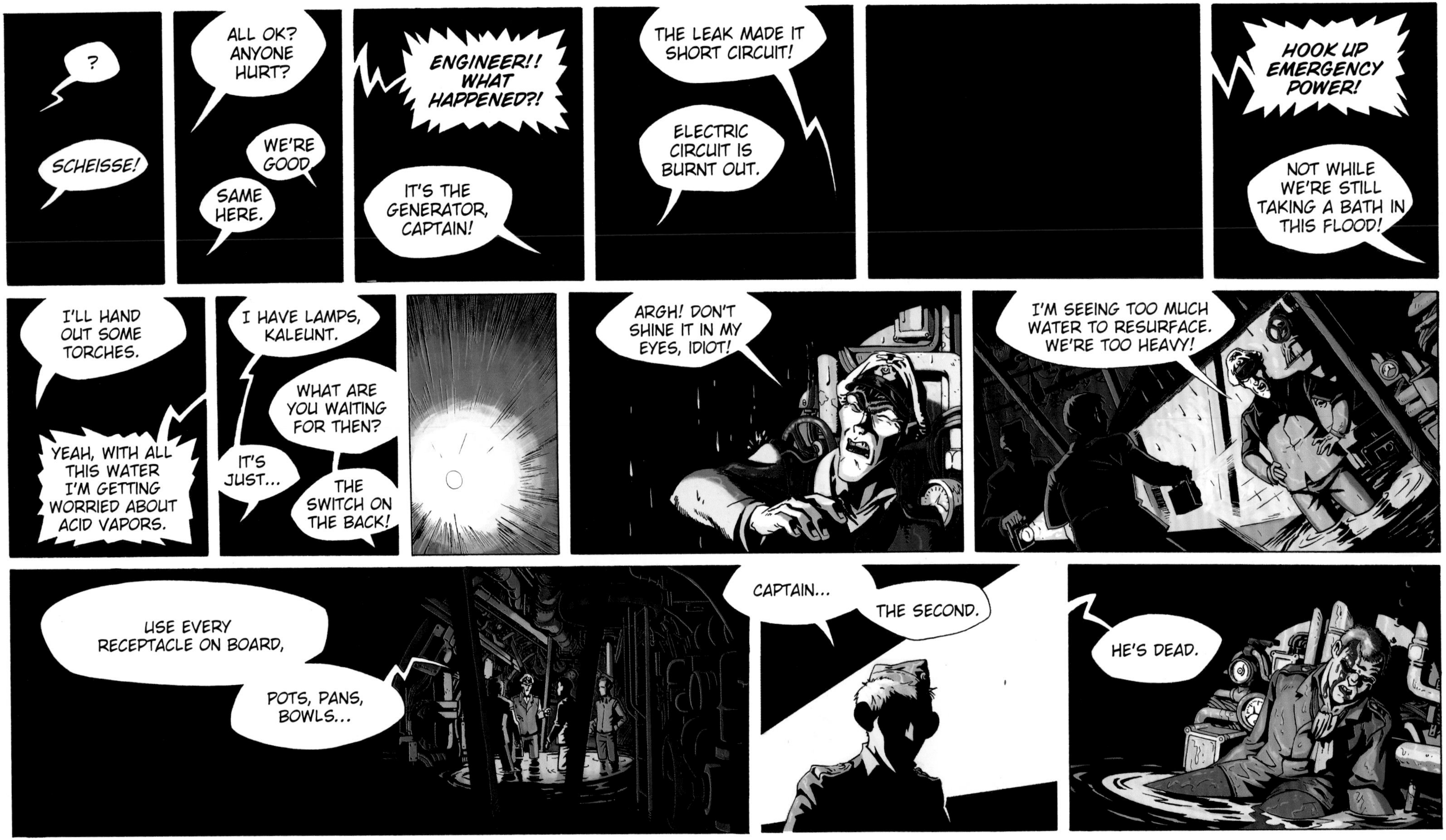
?
SCHEISSE!
ALL OK? ANYONE HURT?
WE'RE GOOD.
SAME HERE.
ENGINEER!! WHAT HAPPENED?!
IT'S THE GENERATOR, CAPTAIN!
THE LEAK MADE IT SHORT CIRCUIT!
ELECTRIC CIRCUIT IS BURNT OUT.
HOOK UP EMERGENCY POWER!
NOT WHILE WE'RE STILL TAKING A BATH IN THIS FLOOD!
I'LL HAND OUT SOME TORCHES.
YEAH, WITH ALL THIS WATER I'M GETTING WORRIED ABOUT ACID VAPORS.
I HAVE LAMPS, KALEUNT.
WHAT ARE YOU WAITING FOR THEN?
IT'S JUST...
THE SWITCH ON THE BACK!
ARGH! DON'T SHINE IT IN MY EYES, IDIOT!
I'M SEEING TOO MUCH WATER TO RESURFACE. WE'RE TOO HEAVY!
USE EVERY RECEPTACLE ON BOARD,
POTS, PANS, BOWLS...
CAPTAIN...
THE SECOND.
HE'S DEAD.

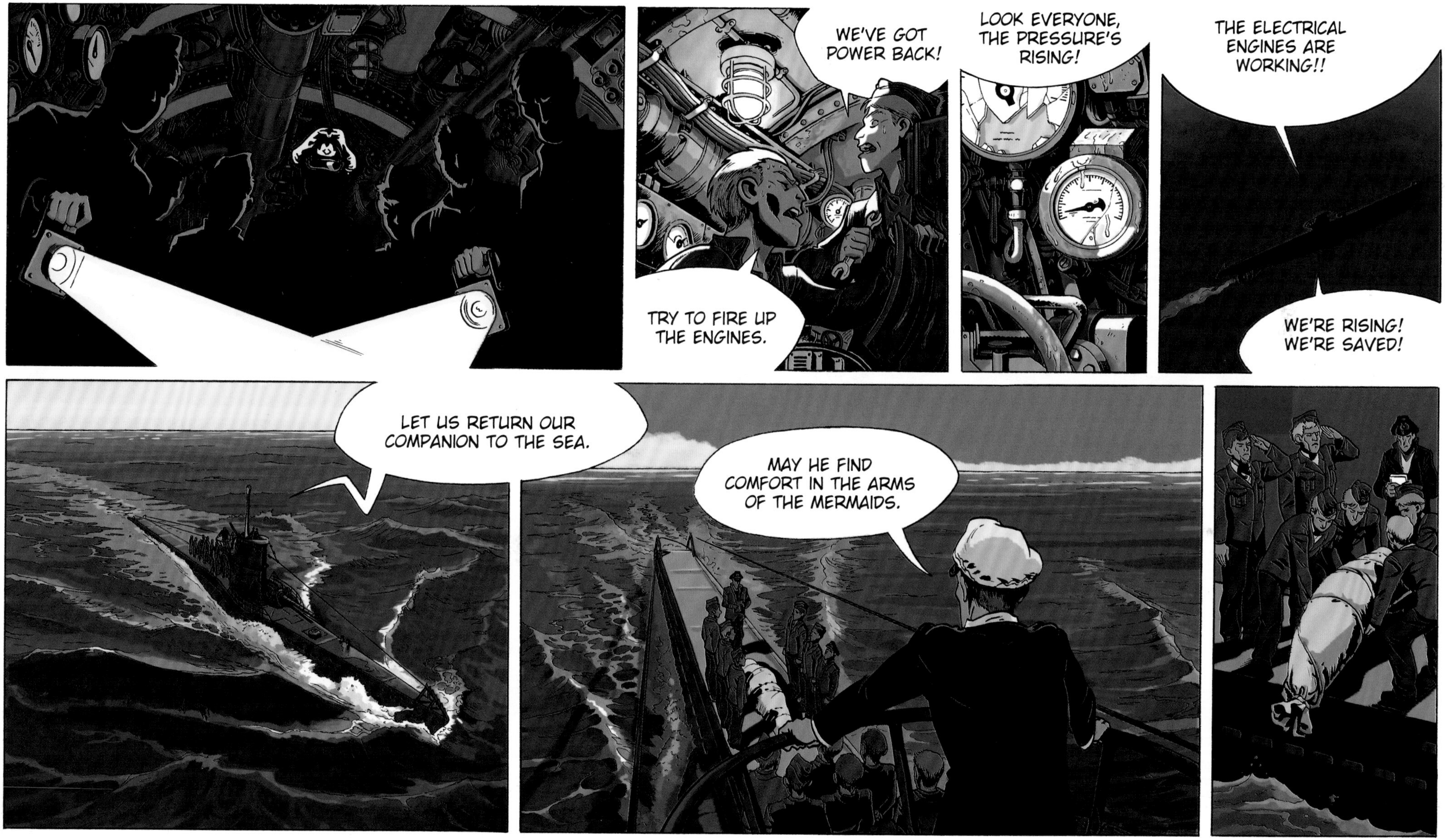
WE'VE GOT POWER BACK!
TRY TO FIRE UP THE ENGINES.
LOOK EVERYONE, THE PRESSURE'S RISING!
THE ELECTRICAL ENGINES ARE WORKING!!
WE'RE RISING! WE'RE SAVED!
LET US RETURN OUR COMPANION TO THE SEA.
MAY HE FIND COMFORT IN THE ARMS OF THE MERMAIDS.

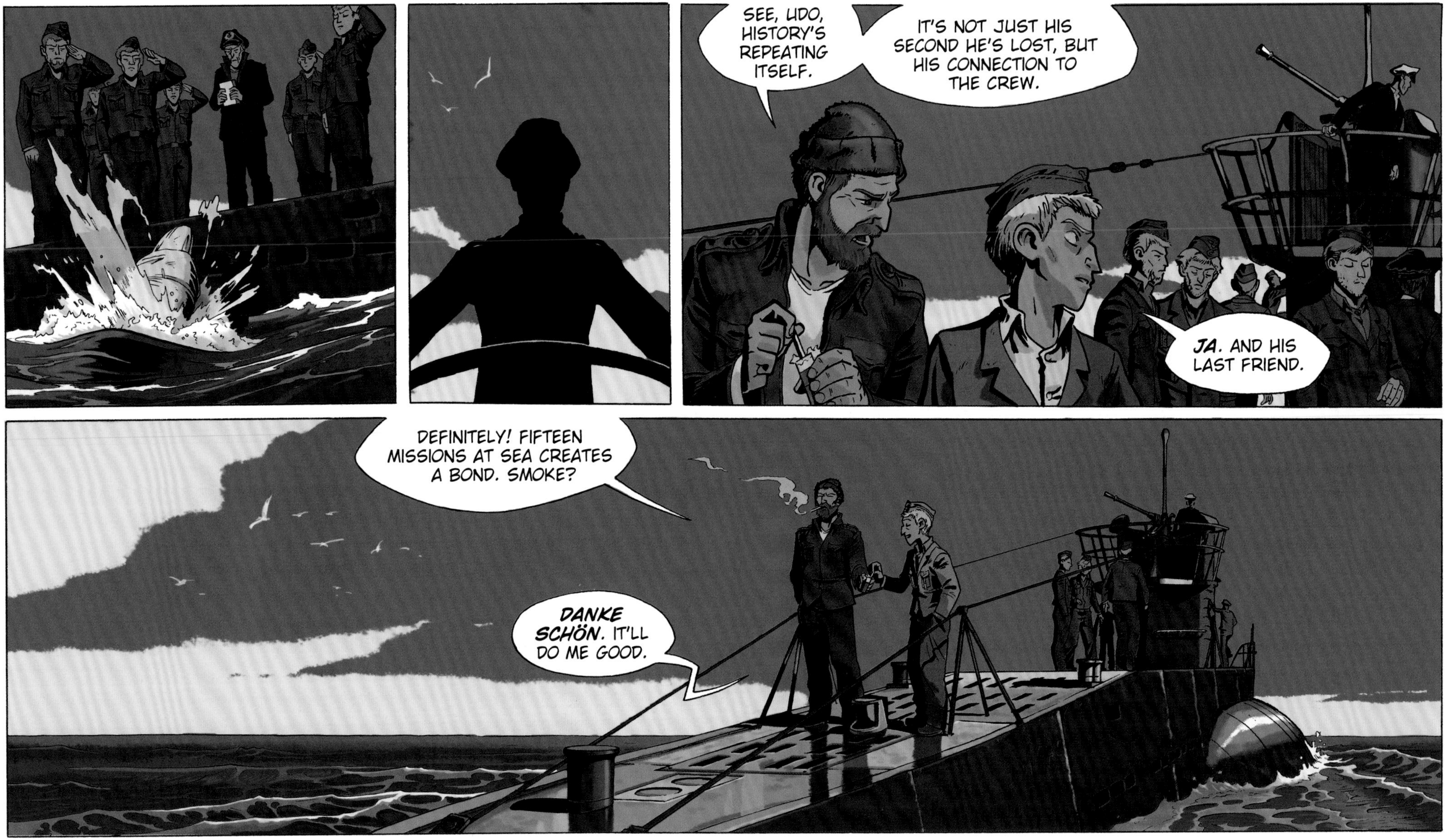
SEE, UDO, HISTORY'S REPEATING ITSELF.
IT'S NOT JUST HIS SECOND HE'S LOST, BUT HIS CONNECTION TO THE CREW.
JA. AND HIS LAST FRIEND.
DEFINITELY! FIFTEEN MISSIONS AT SEA CREATES A BOND. SMOKE?
DANKE SCHÖN. IT'LL DO ME GOOD.

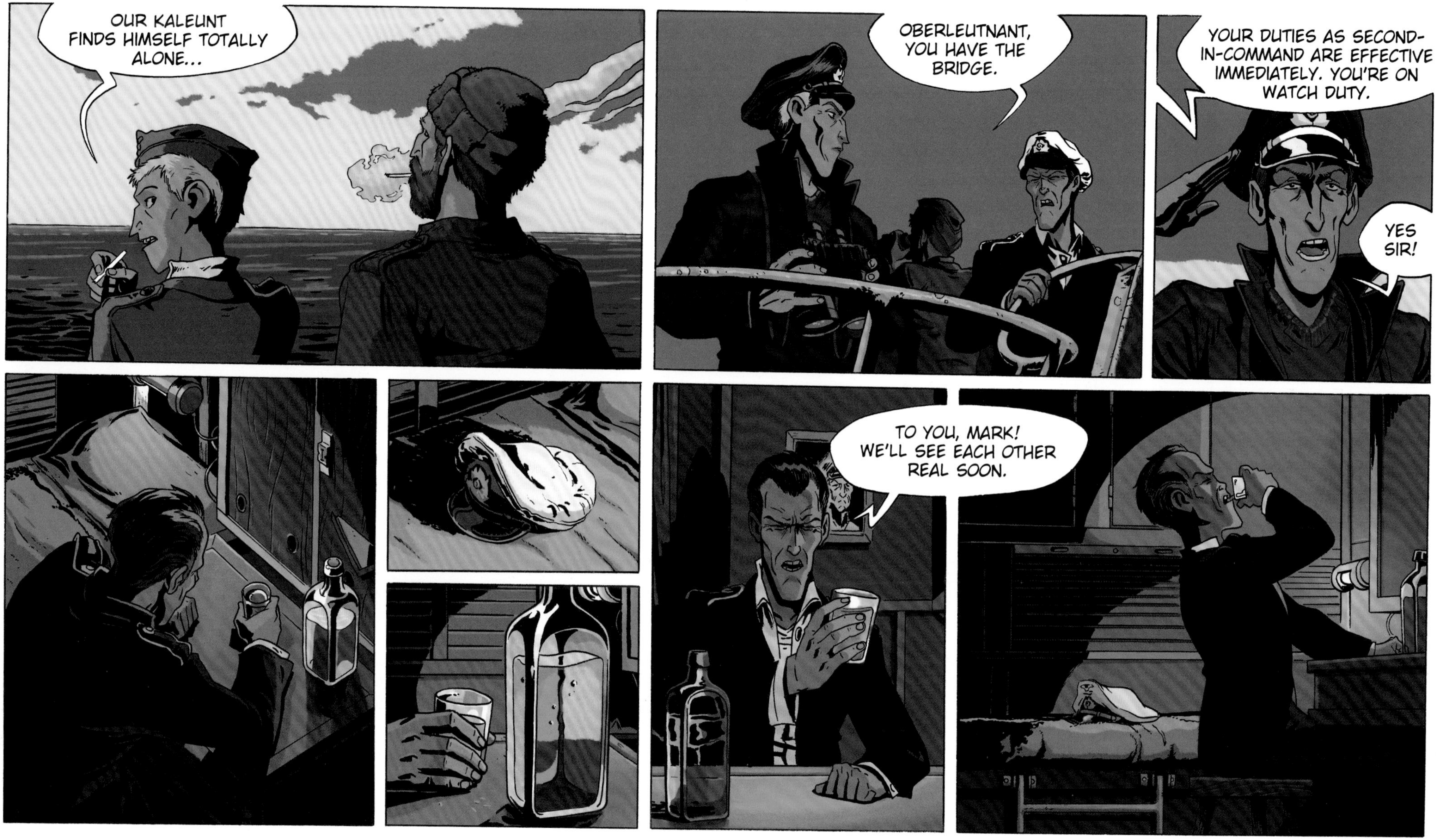
OUR KALEUNT FINDS HIMSELF TOTALLY ALONE...
OBERLEUTNANT, YOU HAVE THE BRIDGE.
YOUR DUTIES AS SECOND-IN-COMMAND ARE EFFECTIVE IMMEDIATELY. YOU'RE ON WATCH DUTY.
YES SIR!
TO YOU, MARK! WE'LL SEE EACH OTHER REAL SOON.

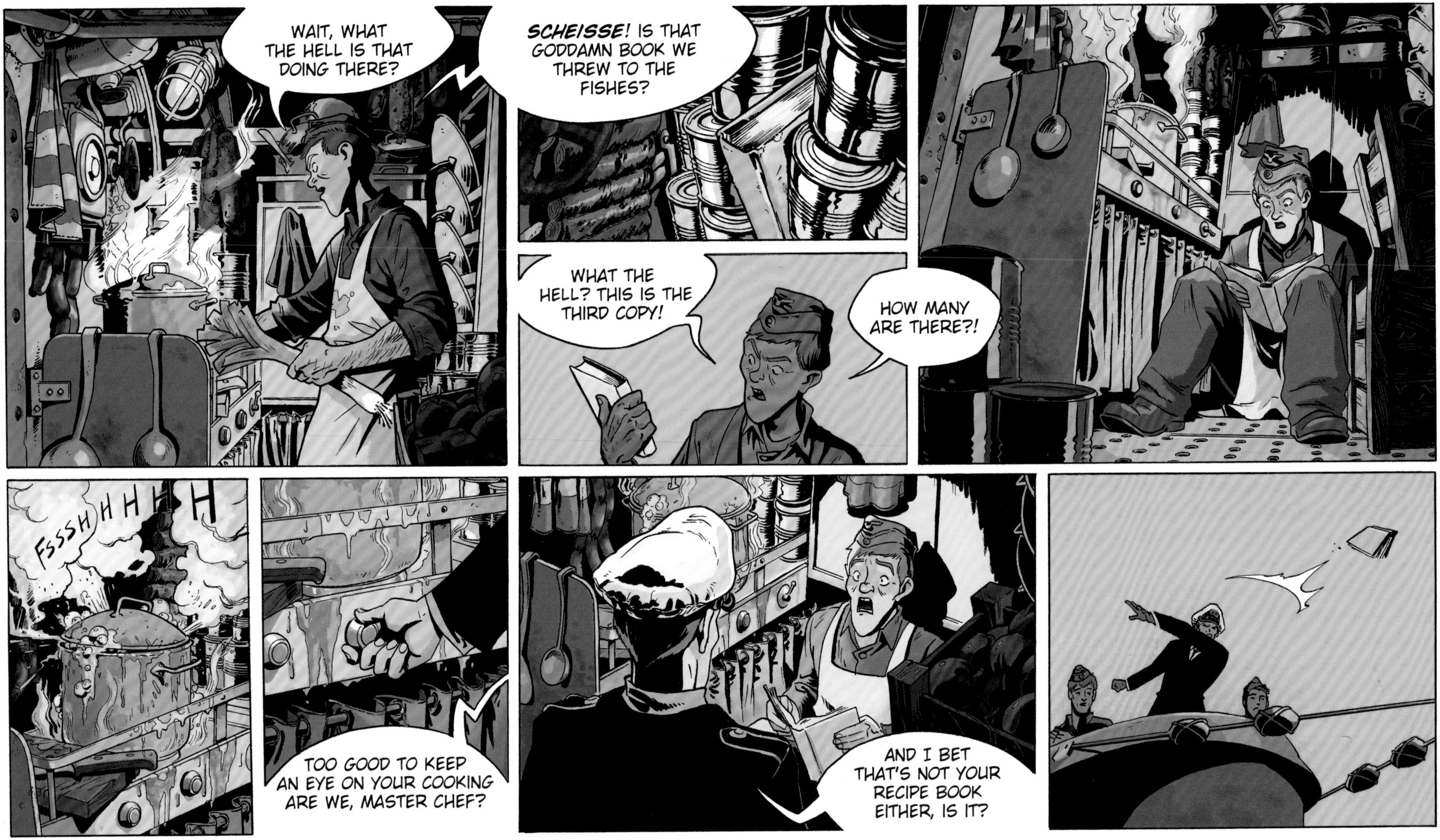
WAIT, WHAT THE HELL IS THAT DOING THERE?
SCHEISSE! IS THAT GODDAMN BOOK WE THREW TO THE FISHES?
WHAT THE HELL? THIS IS THE THIRD COPY!
HOW MANY ARE THERE?!
FSSSHHHHH
TOO GOOD TO KEEP AN EYE ON YOUR COOKING ARE WE, MASTER CHEF?
AND I BET THAT'S NOT YOUR RECIPE BOOK EITHER, IS IT?

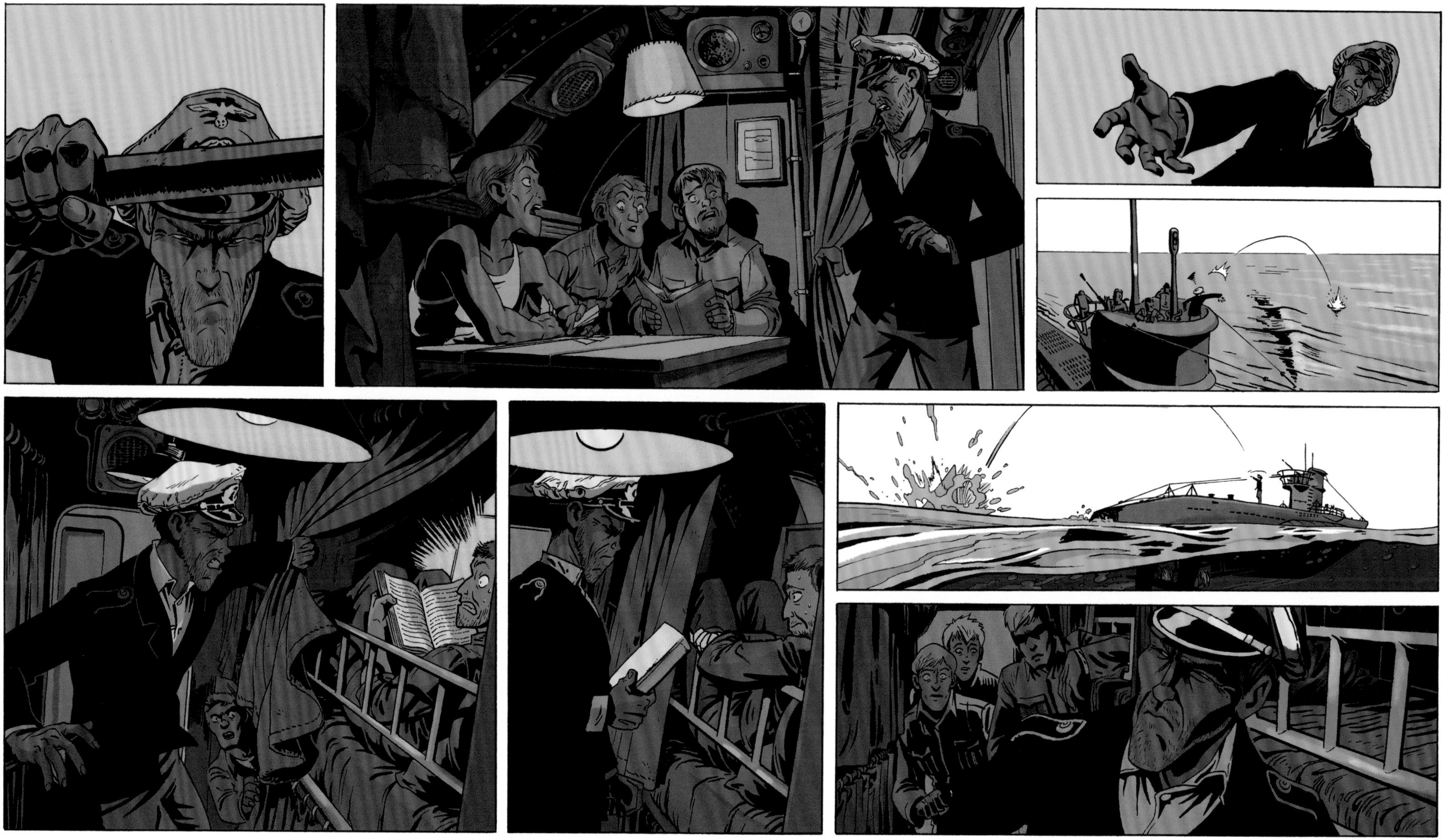

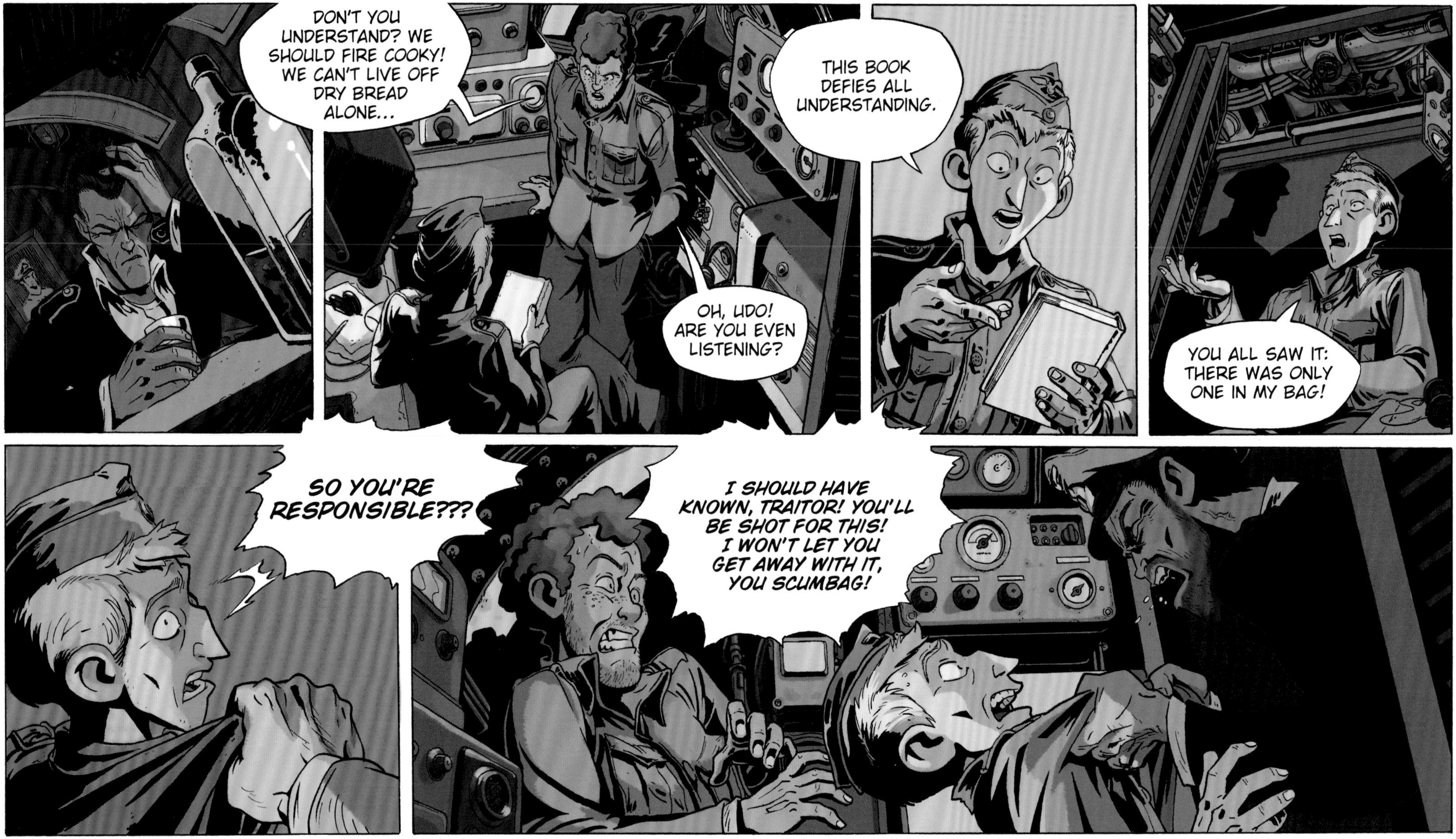
DON'T YOU UNDERSTAND? WE SHOULD FIRE COOKY! WE CAN'T LIVE OFF DRY BREAD ALONE...
OH, UDO! ARE YOU EVEN LISTENING?
THIS BOOK DEFIES ALL UNDERSTANDING.
YOU ALL SAW IT: THERE WAS ONLY ONE IN MY BAG!
SO YOU'RE RESPONSIBLE???
I SHOULD HAVE KNOWN, TRAITOR! YOU'LL BE SHOT FOR THIS! I WON'T LET YOU GET AWAY WITH IT, YOU SCUMBAG!

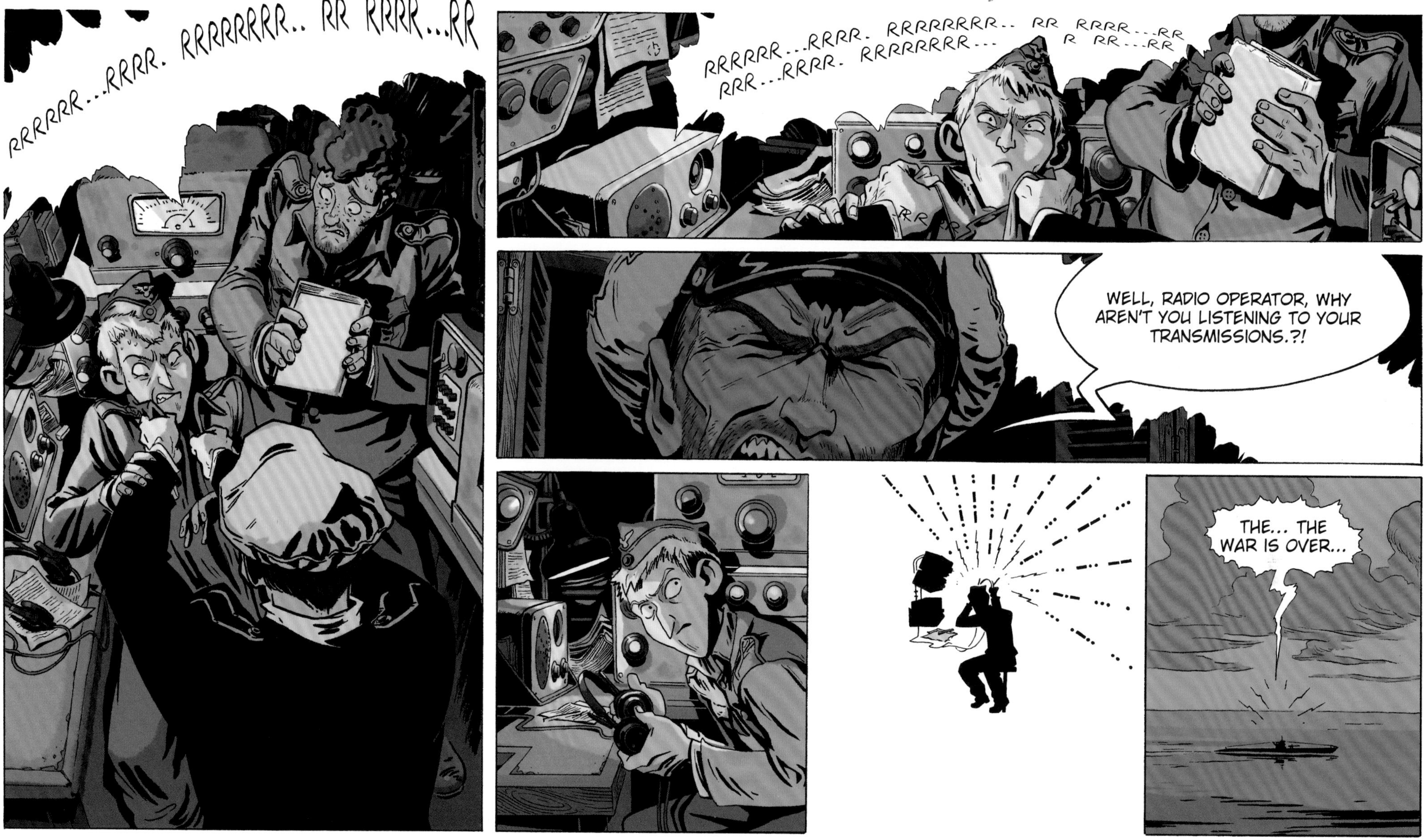
RRRRRR...RRRR. RRRRRRRR.. RR RRRR...RR
RRRRRR...RRRR. RRRRRRRR.. RR RRRR...RR
RRR...RRRR. RRRRRRRR... R RR...RR
WELL, RADIO OPERATOR, WHY AREN'T YOU LISTENING TO YOUR TRANSMISSIONS.?!
THE... THE WAR IS OVER...

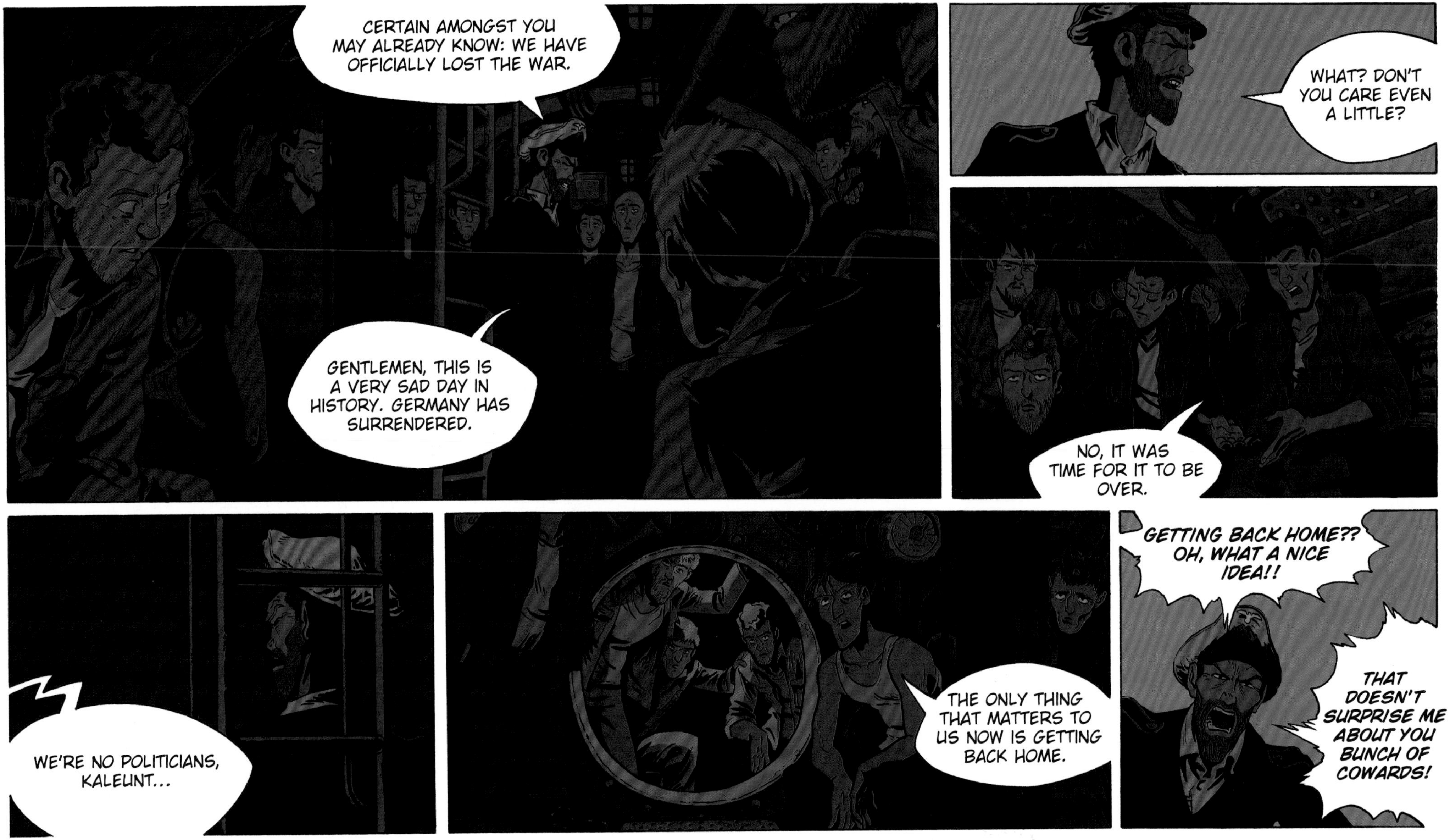

CERTAIN AMONGST YOU MAY ALREADY KNOW: WE HAVE OFFICIALLY LOST THE WAR.
GENTLEMEN, THIS IS A VERY SAD DAY IN HISTORY. GERMANY HAS SURRENDERED.
WHAT? DON'T YOU CARE EVEN A LITTLE?
NO, IT WAS TIME FOR IT TO BE OVER.
WE'RE NO POLITICIANS, KALEUNT...
THE ONLY THING THAT MATTERS TO US NOW IS GETTING BACK HOME.
GETTING BACK HOME?? OH, WHAT A NICE IDEA!!
THAT DOESN'T SURPRISE ME ABOUT YOU BUNCH OF COWARDS!

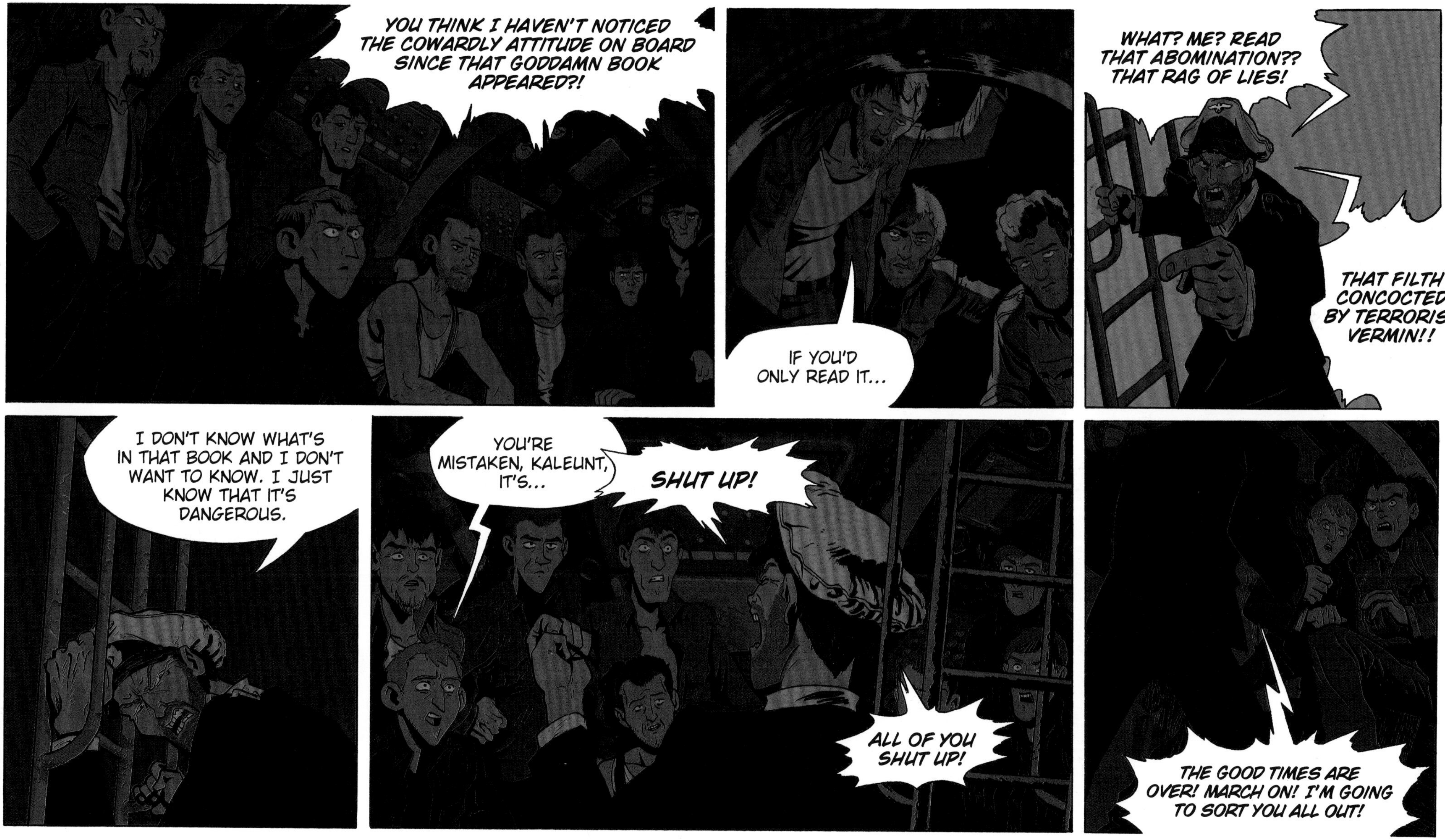
YOU THINK I HAVEN'T NOTICED THE COWARDLY ATTITUDE ON BOARD SINCE THAT GODDAMN BOOK APPEARED?!
IF YOU'D ONLY READ IT...
WHAT? ME? READ THAT ABOMINATION?? THAT RAG OF LIES!
THAT FILTH CONCOCTED BY TERRORIST VERMIN!!
I DON'T KNOW WHAT'S IN THAT BOOK AND I DON'T WANT TO KNOW. I JUST KNOW THAT IT'S DANGEROUS.
YOU'RE MISTAKEN, KALEUNT, IT'S...
SHUT UP!
ALL OF YOU SHUT UP!
THE GOOD TIMES ARE OVER! MARCH ON! I'M GOING TO SORT YOU ALL OUT!

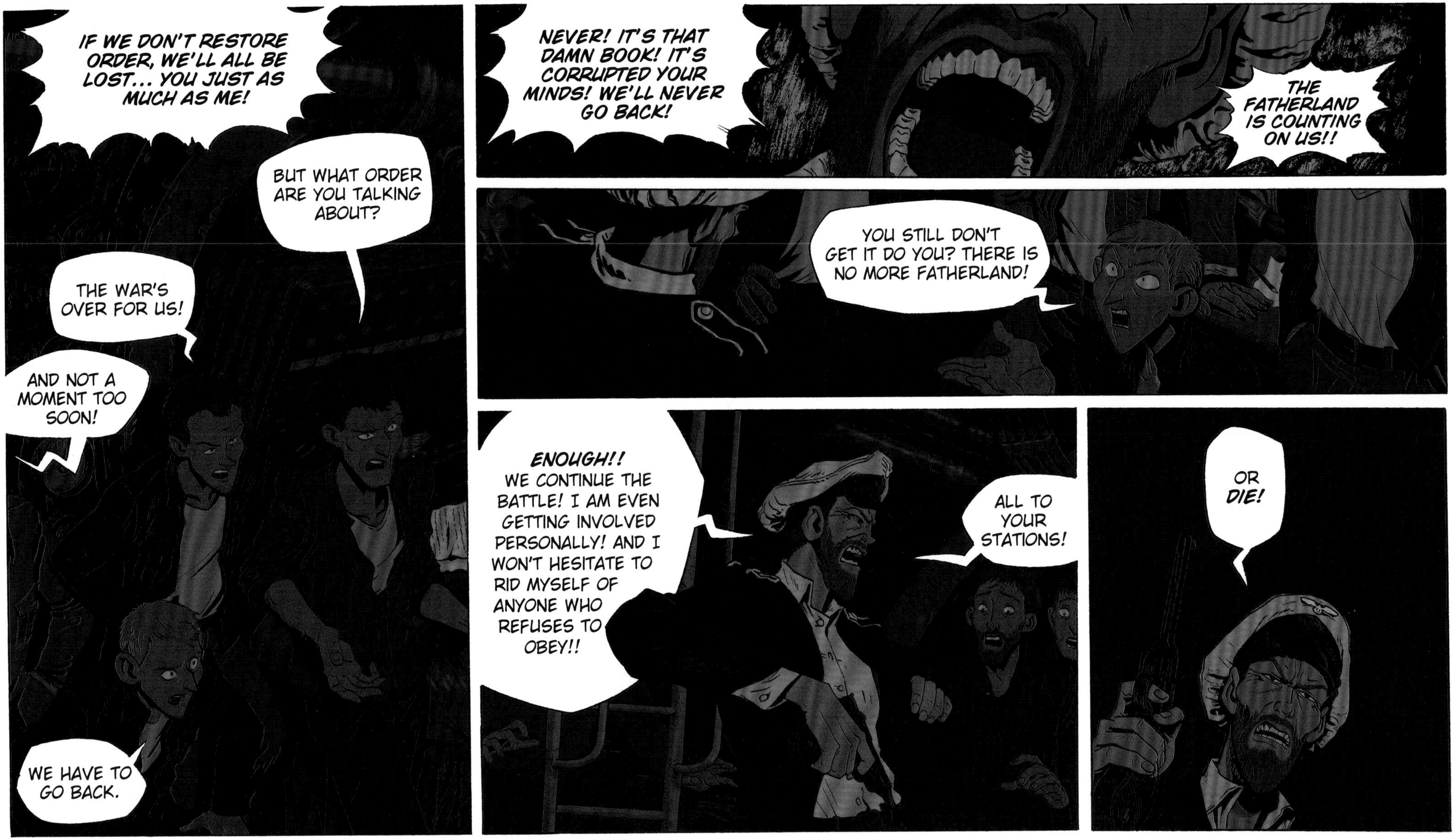
IF WE DON'T RESTORE ORDER, WE'LL ALL BE LOST... YOU JUST AS MUCH AS ME!
BUT WHAT ORDER ARE YOU TALKING ABOUT?
THE WAR'S OVER FOR US!
AND NOT A MOMENT TOO SOON!
WE HAVE TO GO BACK.
NEVER! IT'S THAT DAMN BOOK! IT'S CORRUPTED YOUR MINDS! WE'LL NEVER GO BACK!
THE FATHERLAND IS COUNTING ON US!!
YOU STILL DON'T GET IT DO YOU? THERE IS NO MORE FATHERLAND!
ENOUGH!! WE CONTINUE THE BATTLE! I AM EVEN GETTING INVOLVED PERSONALLY! AND I WON'T HESITATE TO RID MYSELF OF ANYONE WHO REFUSES TO OBEY!!
ALL TO YOUR STATIONS!
OR DIE!

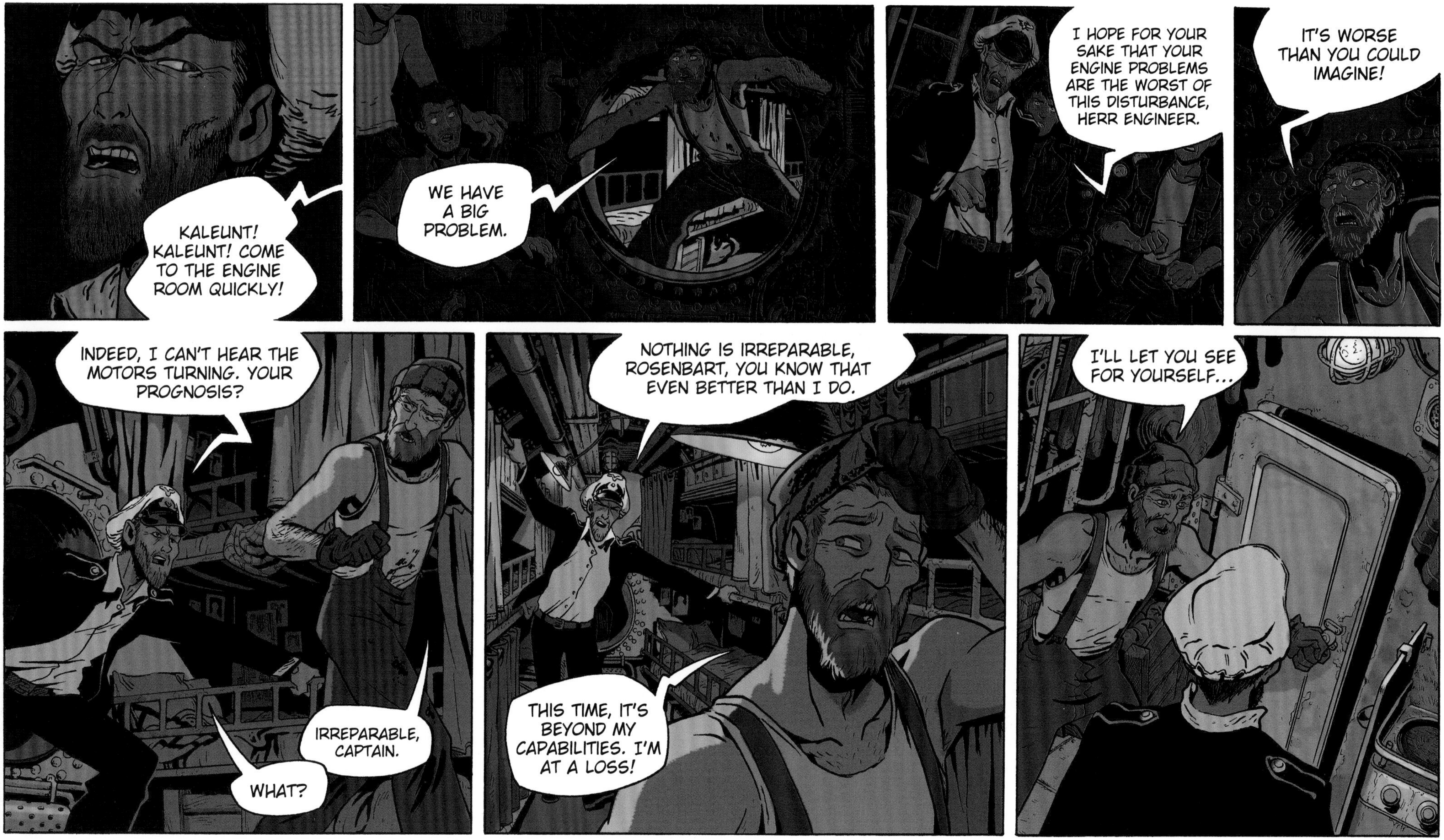
KALEUNT! KALEUNT! COME TO THE ENGINE ROOM QUICKLY!
WE HAVE A BIG PROBLEM.
I HOPE FOR YOUR SAKE THAT YOUR ENGINE PROBLEMS ARE THE WORST OF THIS DISTURBANCE, HERR ENGINEER.
IT'S WORSE THAN YOU COULD IMAGINE!
INDEED, I CAN'T HEAR THE MOTORS TURNING. YOUR PROGNOSIS?
IRREPARABLE, CAPTAIN.
WHAT?
NOTHING IS IRREPARABLE, ROSENBART, YOU KNOW THAT EVEN BETTER THAN I DO.
THIS TIME, IT'S BEYOND MY CAPABILITIES. I'M AT A LOSS!
I'LL LET YOU SEE FOR YOURSELF...

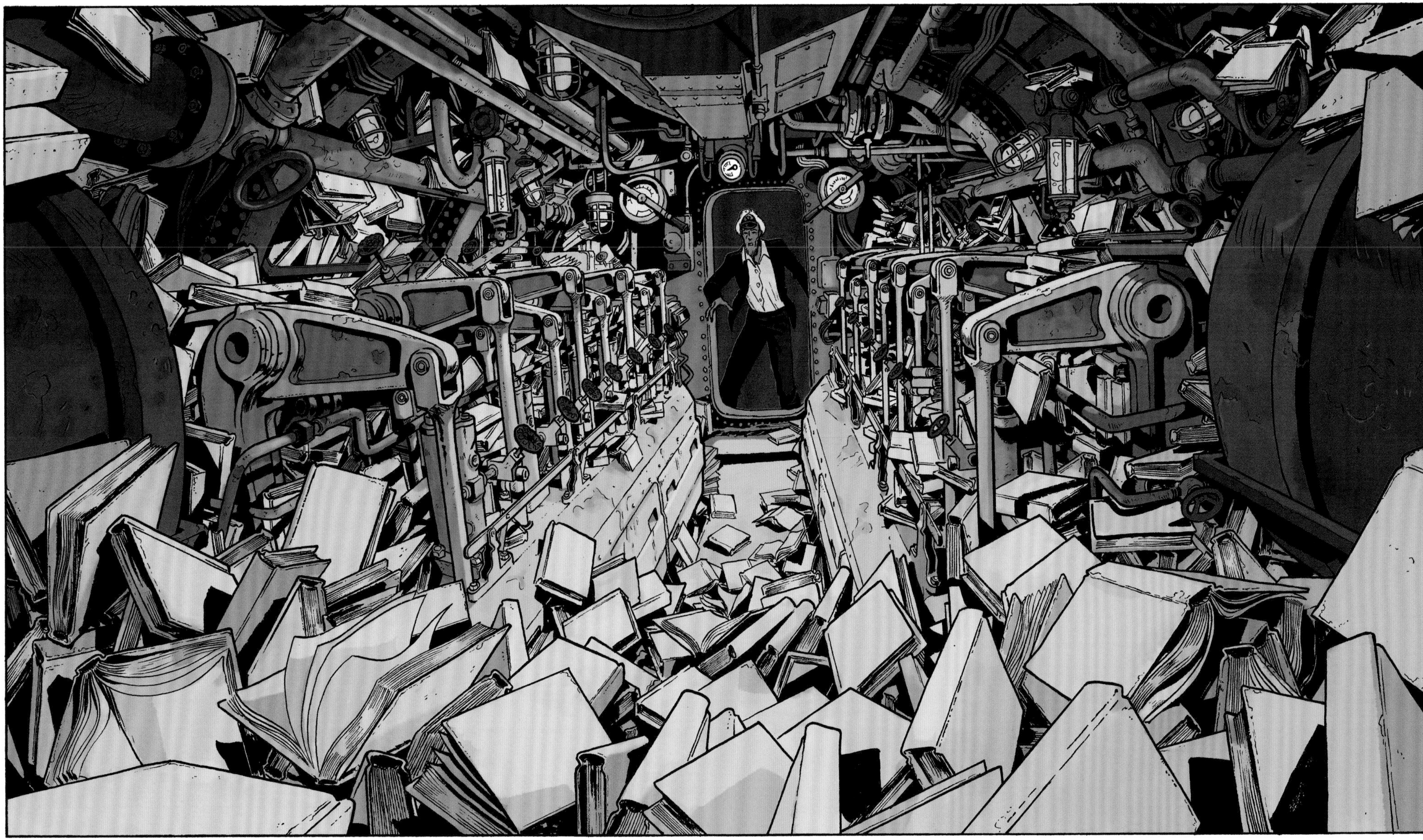

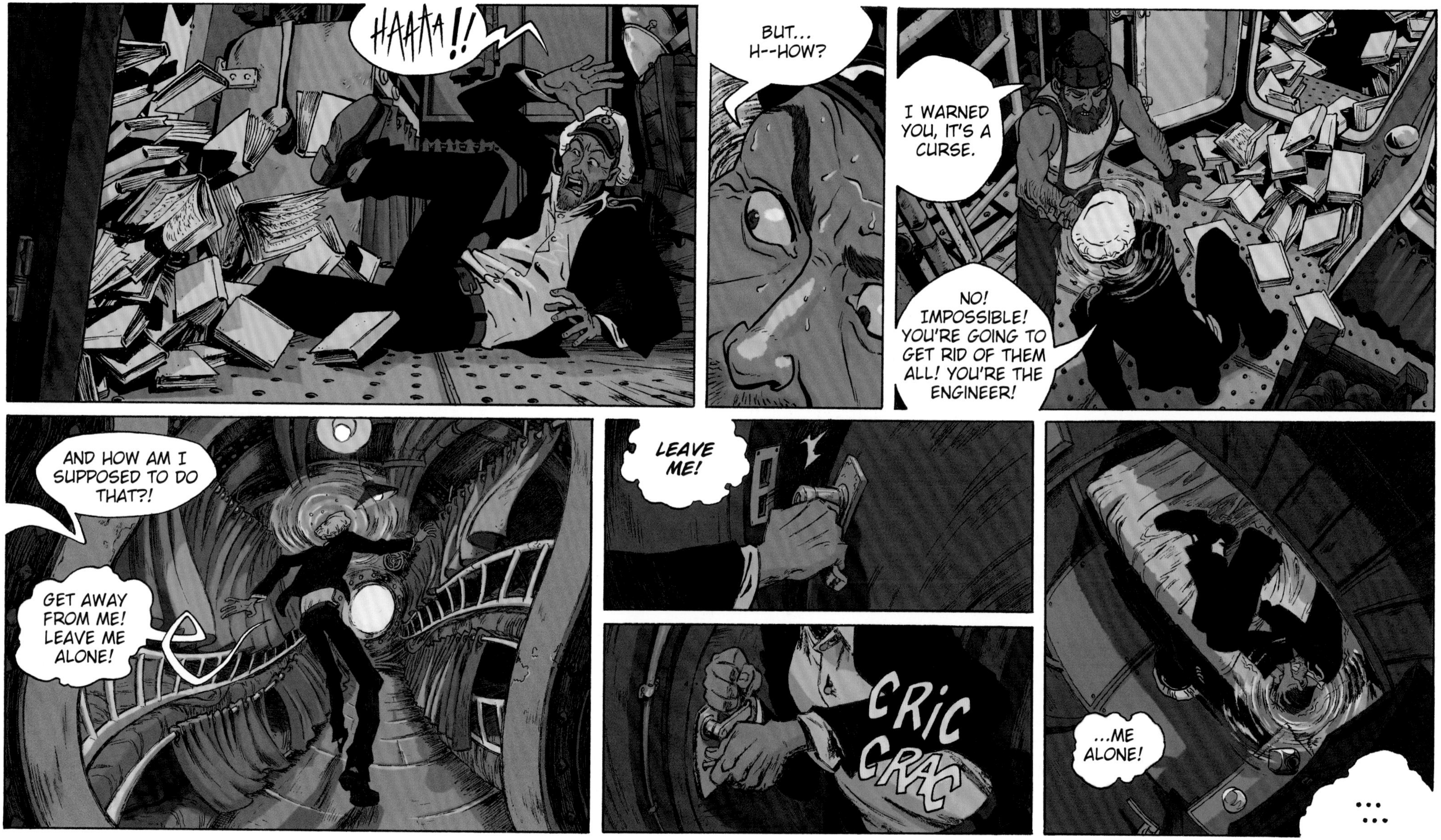
HAAAA!!
BUT... H--HOW?
I WARNED YOU, IT'S A CURSE.
NO! IMPOSSIBLE! YOU'RE GOING TO GET RID OF THEM ALL! YOU'RE THE ENGINEER!
AND HOW AM I SUPPOSED TO DO THAT?!
GET AWAY FROM ME! LEAVE ME ALONE!
LEAVE ME!
CRIC CRAC
...ME ALONE!
...
...

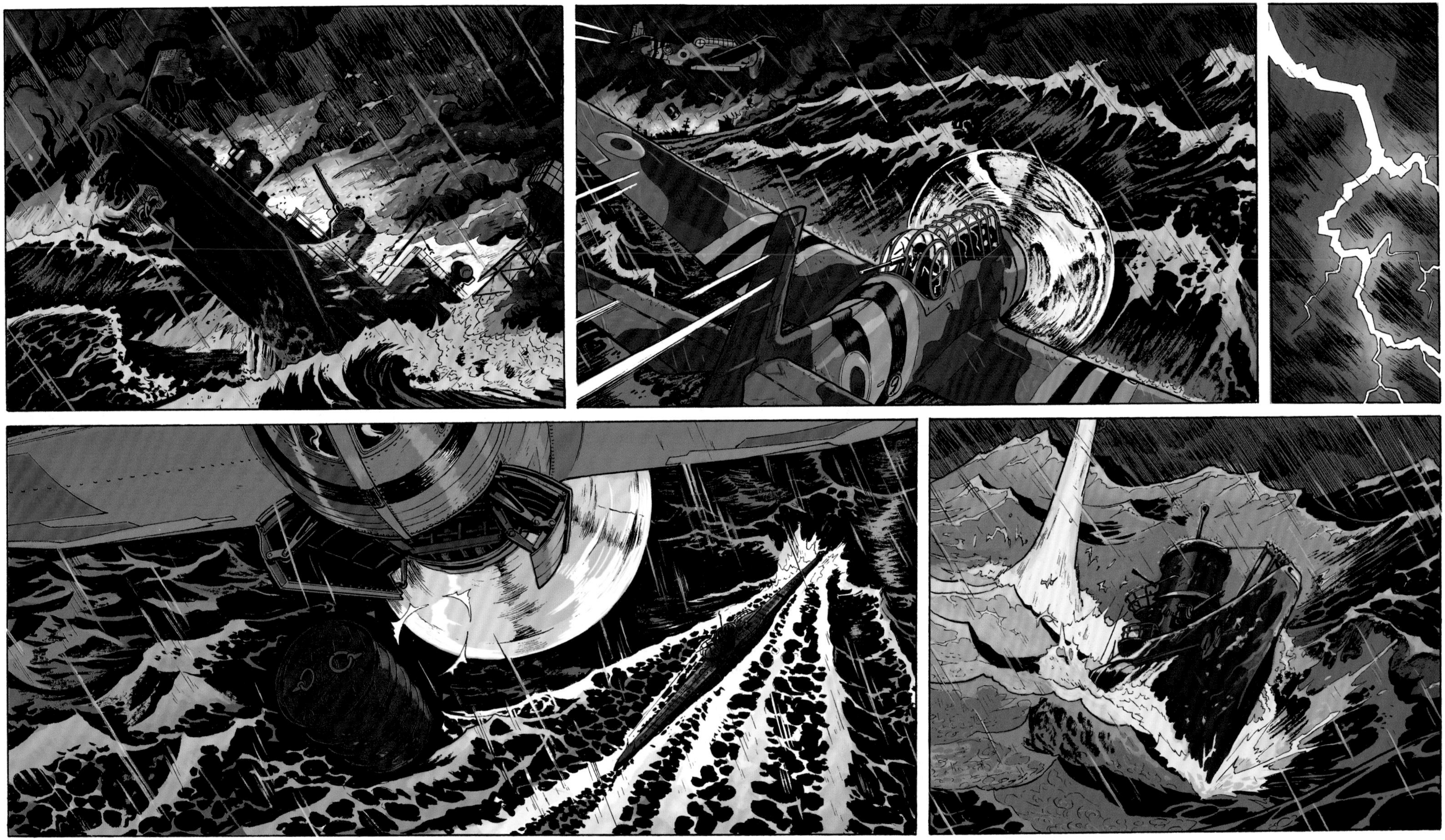

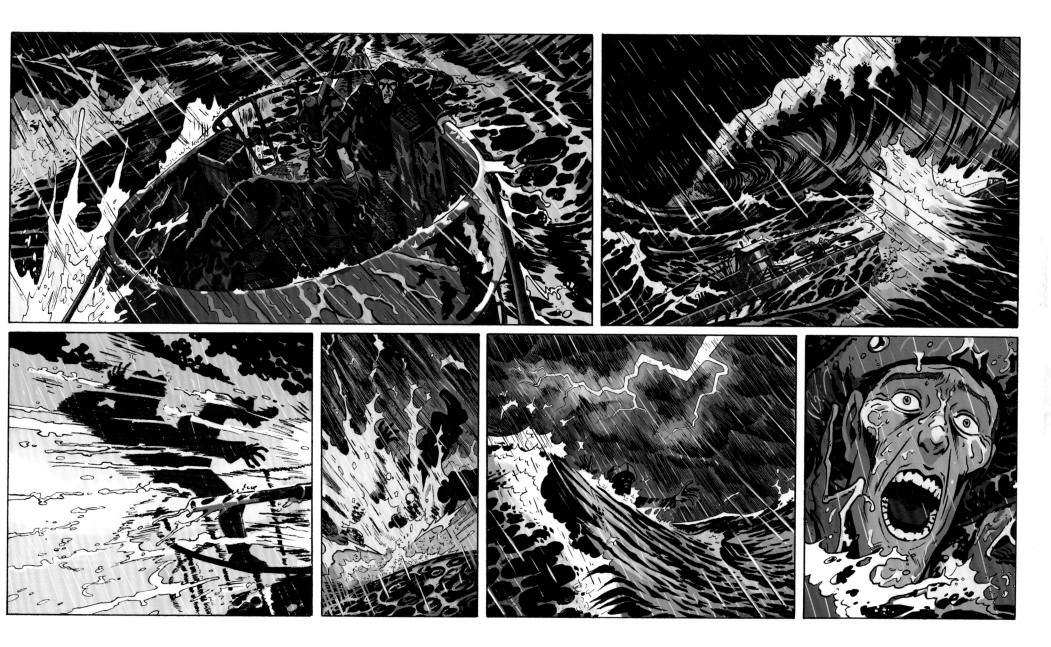

61

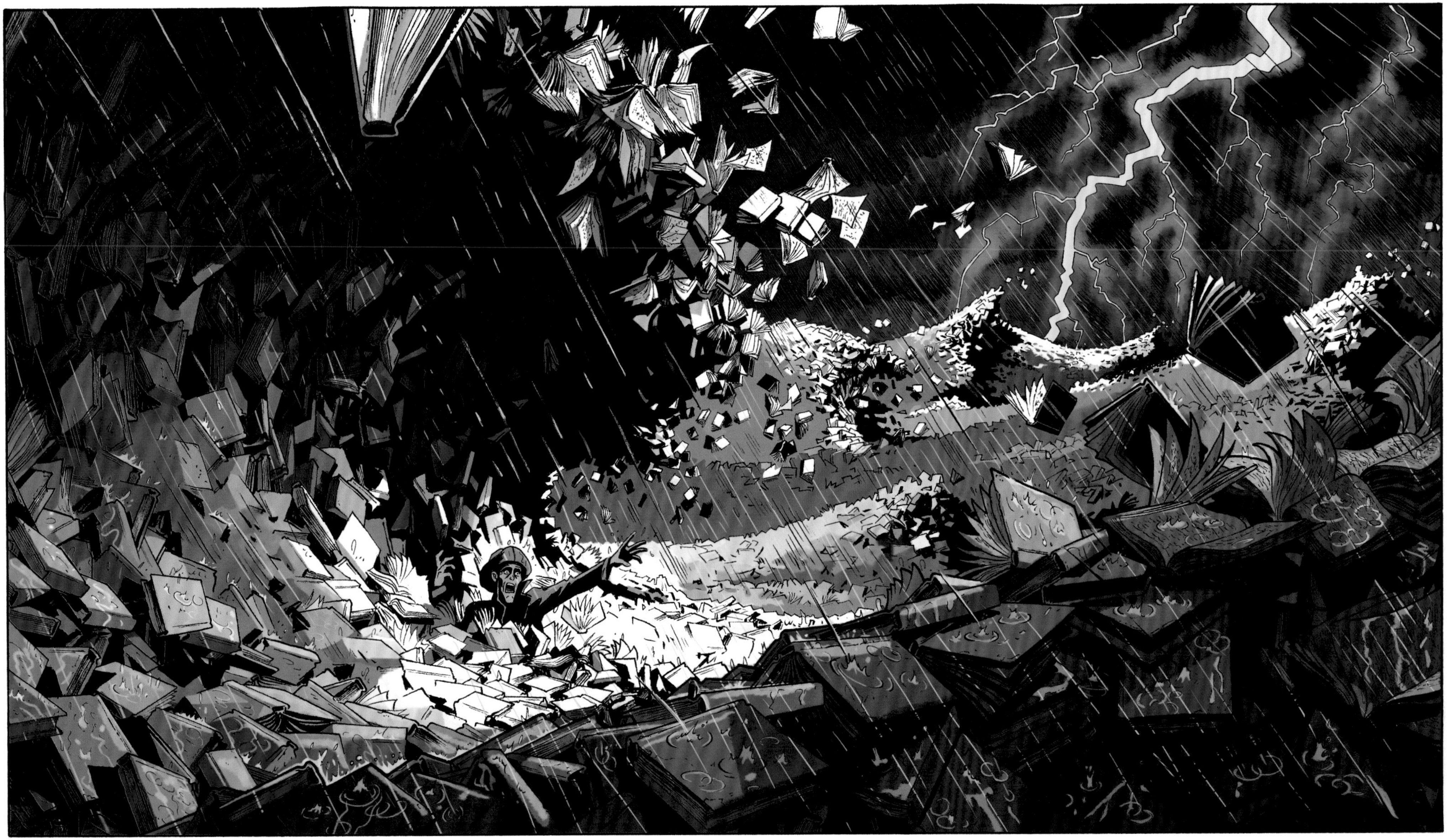

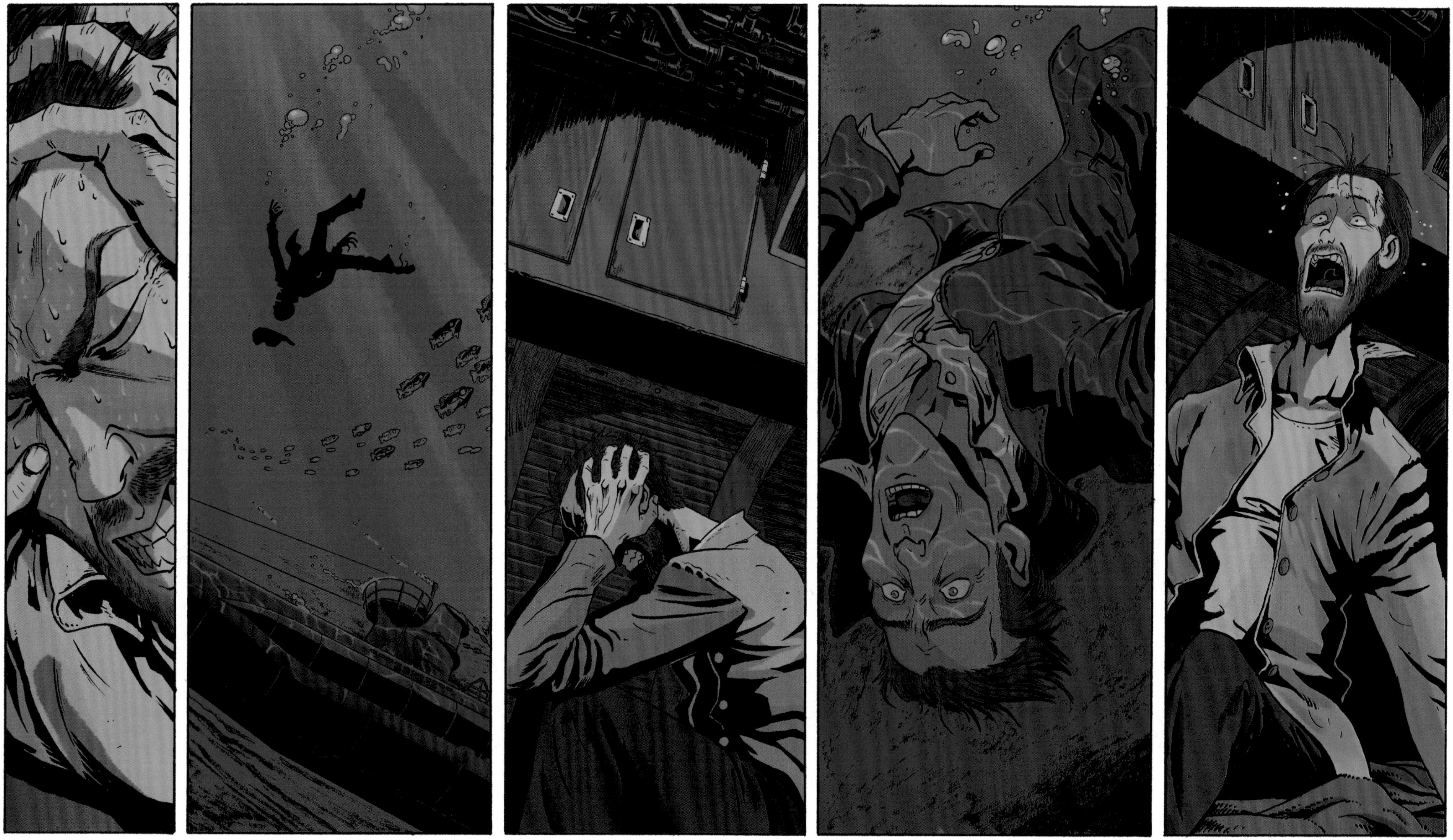

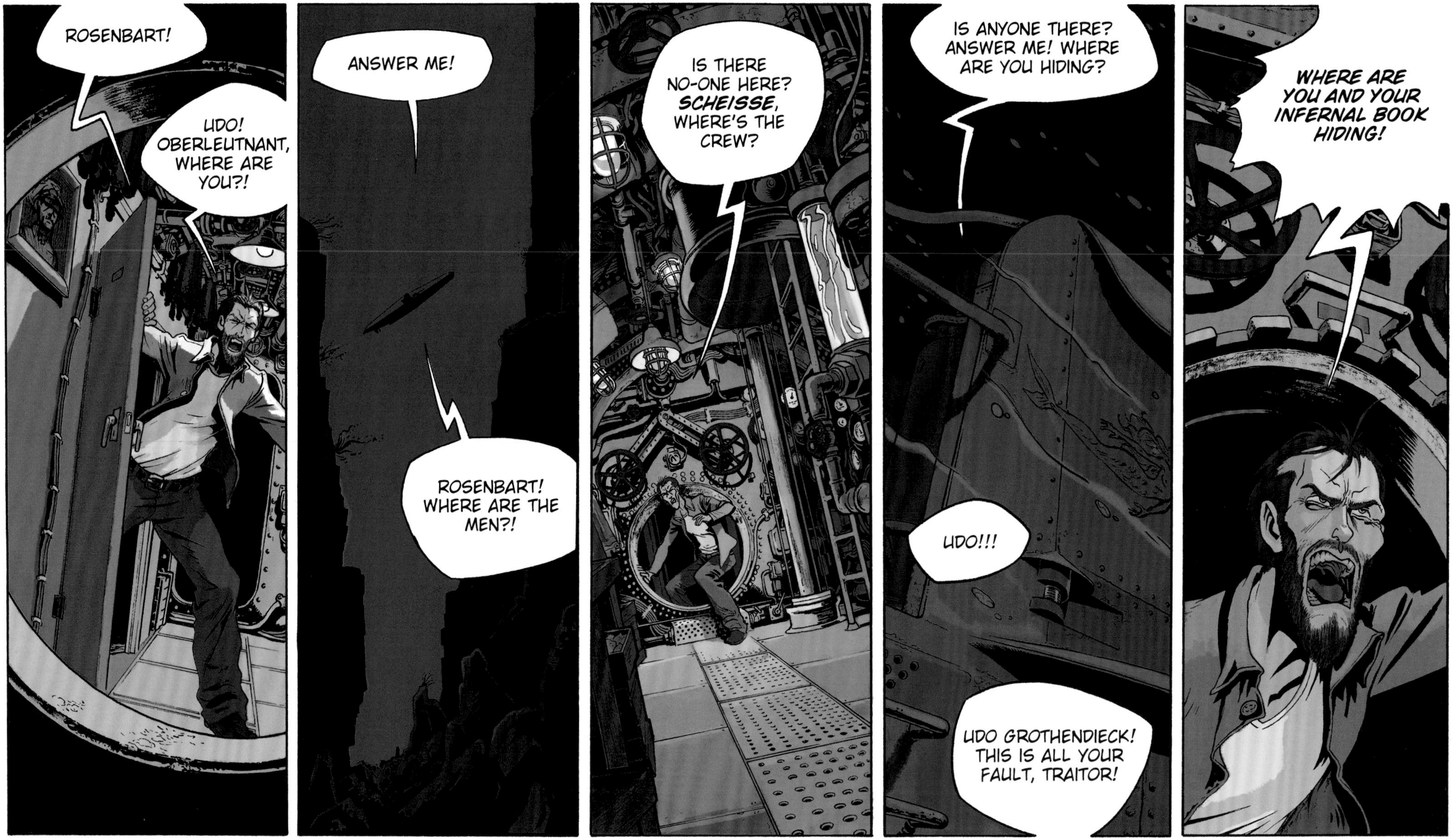
ROSENBART!
UDO! OBERLEUTNANT, WHERE ARE YOU?!
ANSWER ME!
ROSENBART! WHERE ARE THE MEN?!
IS THERE NO-ONE HERE? *SCHEISSE*, WHERE'S THE CREW?
IS ANYONE THERE? ANSWER ME! WHERE ARE YOU HIDING?
UDO!!!
UDO GROTHENDIECK! THIS IS ALL YOUR FAULT, TRAITOR!
WHERE ARE YOU AND YOUR INFERNAL BOOK HIDING!

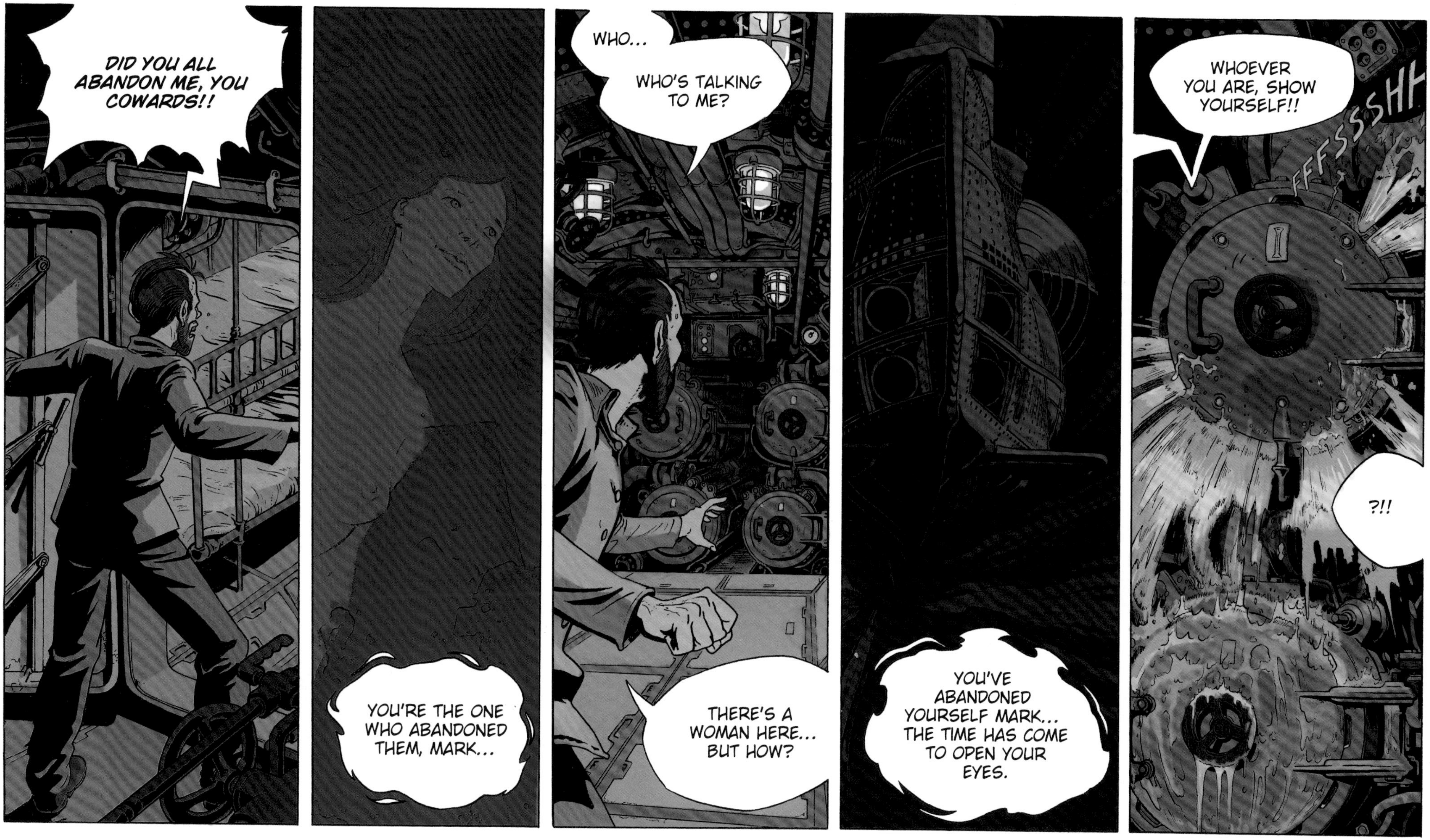
DID YOU ALL ABANDON ME, YOU COWARDS!!
YOU'RE THE ONE WHO ABANDONED THEM, MARK...
WHO...
WHO'S TALKING TO ME?
THERE'S A WOMAN HERE... BUT HOW?
YOU'VE ABANDONED YOURSELF MARK... THE TIME HAS COME TO OPEN YOUR EYES.
WHOEVER YOU ARE, SHOW YOURSELF!!
FFFSSSHH
?!!

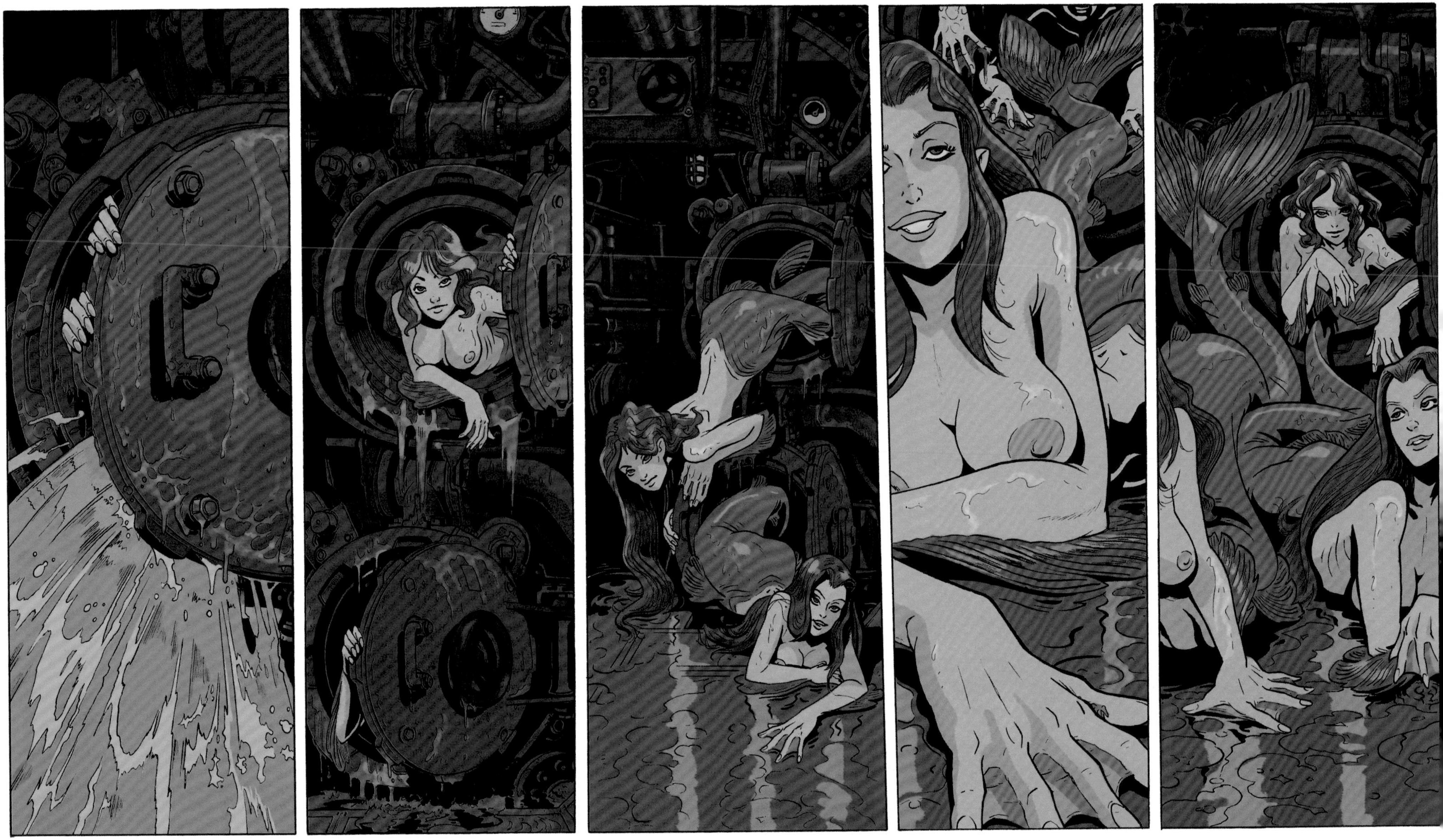

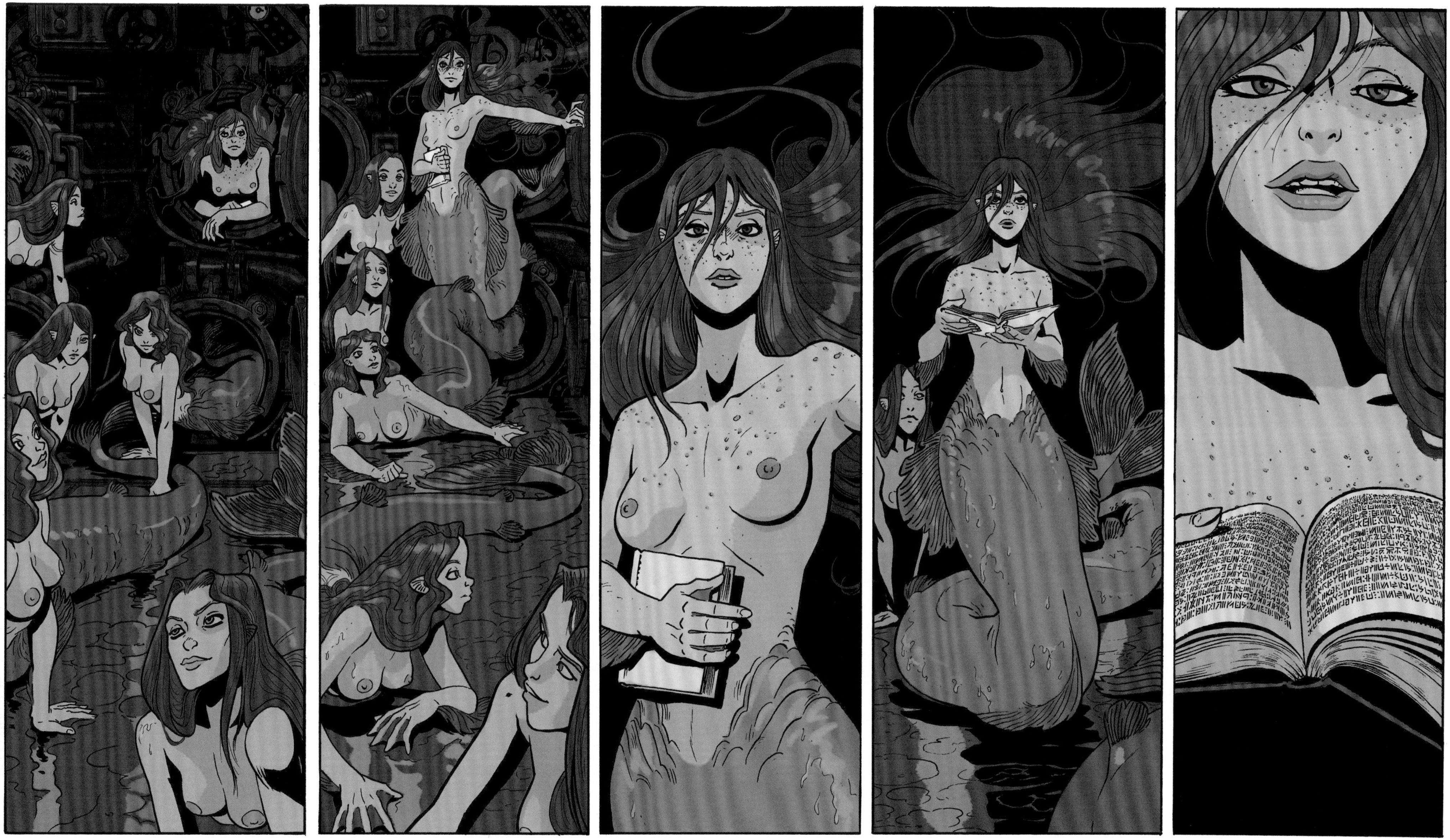

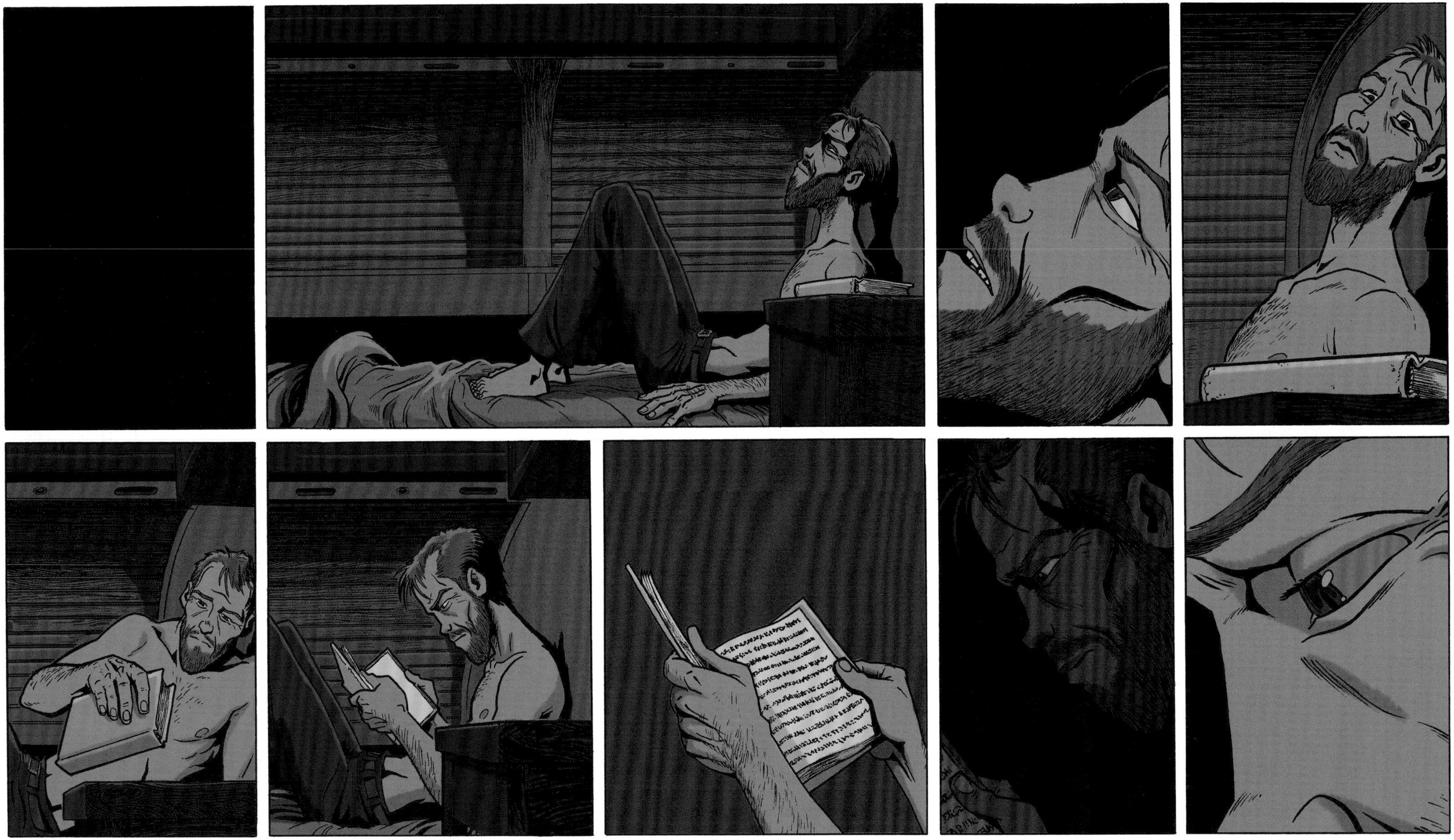

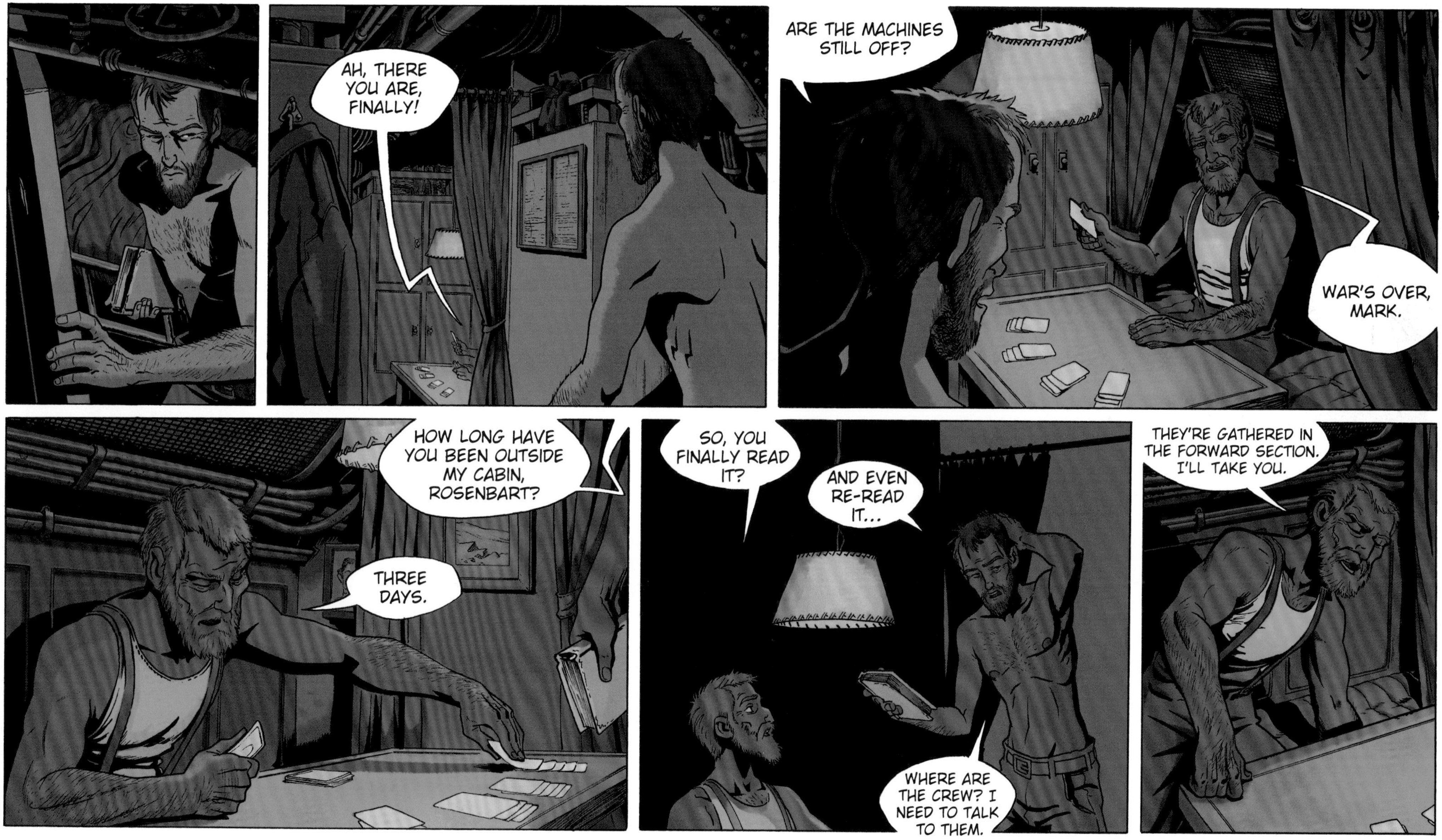
AH, THERE YOU ARE, FINALLY!
ARE THE MACHINES STILL OFF?
WAR'S OVER, MARK.
HOW LONG HAVE YOU BEEN OUTSIDE MY CABIN, ROSENBART?
THREE DAYS.
SO, YOU FINALLY READ IT?
AND EVEN RE-READ IT...
WHERE ARE THE CREW? I NEED TO TALK TO THEM.
THEY'RE GATHERED IN THE FORWARD SECTION. I'LL TAKE YOU.

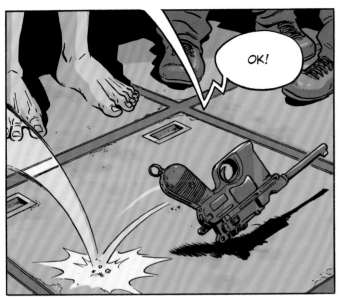

OK!

YOU MUST BE WONDERING WHY I HAD IT IN FOR THAT BOOK SO MUCH... SIMPLE: IT WAS ALLURING ME... SO MUCH SO THAT I WENT OFF THE RAILS...

AND TO THINK I NEARLY KILLED YOU ALL OVER A WAR THAT HAD ENDED... THERE WILL BE NO MORE CAPTAIN ON BOARD!

SO, WHAT ARE WE GOING TO CHOOSE TO DO NOW?

HONESTLY, DO ANY OF YOU REALLY SEE YOURSELVES GOING BACK HOME?

I'D RATHER DIE, YEAH!

NO QUESTION OF LIVING AMIDST THE LIE. ALL THIS SHIT WILL START OVER AND OVER AGAIN.

THIS WORLD LEADS TO NOTHING... LET US GO FIND OUR TRUTH, ACCEPT THE MESSAGE OF A BETTER LIFE AS OUTLINED IN THE BOOK...

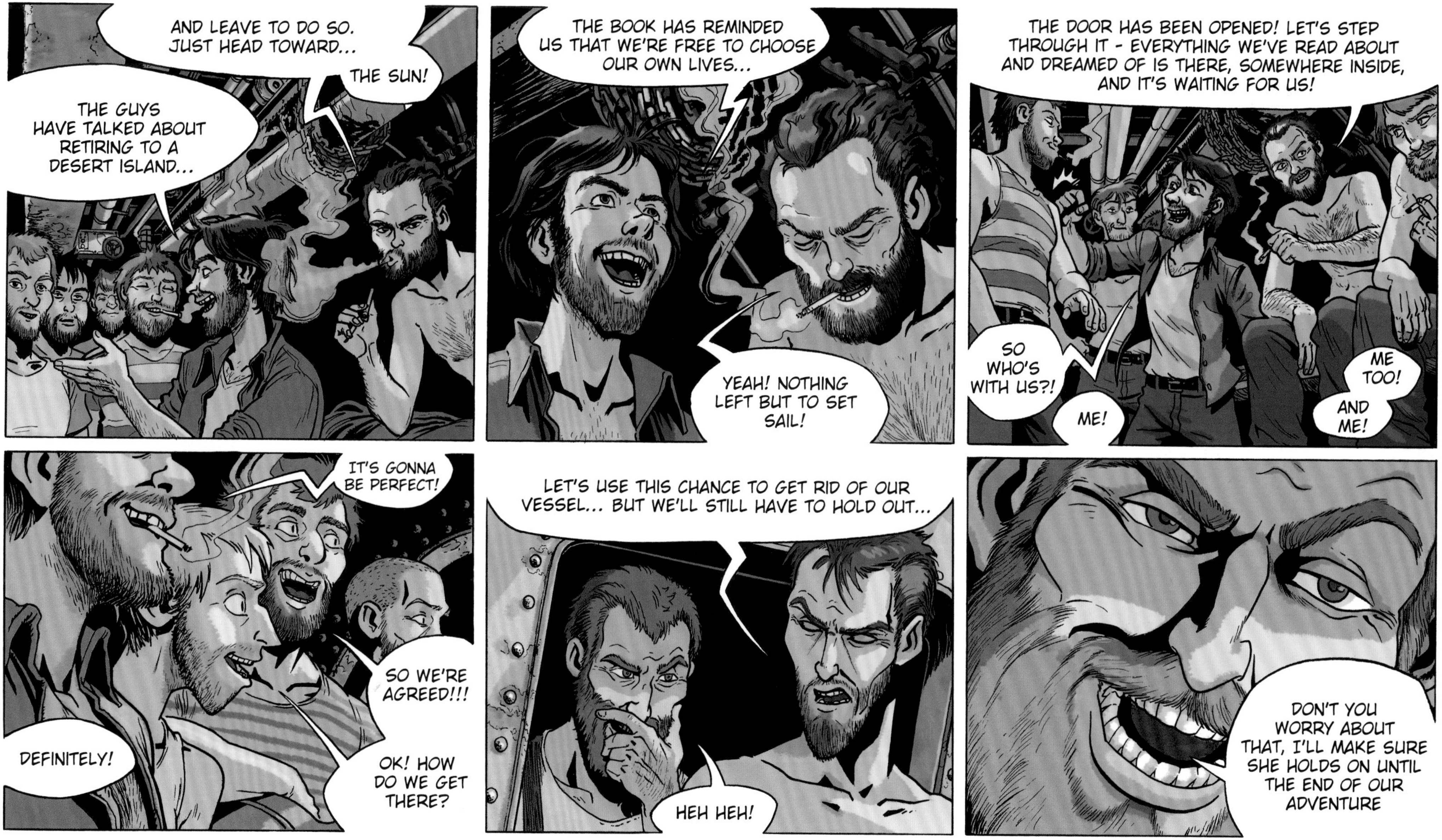
AND LEAVE TO DO SO. JUST HEAD TOWARD...
THE SUN!
THE GUYS HAVE TALKED ABOUT RETIRING TO A DESERT ISLAND...
THE BOOK HAS REMINDED US THAT WE'RE FREE TO CHOOSE OUR OWN LIVES...
YEAH! NOTHING LEFT BUT TO SET SAIL!
THE DOOR HAS BEEN OPENED! LET'S STEP THROUGH IT - EVERYTHING WE'VE READ ABOUT AND DREAMED OF IS THERE, SOMEWHERE INSIDE, AND IT'S WAITING FOR US!
SO WHO'S WITH US?!
ME!
ME TOO!
AND ME!
IT'S GONNA BE PERFECT!
SO WE'RE AGREED!!!
DEFINITELY!
OK! HOW DO WE GET THERE?
LET'S USE THIS CHANCE TO GET RID OF OUR VESSEL... BUT WE'LL STILL HAVE TO HOLD OUT...
HEH HEH!
DON'T YOU WORRY ABOUT THAT, I'LL MAKE SURE SHE HOLDS ON UNTIL THE END OF OUR ADVENTURE

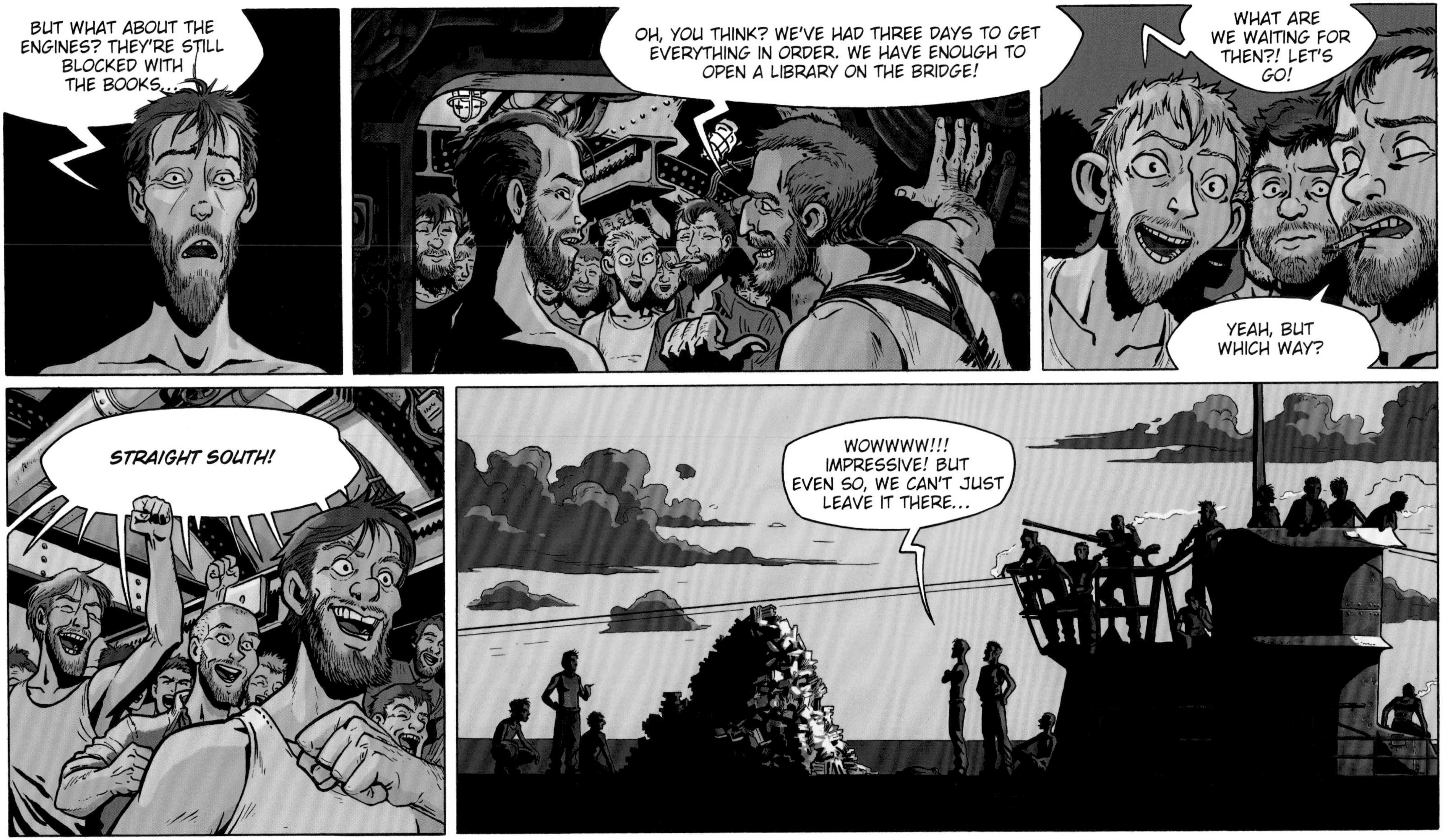

BUT WHAT ABOUT THE ENGINES? THEY'RE STILL BLOCKED WITH THE BOOKS...
OH, YOU THINK? WE'VE HAD THREE DAYS TO GET EVERYTHING IN ORDER. WE HAVE ENOUGH TO OPEN A LIBRARY ON THE BRIDGE!
WHAT ARE WE WAITING FOR THEN?! LET'S GO!
YEAH, BUT WHICH WAY?
STRAIGHT SOUTH!
WOWWWW!!! IMPRESSIVE! BUT EVEN SO, WE CAN'T JUST LEAVE IT THERE...

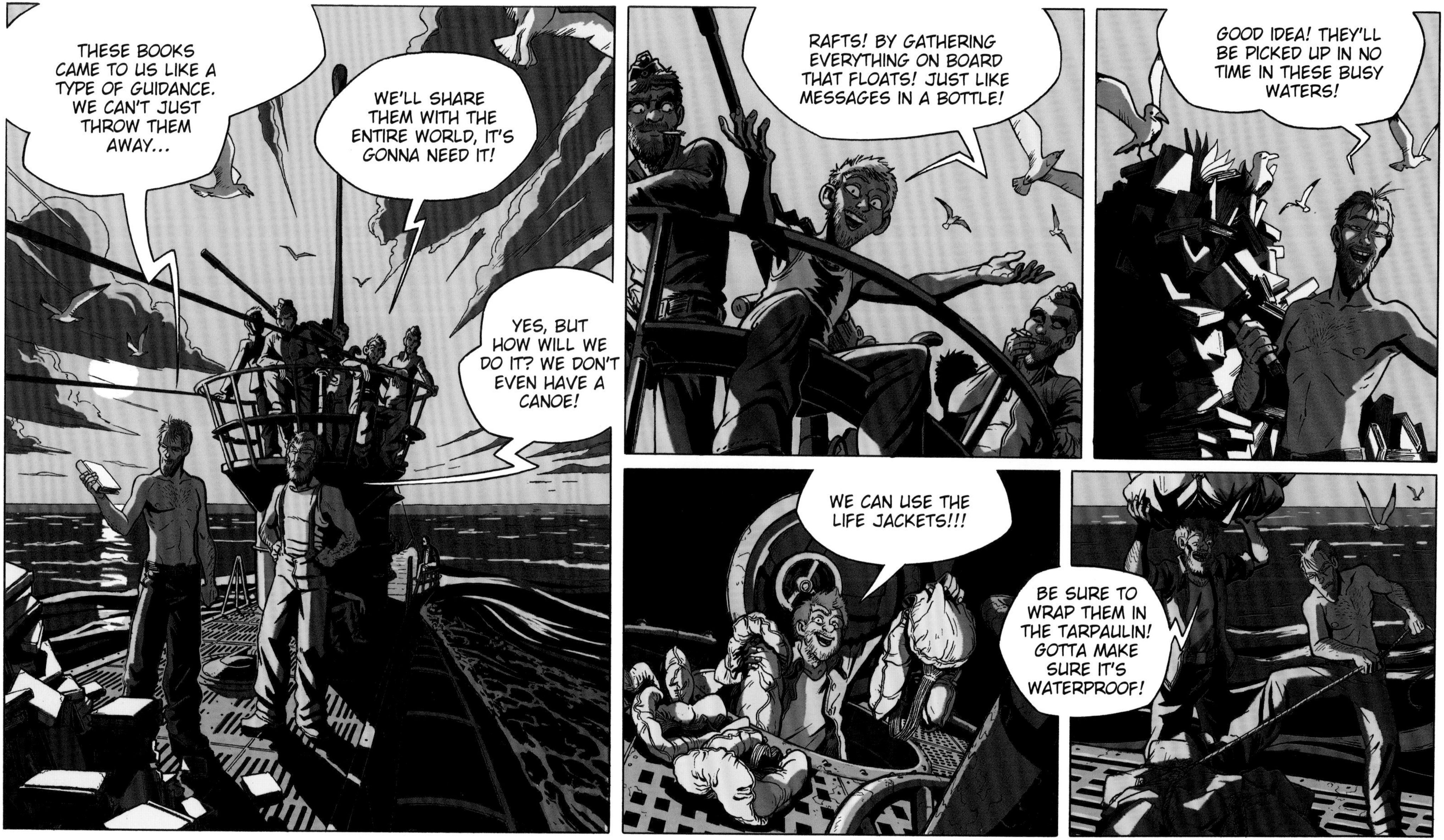
THESE BOOKS CAME TO US LIKE A TYPE OF GUIDANCE. WE CAN'T JUST THROW THEM AWAY...
WE'LL SHARE THEM WITH THE ENTIRE WORLD, IT'S GONNA NEED IT!
YES, BUT HOW WILL WE DO IT? WE DON'T EVEN HAVE A CANOE!
RAFTS! BY GATHERING EVERYTHING ON BOARD THAT FLOATS! JUST LIKE MESSAGES IN A BOTTLE!
GOOD IDEA! THEY'LL BE PICKED UP IN NO TIME IN THESE BUSY WATERS!
WE CAN USE THE LIFE JACKETS!!!
BE SURE TO WRAP THEM IN THE TARPAULIN! GOTTA MAKE SURE IT'S WATERPROOF!

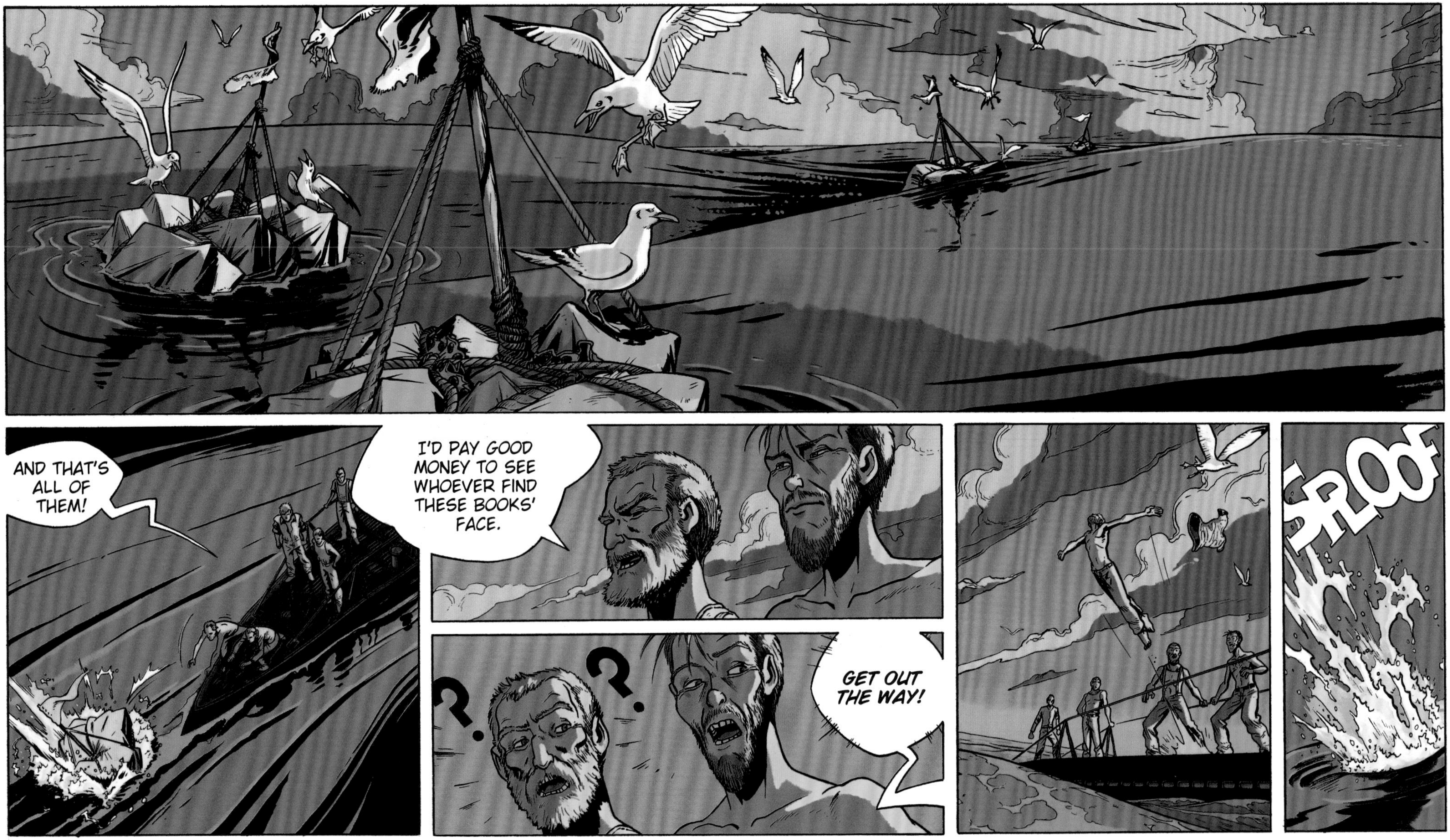
AND THAT'S ALL OF THEM!
I'D PAY GOOD MONEY TO SEE WHOEVER FIND THESE BOOKS' FACE.
?
?
GET OUT THE WAY!
SPLOOF

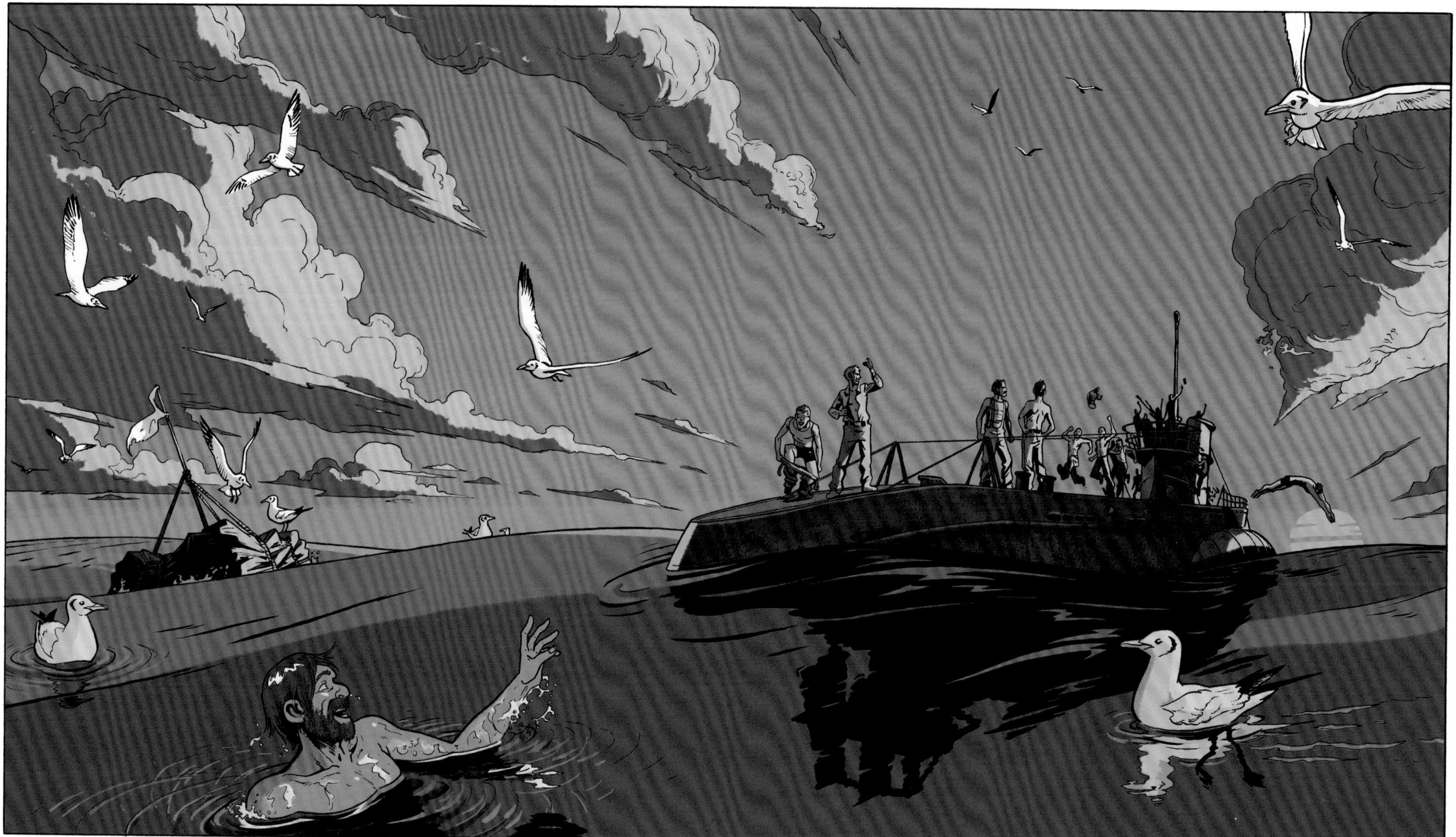

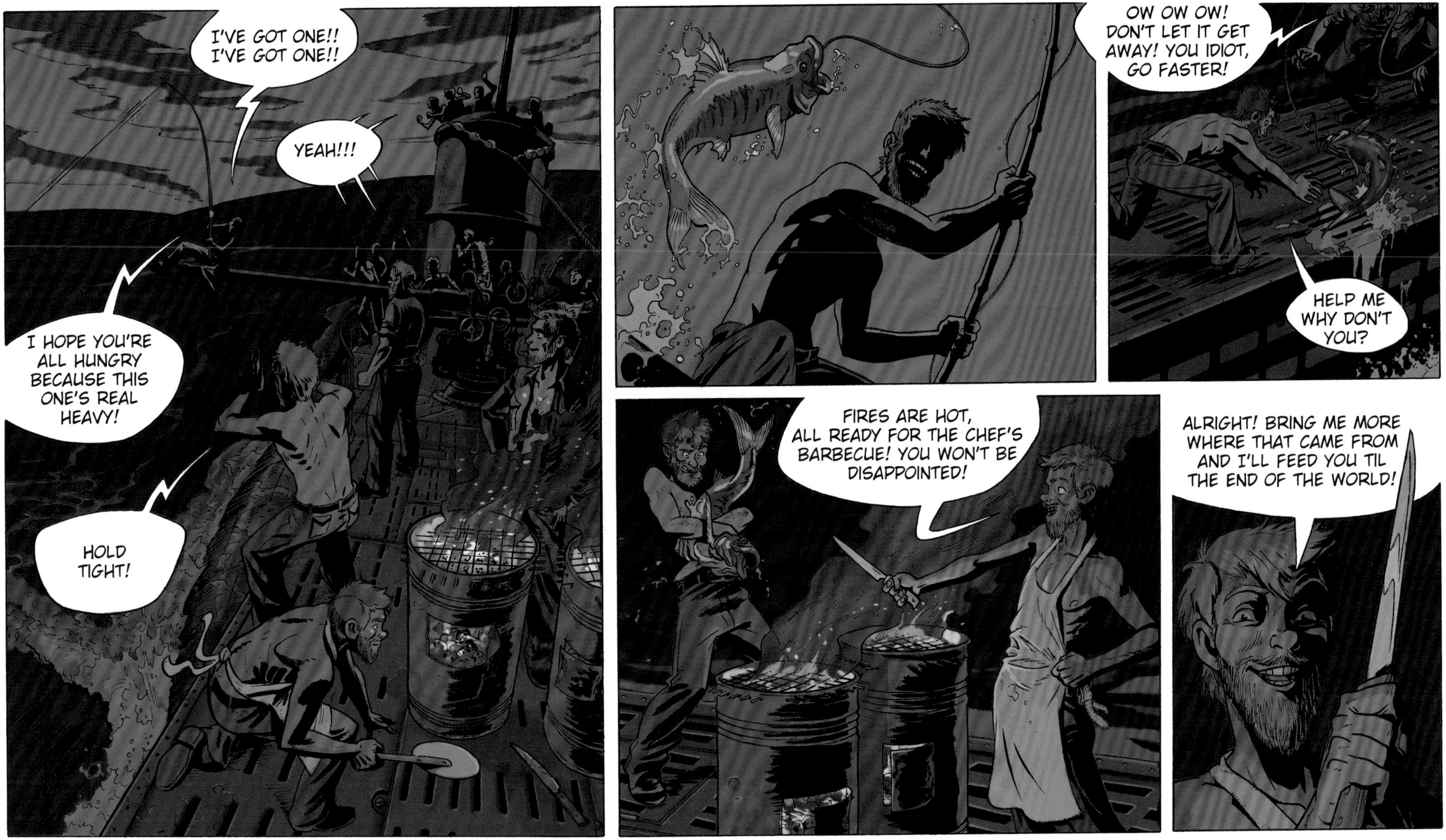
I'VE GOT ONE!! I'VE GOT ONE!!
YEAH!!!
I HOPE YOU'RE ALL HUNGRY BECAUSE THIS ONE'S REAL HEAVY!
HOLD TIGHT!
OW OW OW! DON'T LET IT GET AWAY! YOU IDIOT, GO FASTER!
HELP ME WHY DON'T YOU?
FIRES ARE HOT, ALL READY FOR THE CHEF'S BARBECUE! YOU WON'T BE DISAPPOINTED!
ALRIGHT! BRING ME MORE WHERE THAT CAME FROM AND I'LL FEED YOU TIL THE END OF THE WORLD!

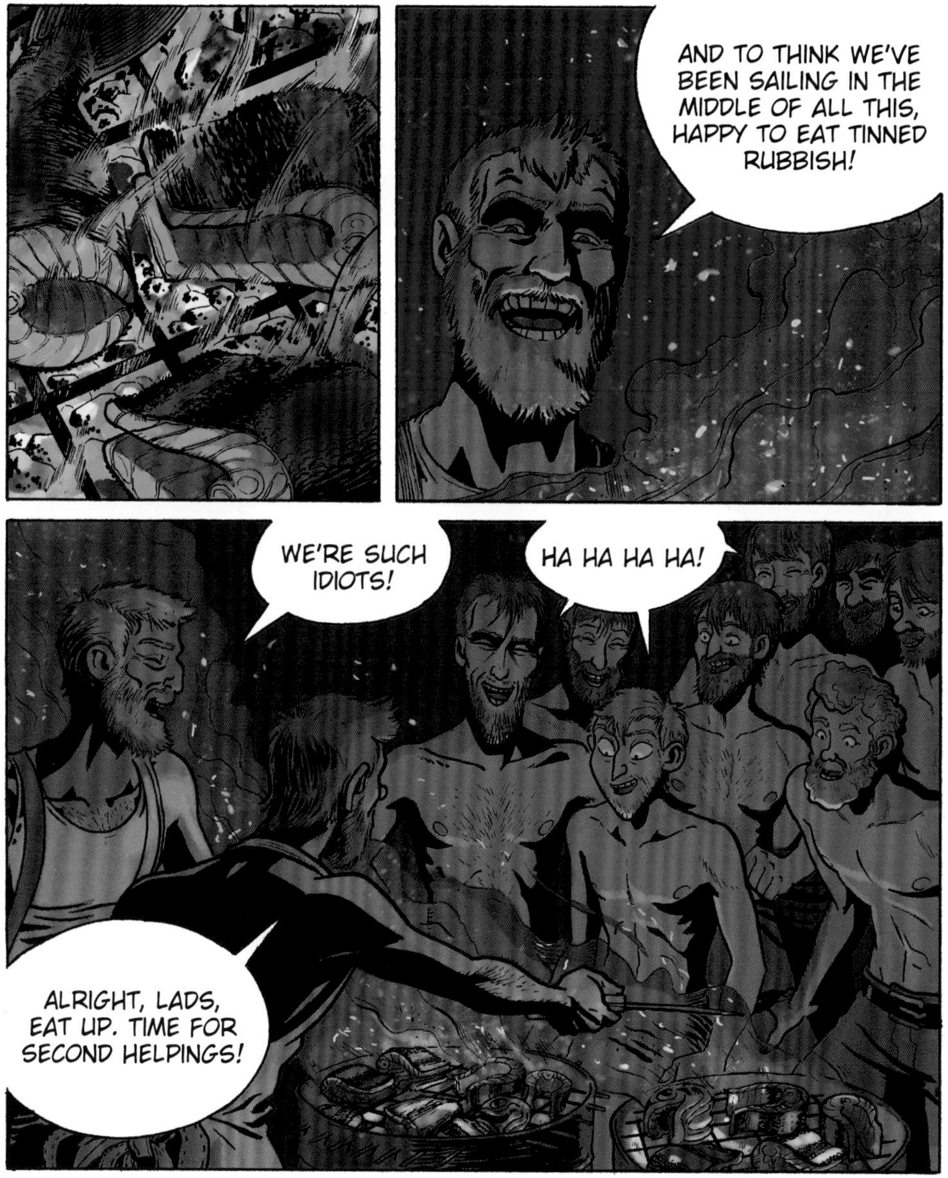
AND TO THINK WE'VE BEEN SAILING IN THE MIDDLE OF ALL THIS, HAPPY TO EAT TINNED RUBBISH!
WE'RE SUCH IDIOTS!
HA HA HA HA!
ALRIGHT, LADS, EAT UP. TIME FOR SECOND HELPINGS!

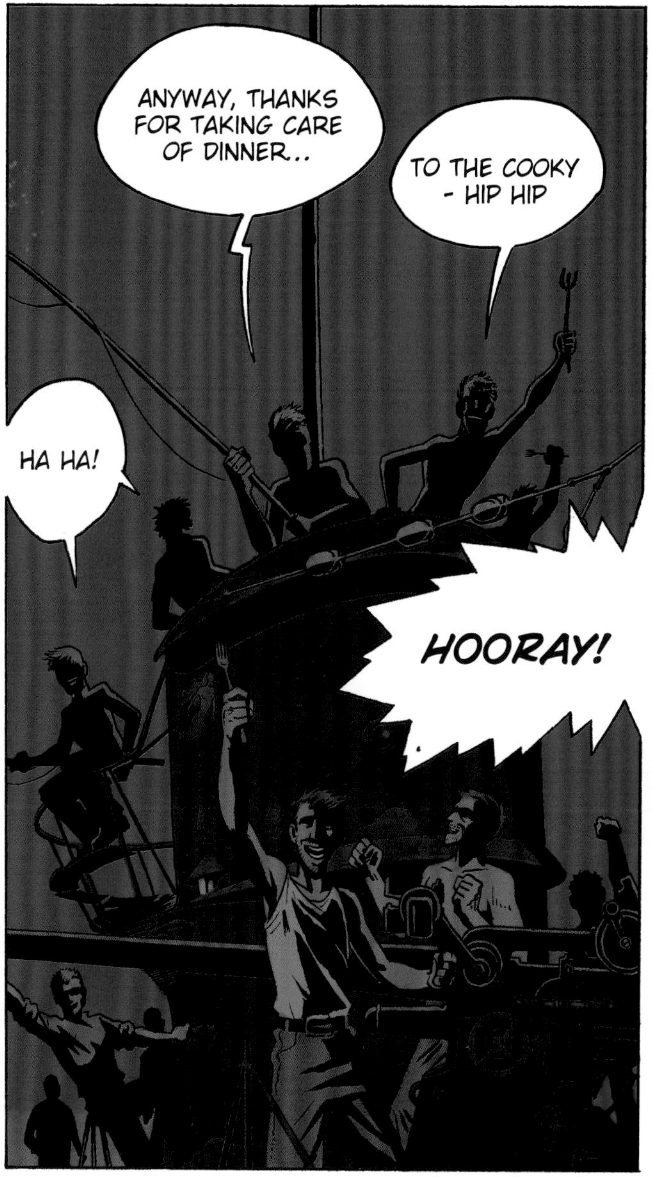
ANYWAY, THANKS FOR TAKING CARE OF DINNER...
TO THE COOKY - HIP HIP
HA HA!
HOORAY!

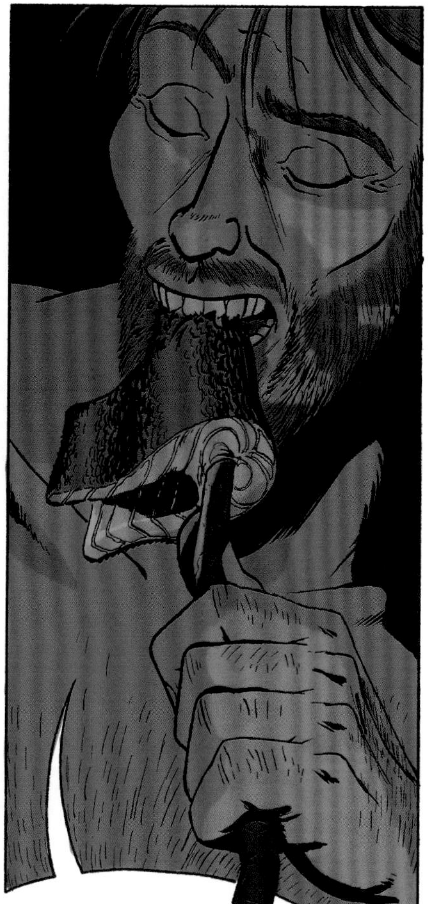

FOR THE SURVIVORS THAT SHOULD BE ENOUGH, FISHING WOULD FILL OUR BELLIES. OUR WATER CONTAINERS ARE STILL HALF FULL, SO IT SHOULD BE ENOUGH TO LAST UNTIL WE REACH OUR DESTINATION...

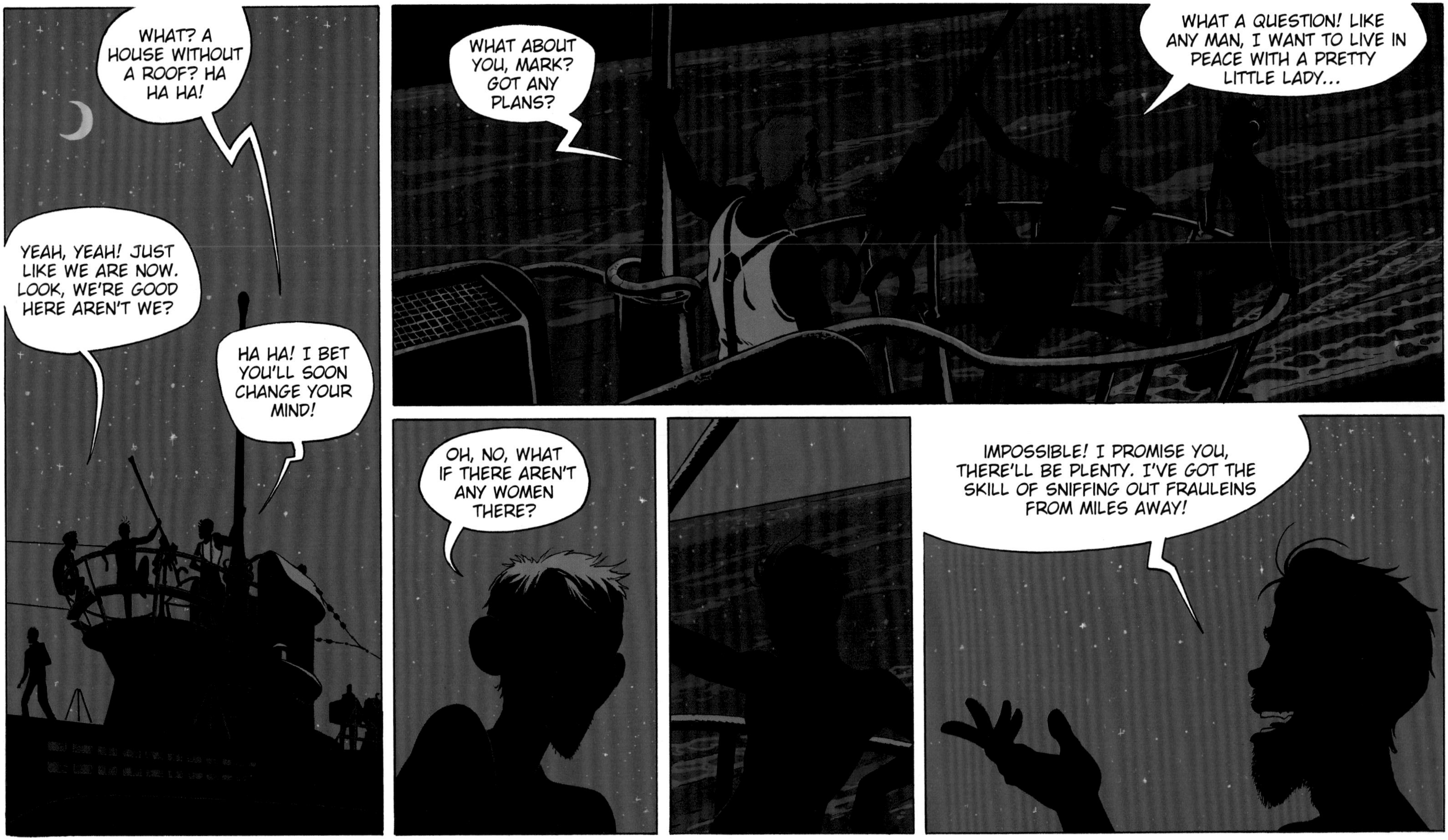
WHAT? A HOUSE WITHOUT A ROOF? HA HA HA!
YEAH, YEAH! JUST LIKE WE ARE NOW. LOOK, WE'RE GOOD HERE AREN'T WE?
HA HA! I BET YOU'LL SOON CHANGE YOUR MIND!
WHAT ABOUT YOU, MARK? GOT ANY PLANS?
WHAT A QUESTION! LIKE ANY MAN, I WANT TO LIVE IN PEACE WITH A PRETTY LITTLE LADY...
OH, NO, WHAT IF THERE AREN'T ANY WOMEN THERE?
IMPOSSIBLE! I PROMISE YOU, THERE'LL BE PLENTY. I'VE GOT THE SKILL OF SNIFFING OUT FRAULEINS FROM MILES AWAY!

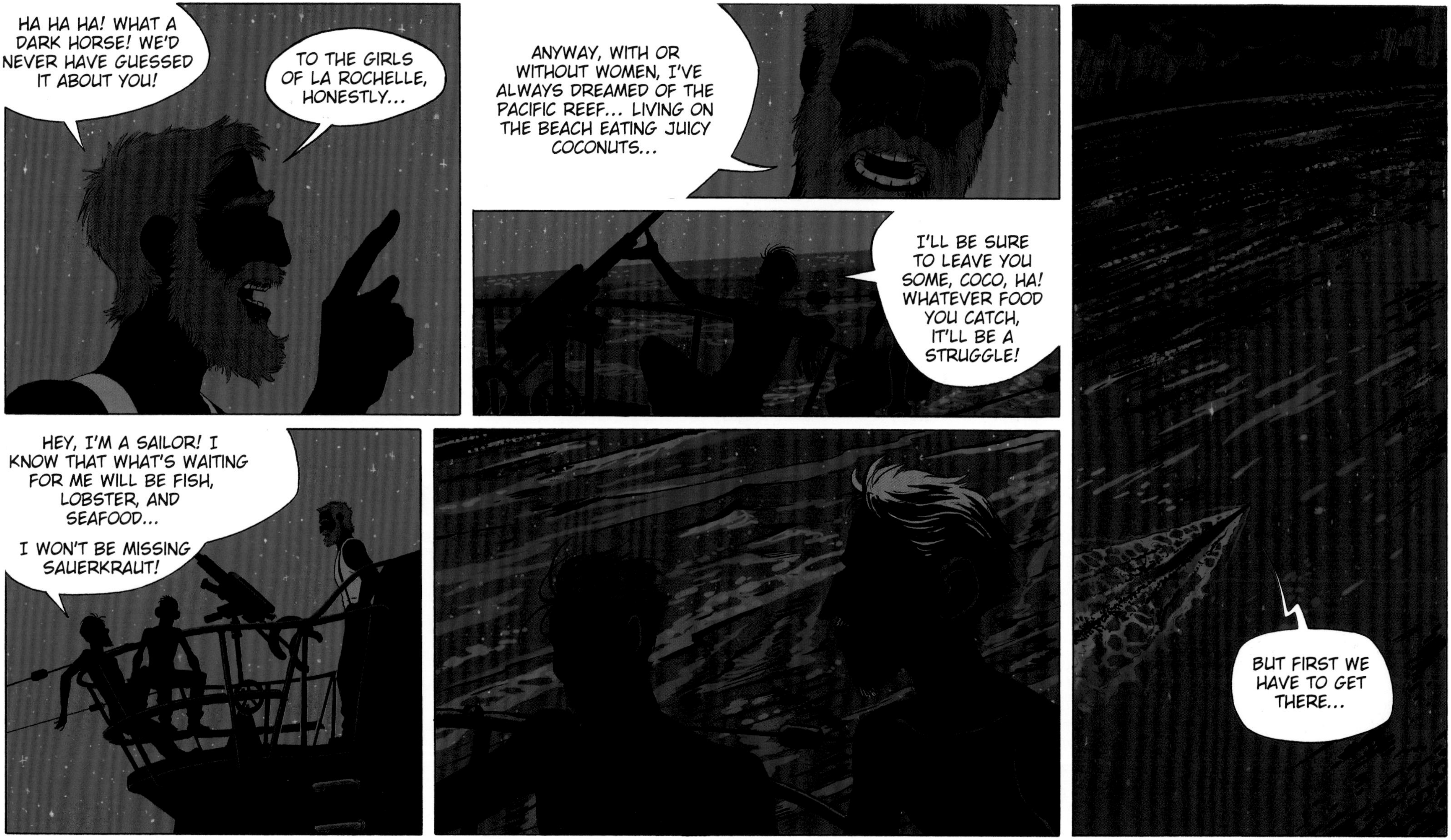
HA HA HA! WHAT A DARK HORSE! WE'D NEVER HAVE GUESSED IT ABOUT YOU!
TO THE GIRLS OF LA ROCHELLE, HONESTLY...
ANYWAY, WITH OR WITHOUT WOMEN, I'VE ALWAYS DREAMED OF THE PACIFIC REEF... LIVING ON THE BEACH EATING JUICY COCONUTS...
I'LL BE SURE TO LEAVE YOU SOME, COCO, HA! WHATEVER FOOD YOU CATCH, IT'LL BE A STRUGGLE!
HEY, I'M A SAILOR! I KNOW THAT WHAT'S WAITING FOR ME WILL BE FISH, LOBSTER, AND SEAFOOD...
I WON'T BE MISSING SAUERKRAUT!
BUT FIRST WE HAVE TO GET THERE...

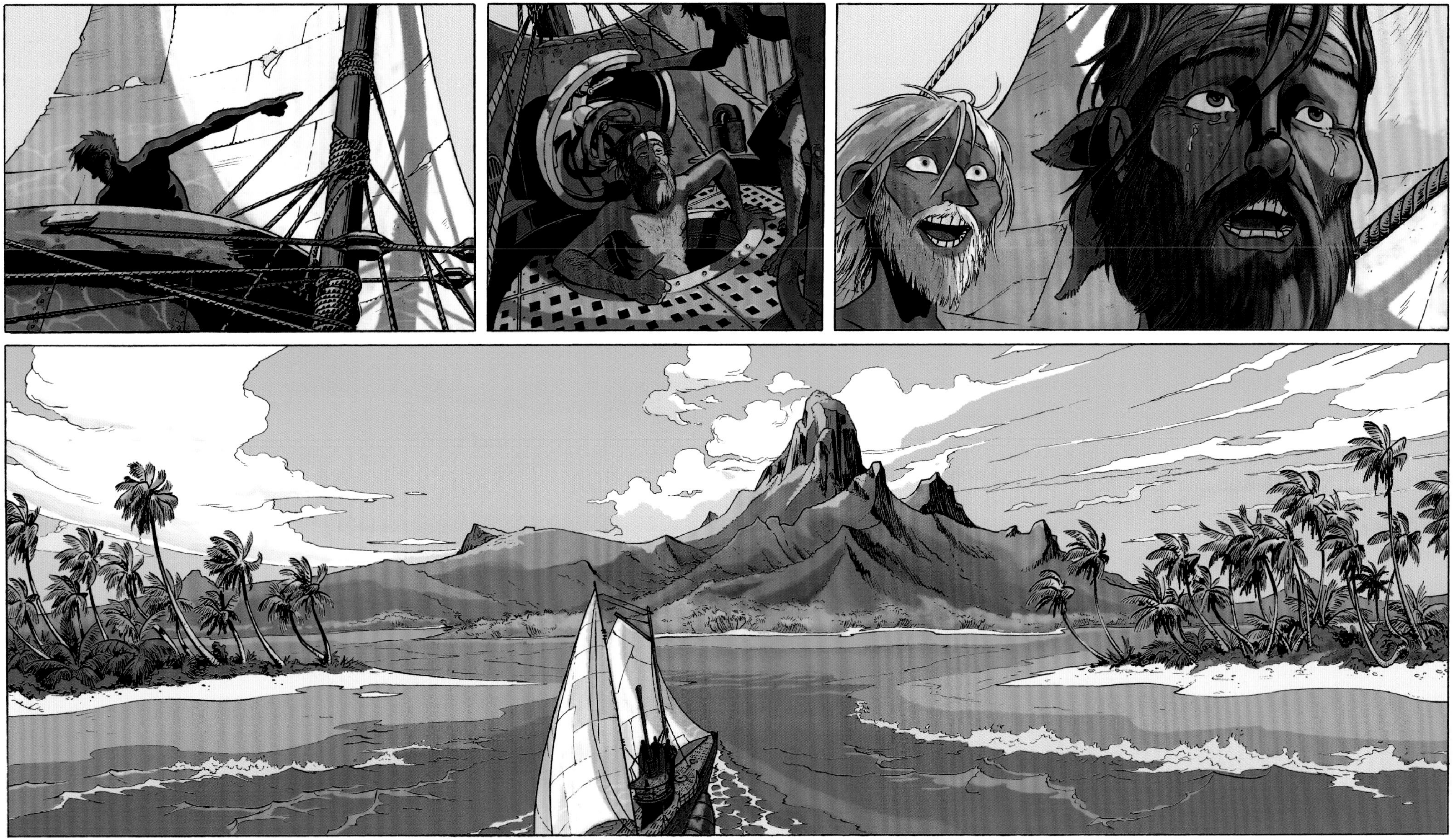

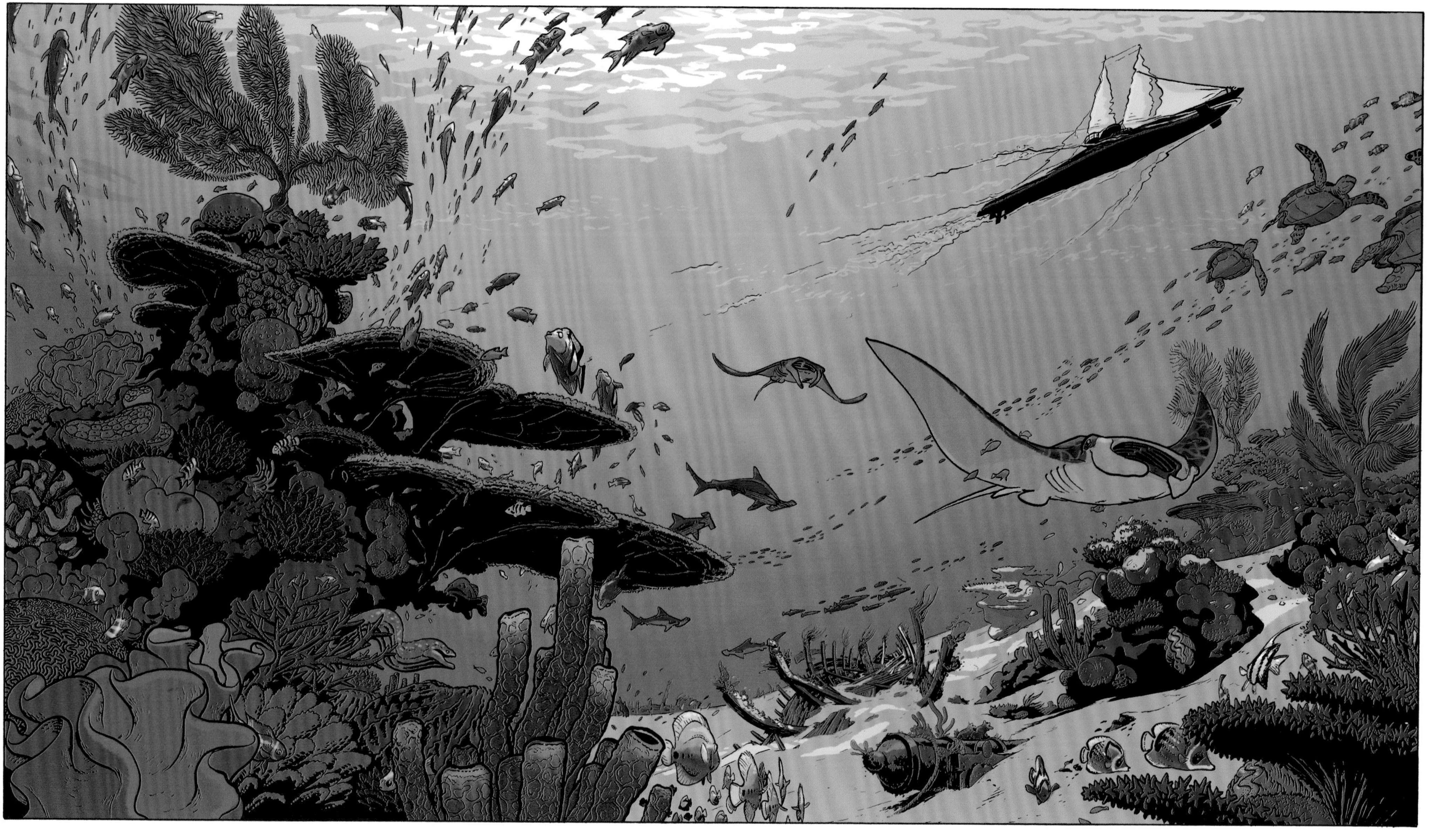

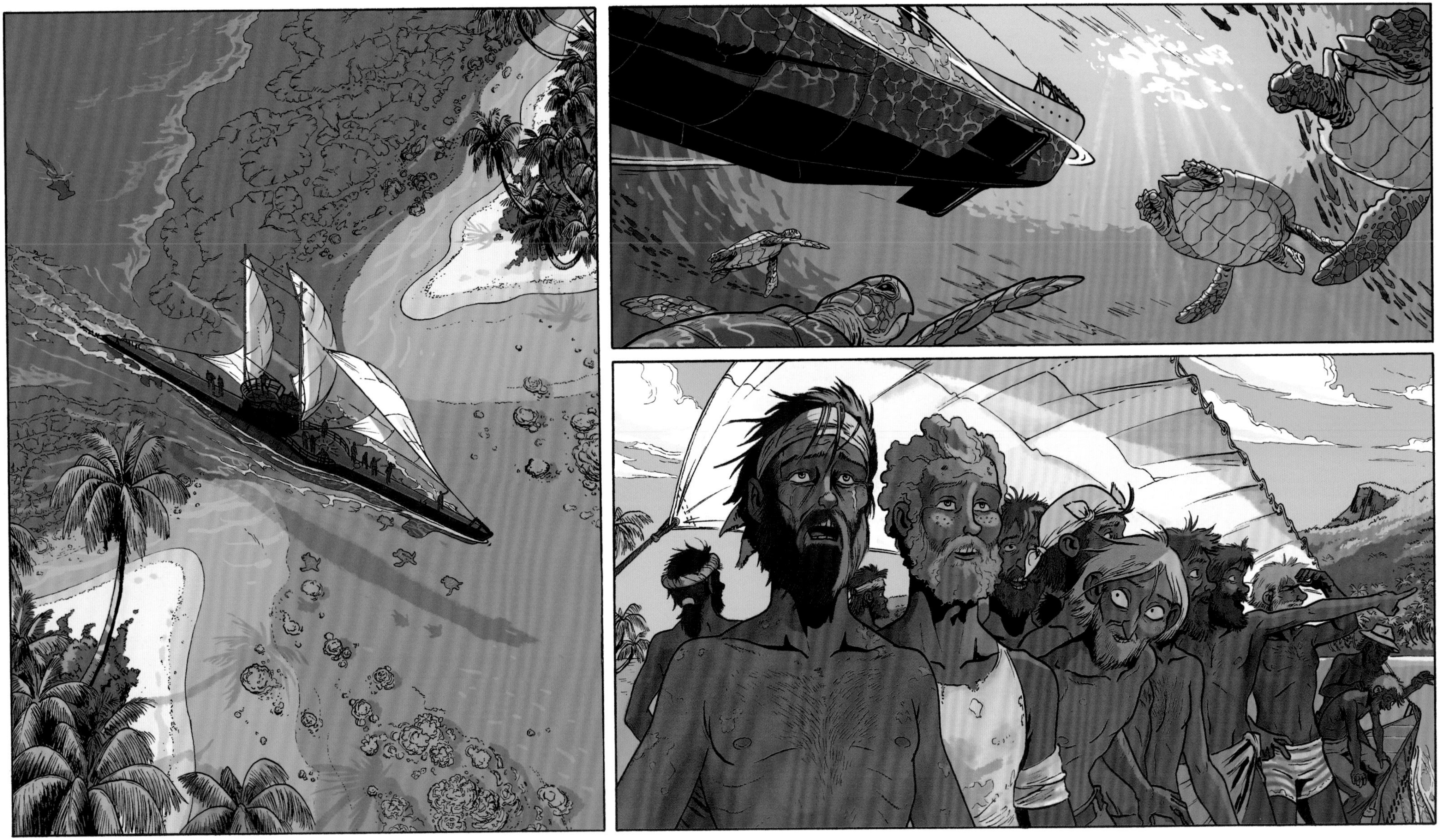

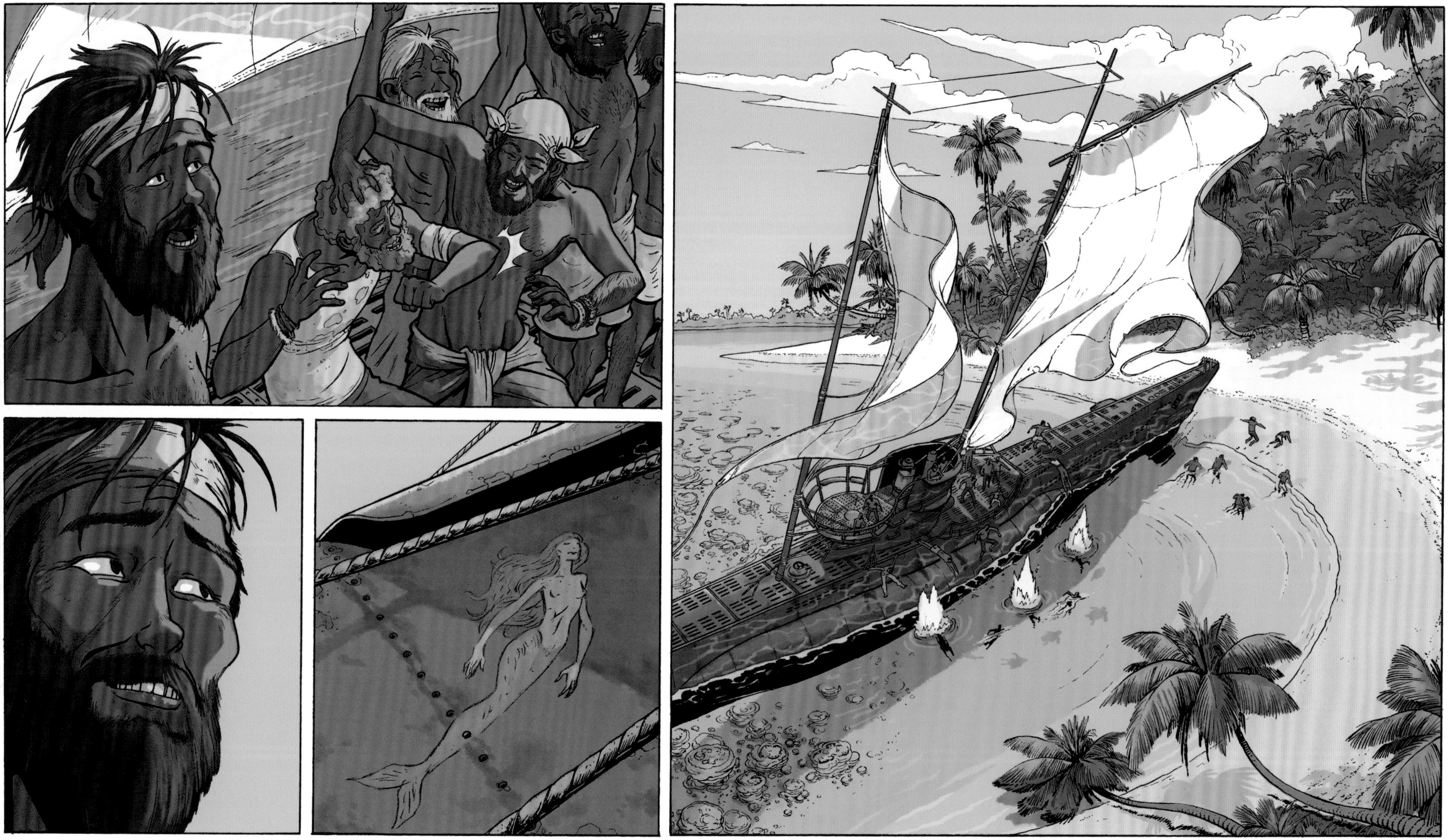

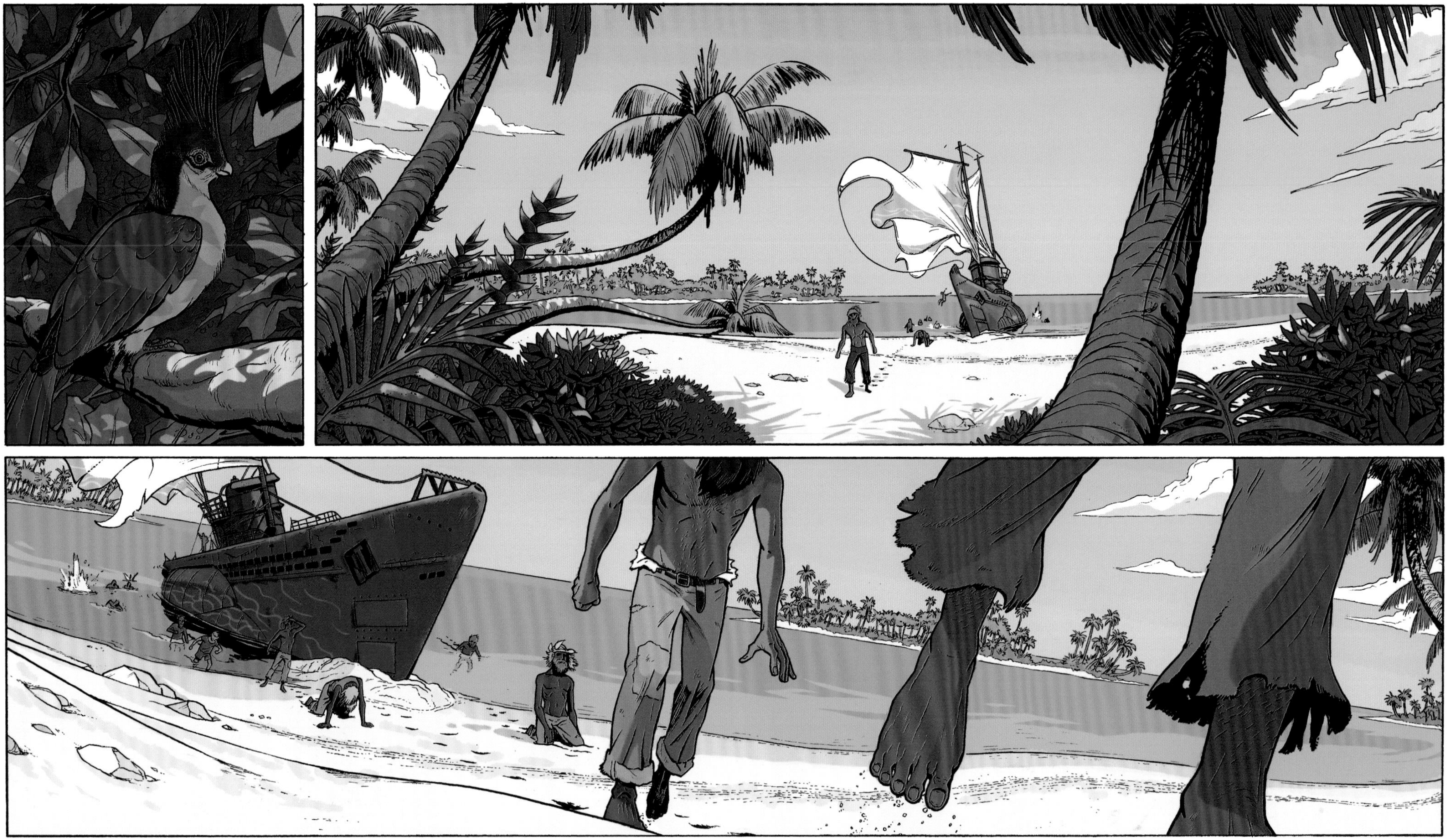

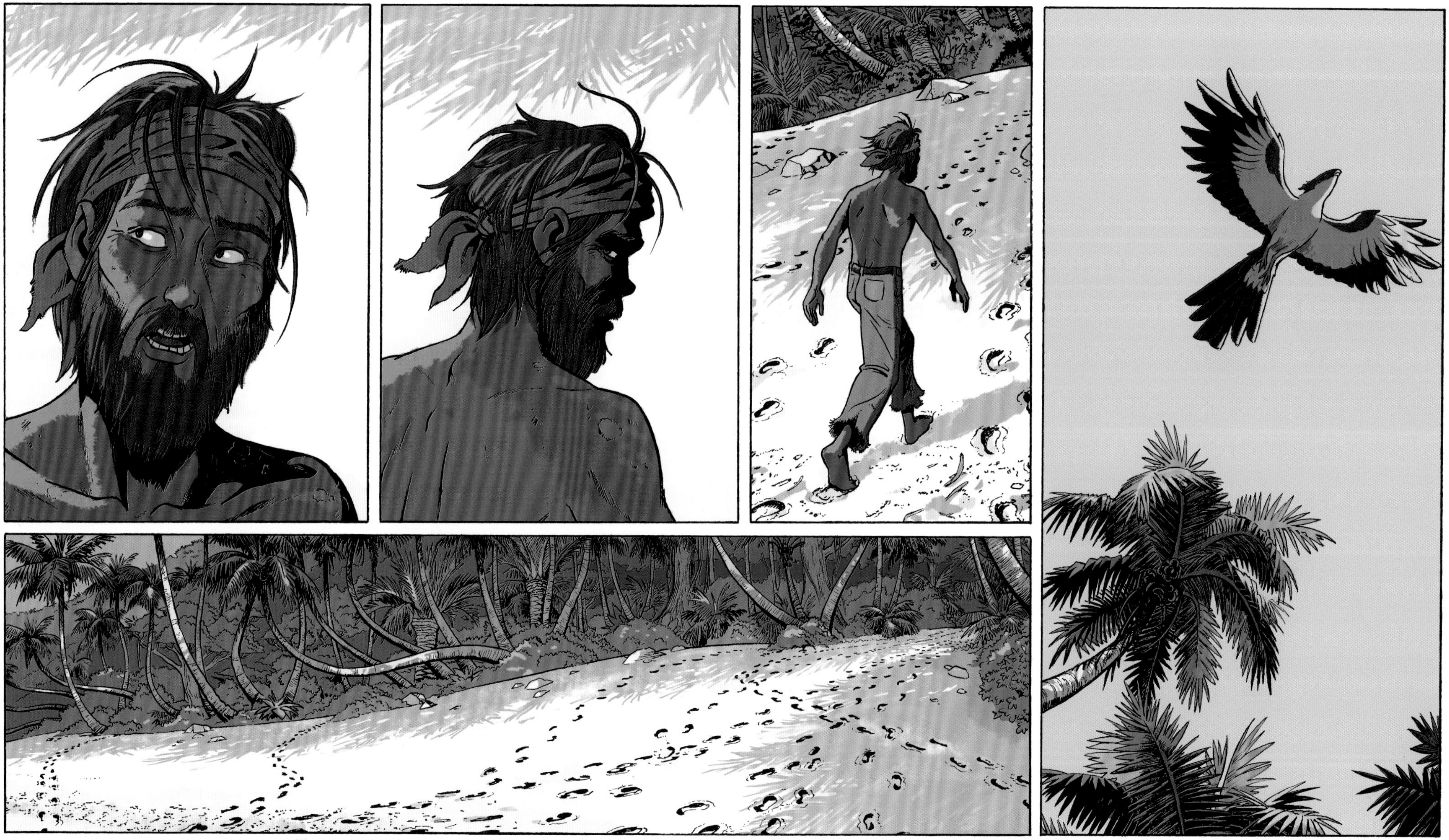

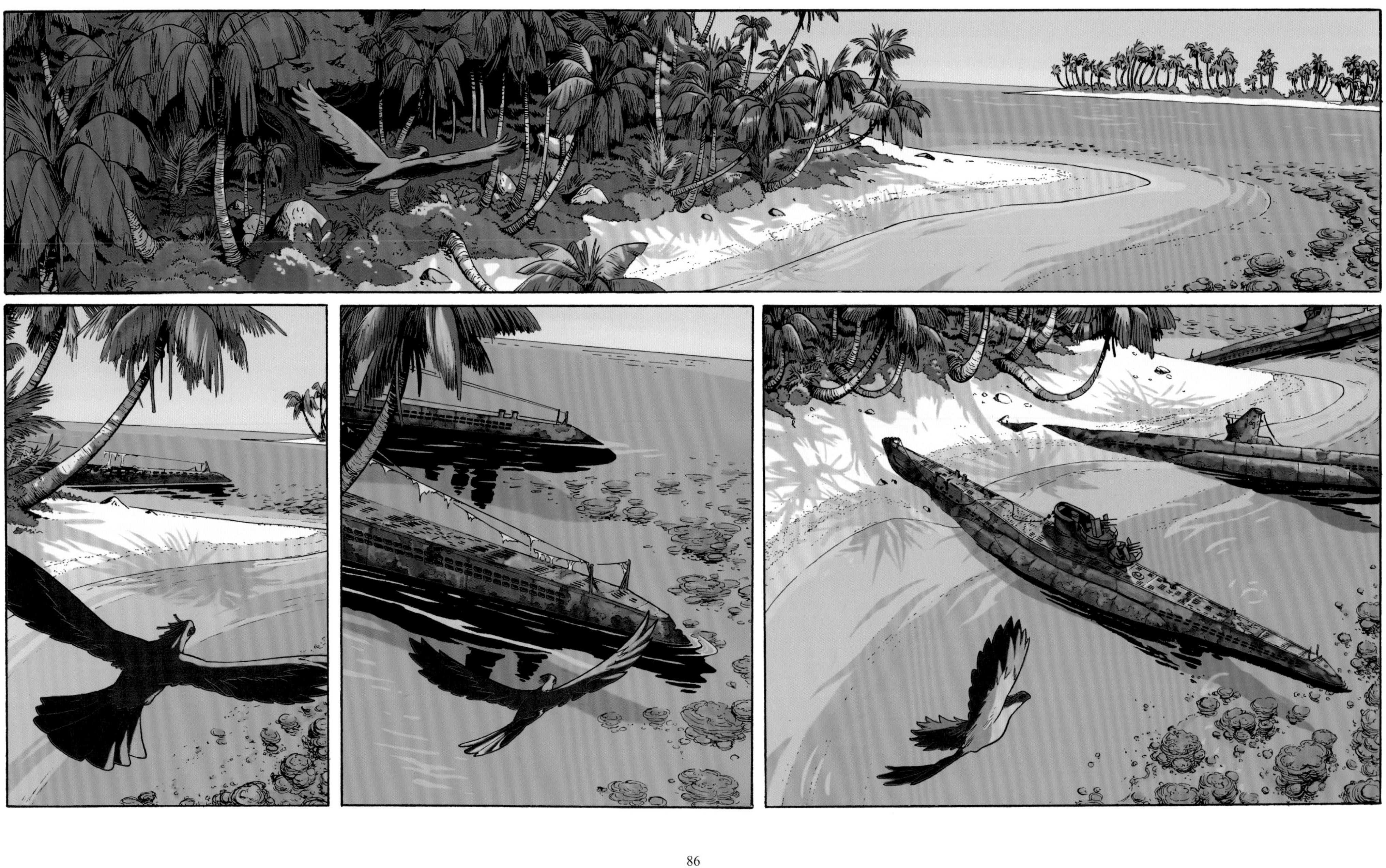

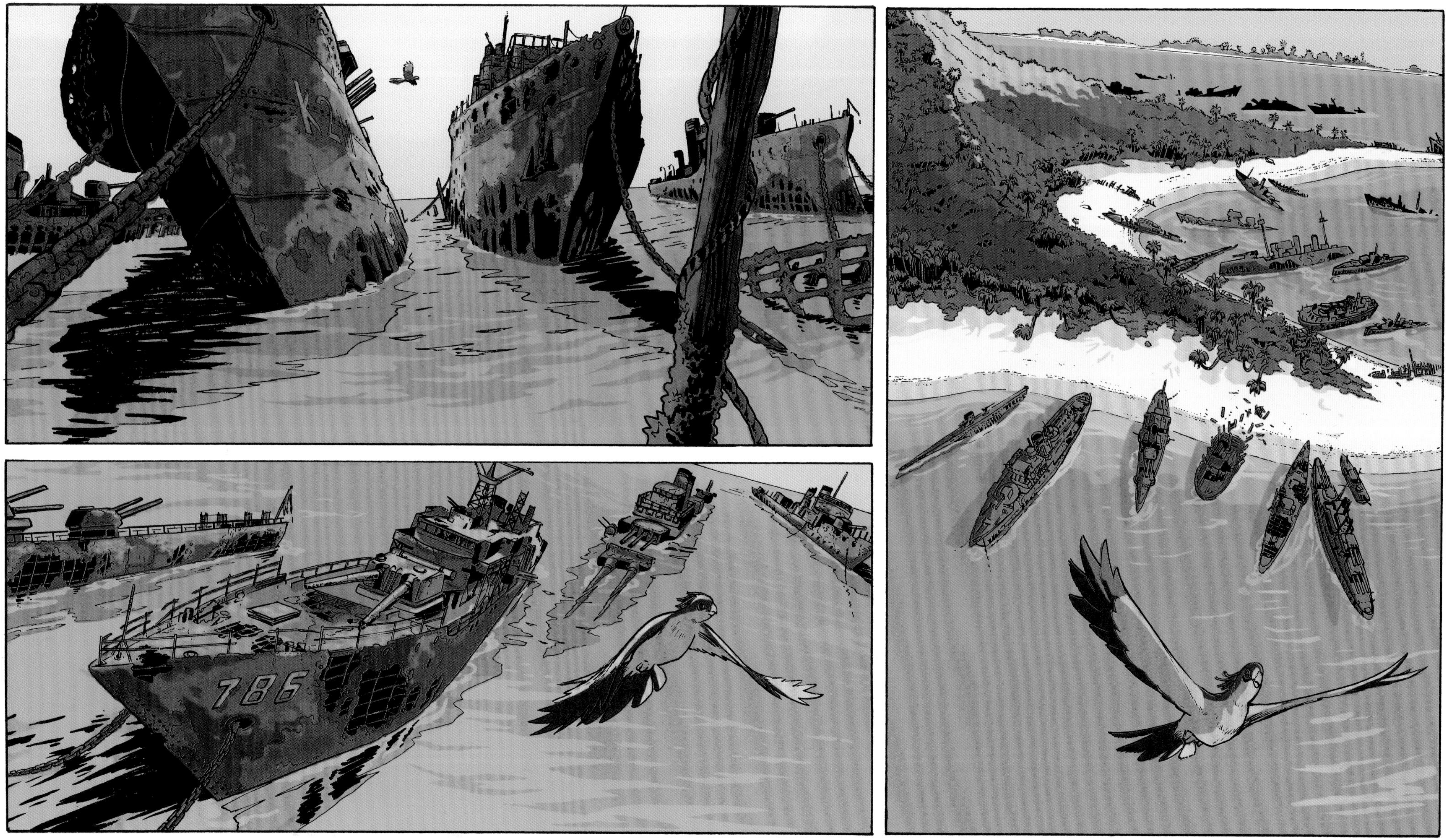
786

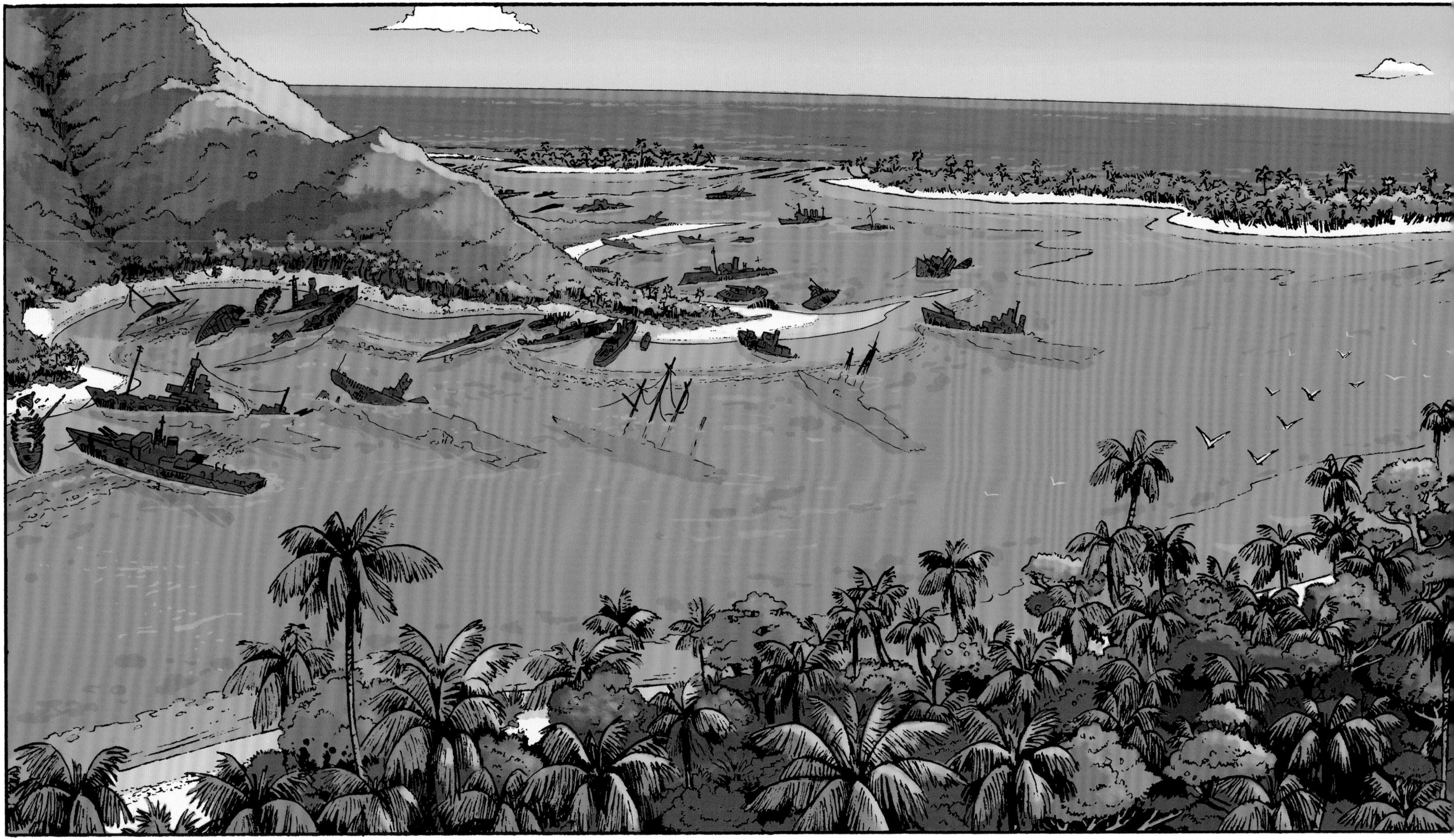

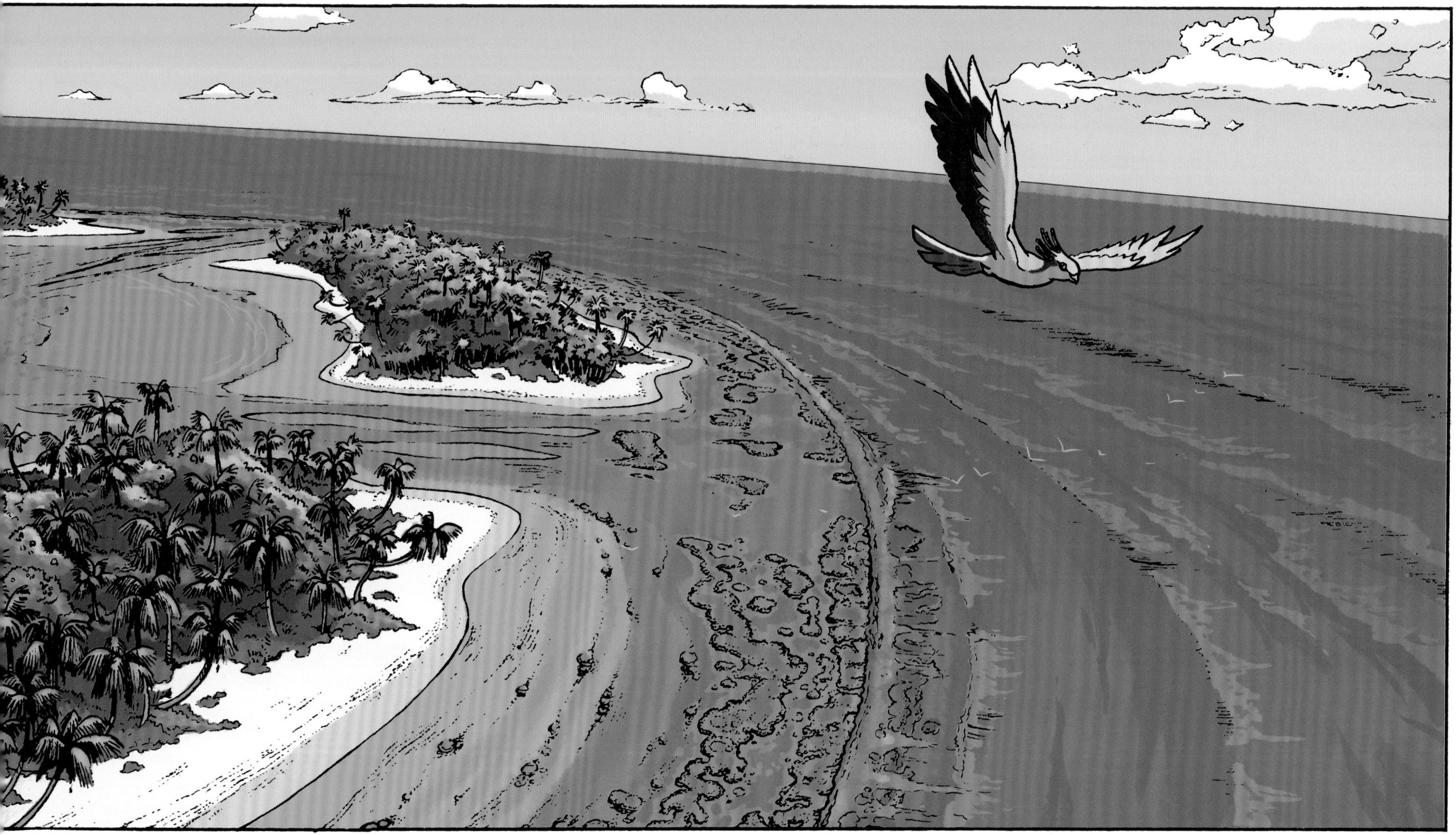

DESIGN PROCESS

Pacific is the work of four sets of hands.
Martin first designed the storyboards and the pencils. These were refined and inked by Romain. Finally, the colours were done by Martin with the assistance of Kyung.

The collaboration resulted in a hybrid style that is neither purely Martin, nor purely Romain. This was the case for the collection of the reference material, as well as for writing the final story.

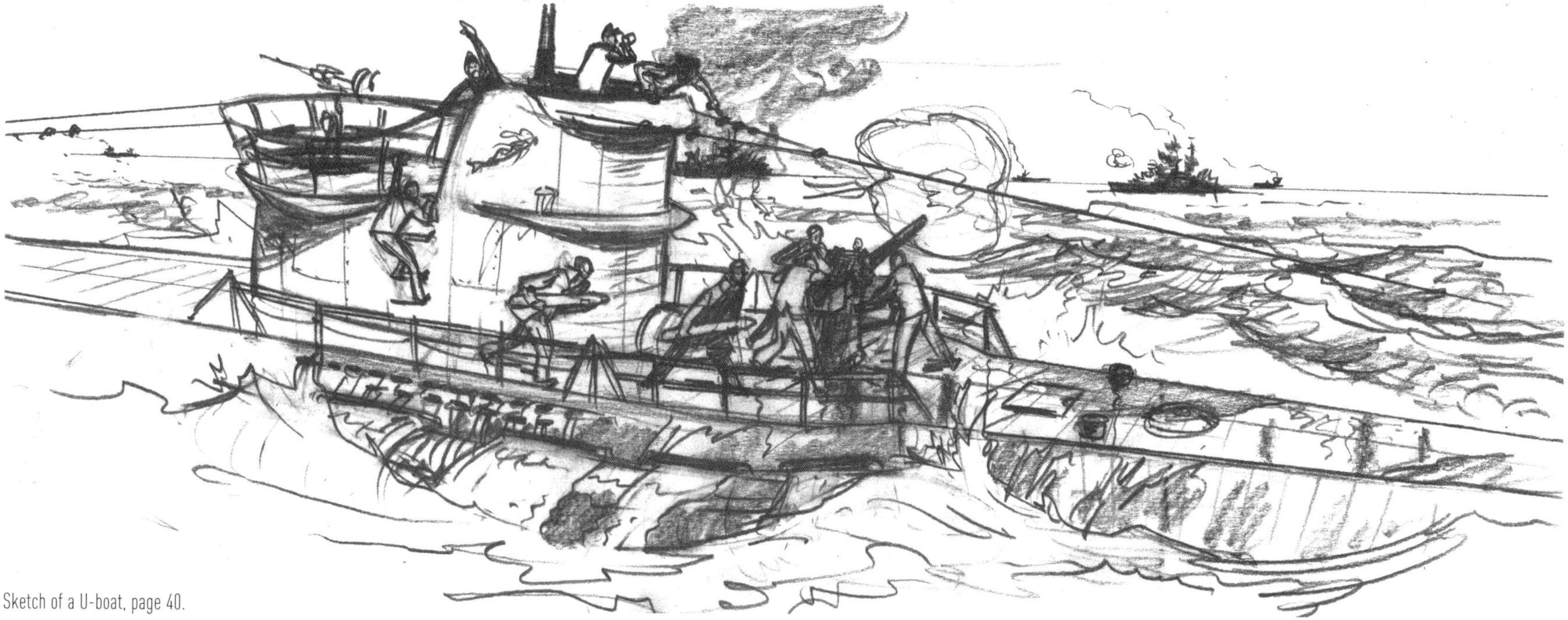

Sketch of a U-boat, page 40.

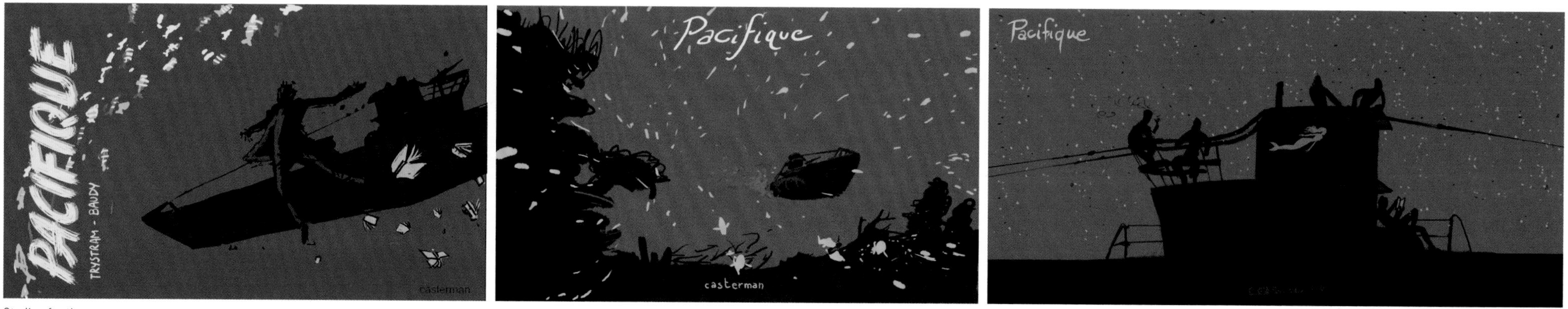
PACIFIQUE
TRYSTRAM - BAUDY
casterman
Pacifique
casterman
Pacifique

Studies for the cover.

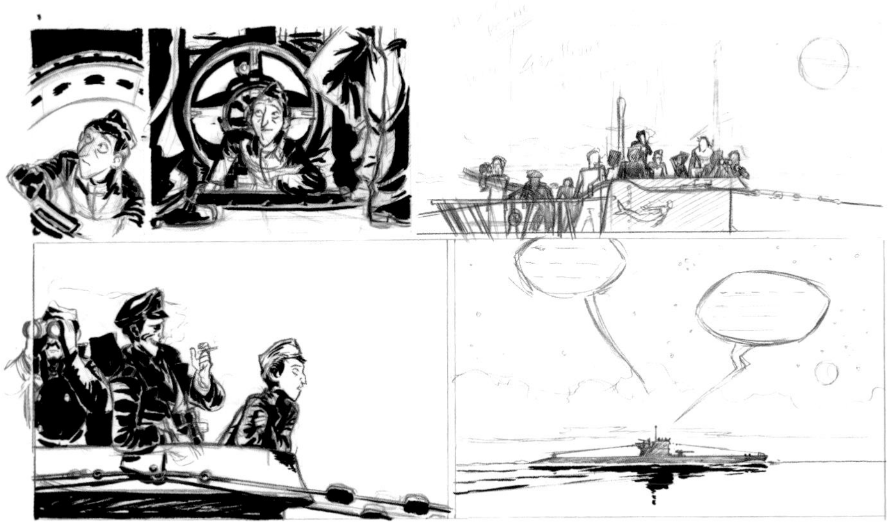

P. 26 – In progress.

The same page, at the storyboard stage.

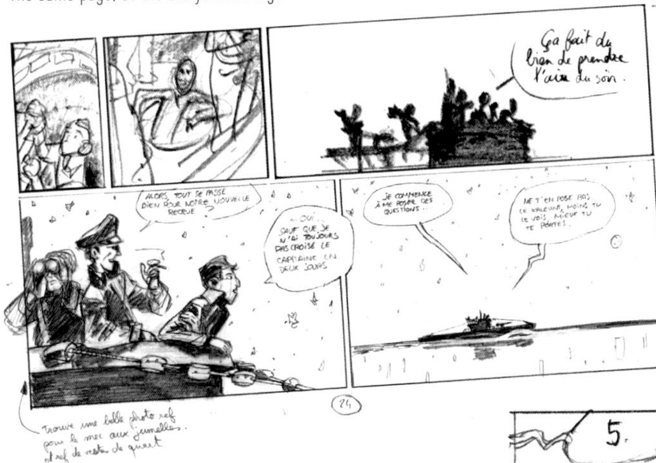

Ça fait du bien de prendre l'air du soir.
ALORS, TOUT SE PASSE BIEN POUR NOTRE NOUVELLE RECRUE ?
... OUI... SAUF QUE JE N'AI TOUJOURS PAS CROISÉ LE CAPITAINE EN DEUX JOURS
JE COMMENCE À ME POSER DES QUESTIONS...
NE T'EN POSE PAS LE KALEUN, MOINS TU LE VOIS, MIEUX TU TE PORTES.
24
Trouve une belle photo ref pour le mec aux jumelles. et ref de vestes de quart

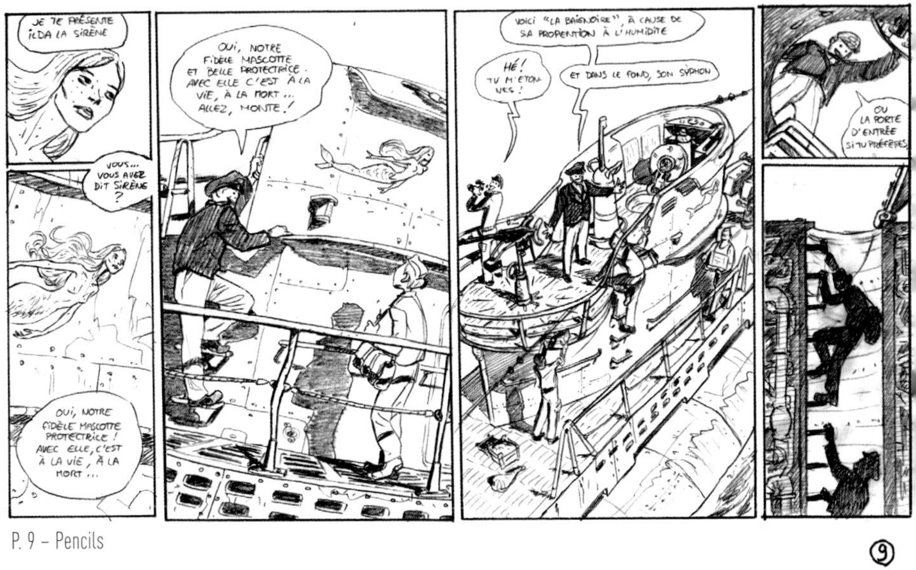

JE TE PRÉSENTE ILDA LA SIRÈNE
VOUS... VOUS AVEZ DIT SIRÈNE ?
OUI, NOTRE FIDÈLE MASCOTTE PROTECTRICE ! AVEC ELLE, C'EST À LA VIE, À LA MORT...
OUI, NOTRE FIDÈLE MASCOTTE ET BELLE PROTECTRICE. AVEC ELLE C'EST À LA VIE, À LA MORT... ALLEZ, MONTE !
VOICI "LA BAIGNOIRE", À CAUSE DE SA PROPENTION À L'HUMIDITE
HÉ ! TU M'ÉTONNES !
ET DANS LE FOND, SON SYPHON
OU LA PORTE D'ENTRÉE SI TU PRÉFÈRES
9

P. 9 – Pencils

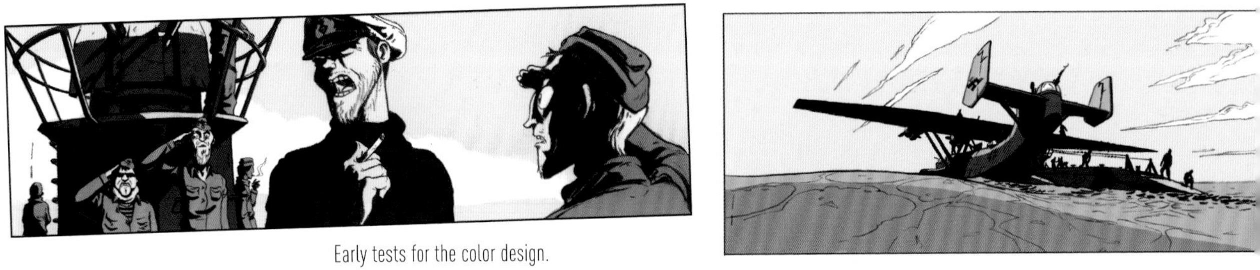

Early tests for the color design.

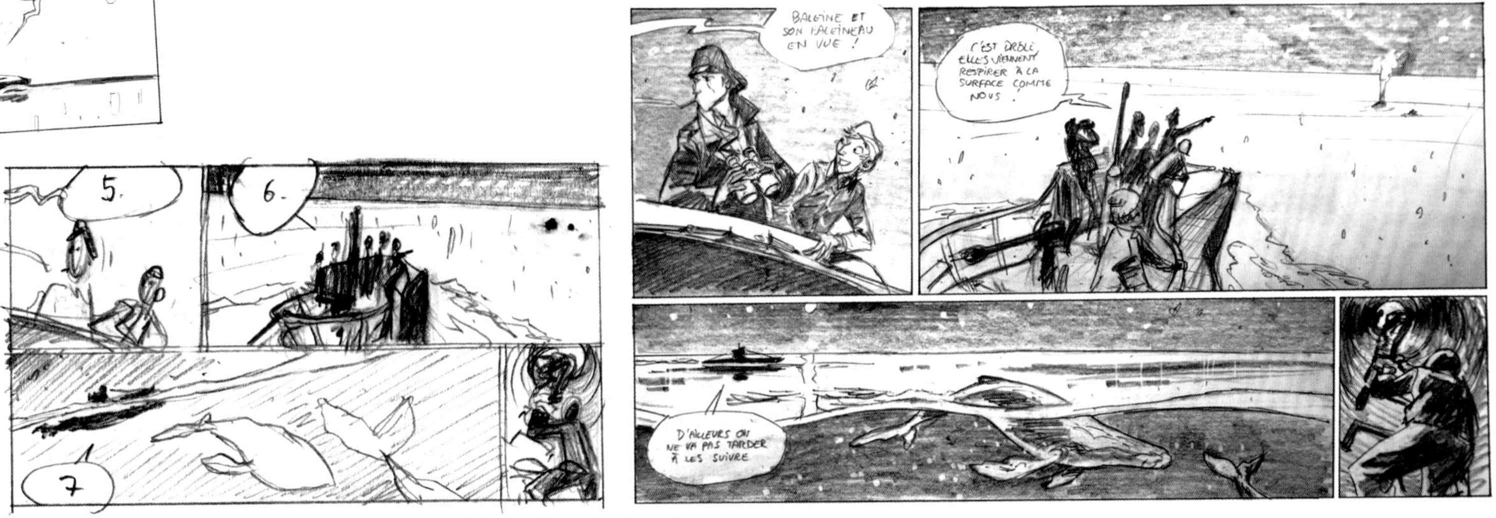

5.
6.
7
BALEINE ET SON BALEINEAU EN VUE !
C'EST DRÔLE, ELLES VIENNENT RESPIRER À LA SURFACE COMME NOUS.
D'AILLEURS ON NE VA PAS TARDER À LES SUIVRE

P. 25 – The storyboard... in pencil.

Design test for the character Rossenbart. Number 12 was the final chosen look.

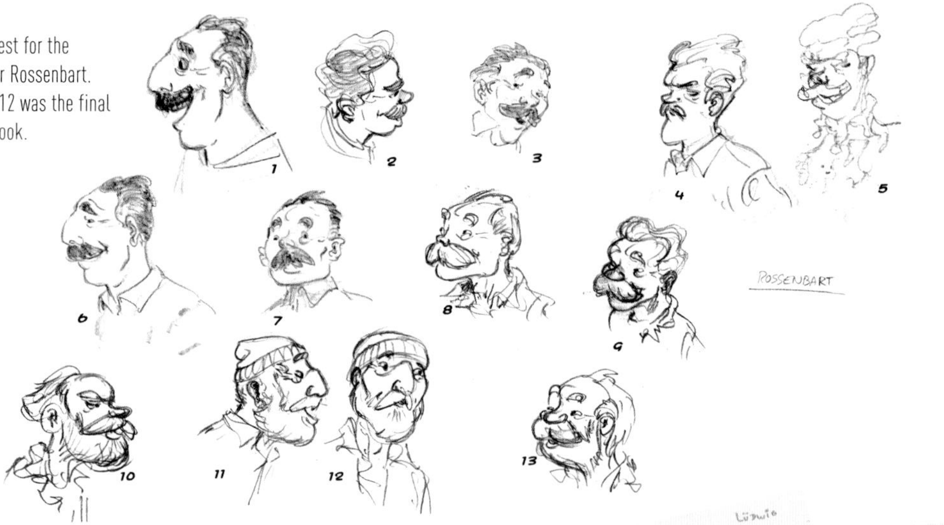
1
2
3
4
5
6
7
8
9
ROSSENBART
10
11
12
13

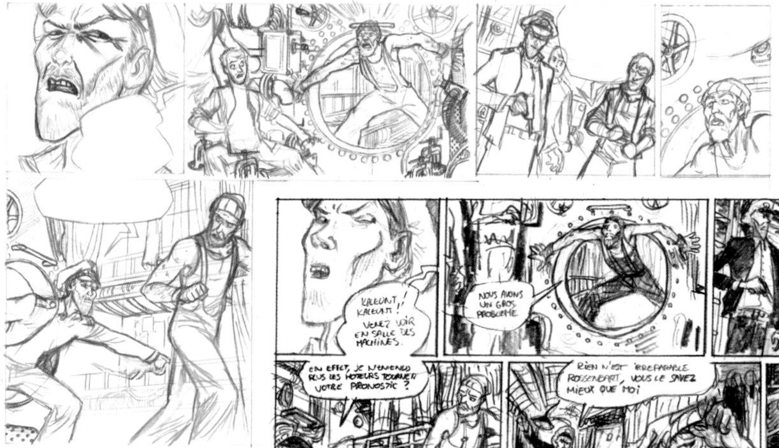

P. 55 – Tight pencils

P. 55 – Preliminary pencils

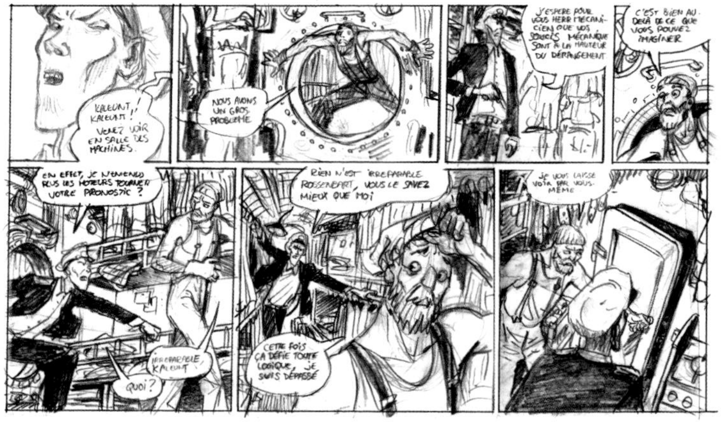
KALEUNT, KALEUNT ! VENEZ VOIR EN SALLE DES MACHINES.
NOUS AVONS UN GROS PROBLEME
J'ESPERE POUR VOUS HERR MÉCANICIEN QUE VOS SOUCIS MÉCANIQUE SONT À LA HAUTEUR DU DÉRANGEMENT
C'EST BIEN AU-DELÀ DE CE QUE VOUS POUVEZ IMAGINER
EN EFFET, JE N'ENTENDS PLUS LES MOTEURS TOURNER VOTRE PRONOSTIC ?
IRREPARABLE, KALEUNT
QUOI ?
RIEN N'EST IRREPARABLE ROSSENBART, VOUS LE SAVEZ MIEUX QUE MOI
CETTE FOIS ÇA DÉFIE TOUTE LOGIQUE, JE SUIS DÉPASSÉ
JE VOUS LAISSE VOIR PAR VOUS-MÊME

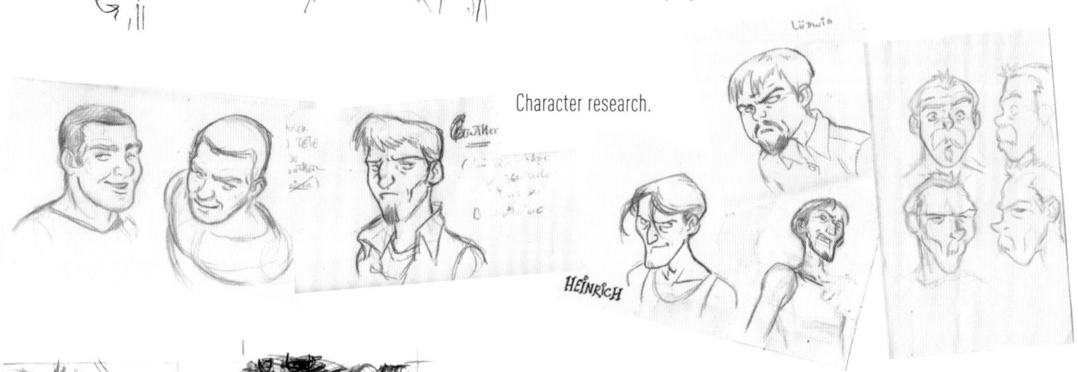
HEINRICH

Character research.

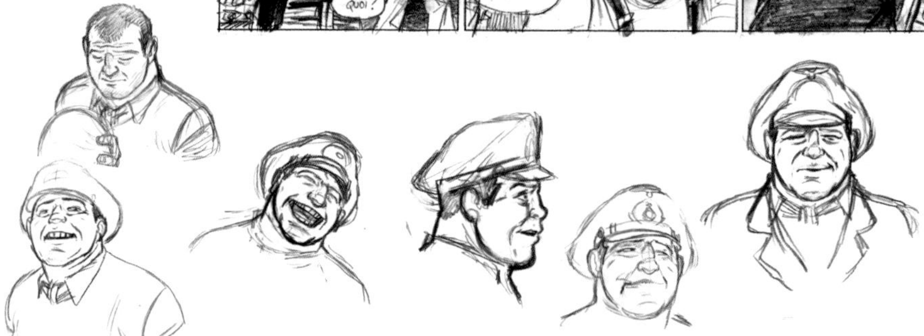

The Second in Command, a study.

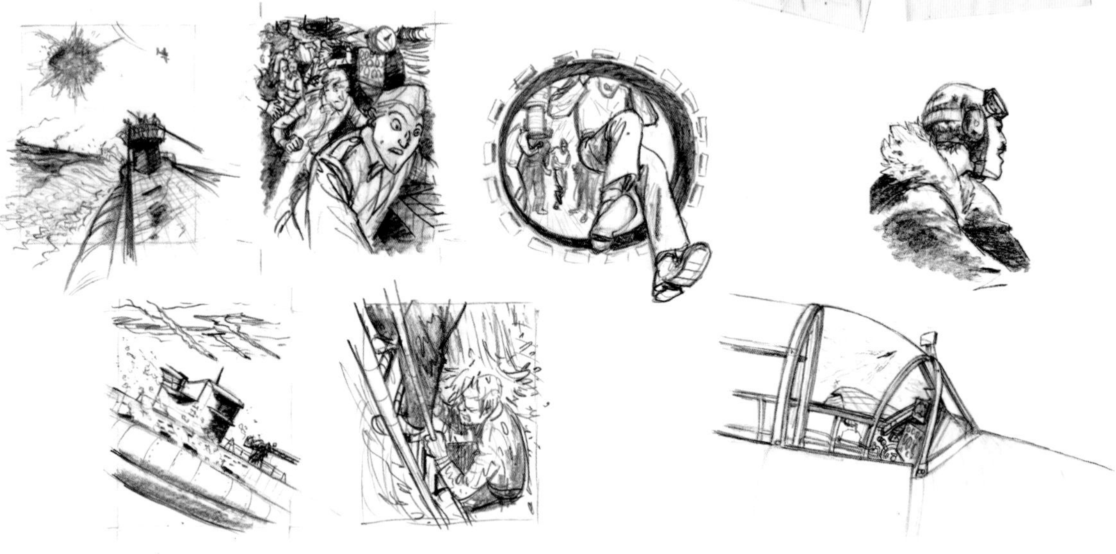

Separate research for p. 41, one of the few action scenes.

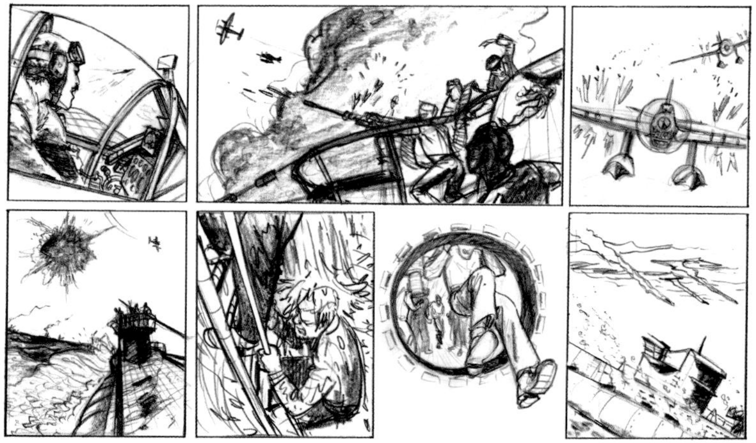

Page 41, pencils.

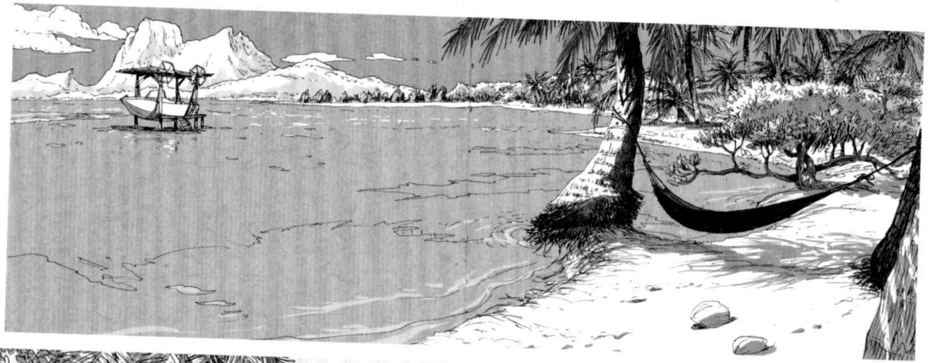

Martin's sketches from a visit to French Polynesia.

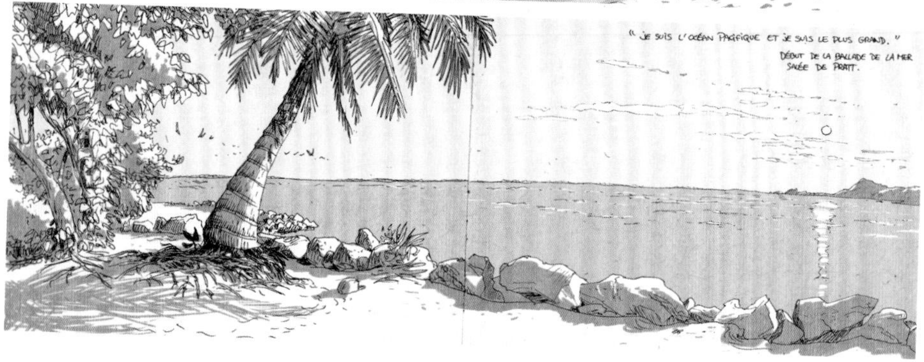

« JE SUIS L'OCÉAN PACIFIQUE ET JE SUIS LE PLUS GRAND. »
DÉBUT DE LA BALLADE DE LA MER SALÉE DE PRATT.

Color test for the ambience of the book. One sequence (p48 to 63).

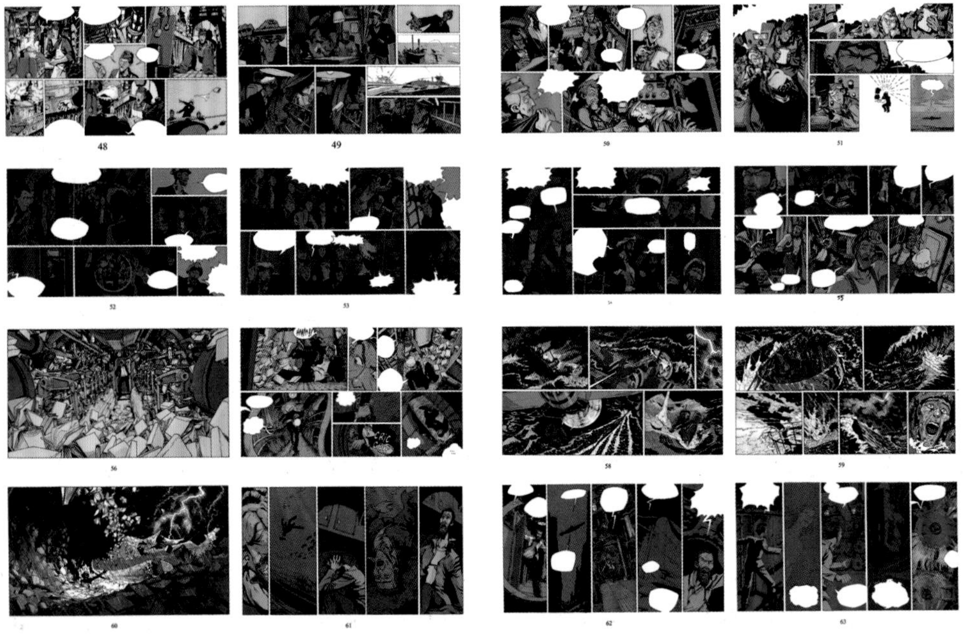

1 – Finding the balance by Martin, p. 79.

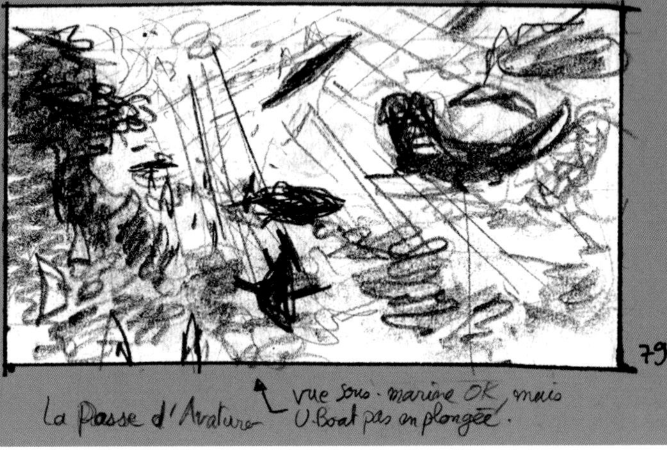

79
La Passe d'Avature
vue sous-marine OK, mais U.Boat pas en plongée.

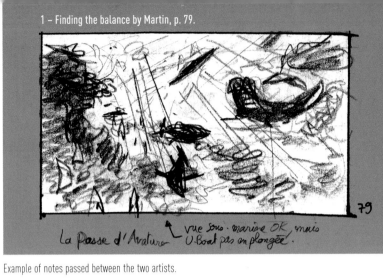

Example of notes passed between the two artists.

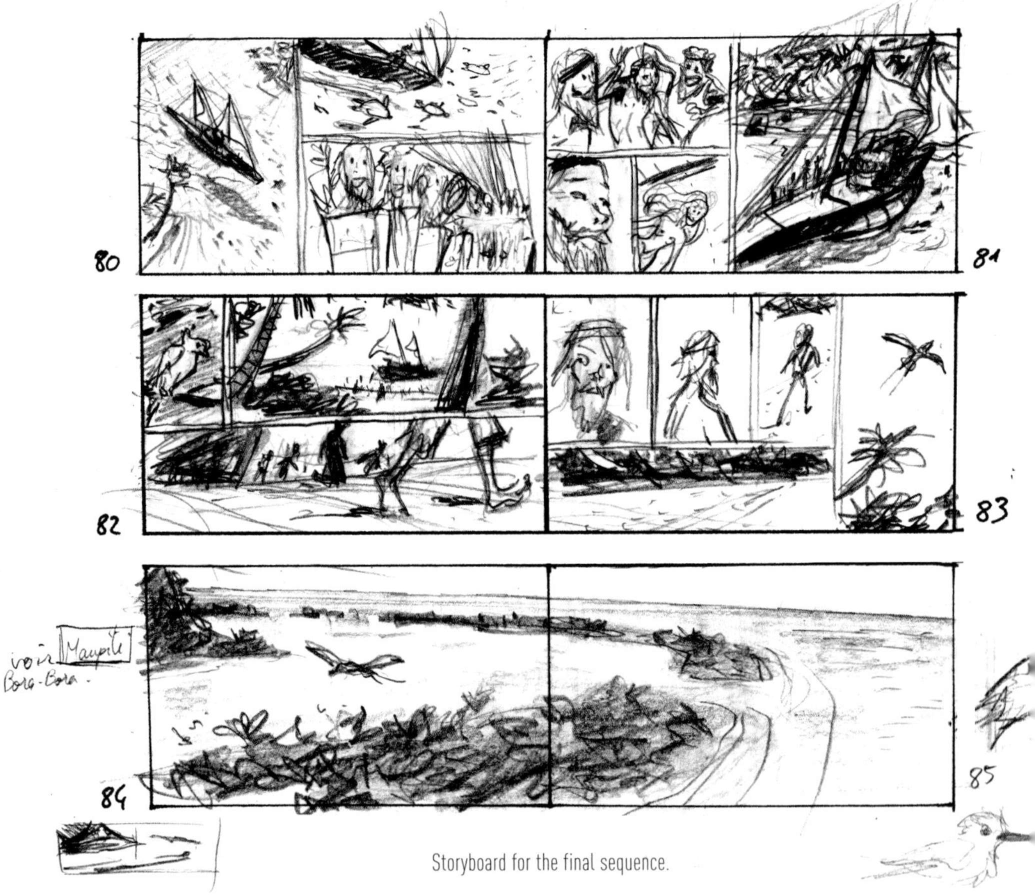

80
81
82
83
voir Maupiti
Bora-Bora.
84
85

Storyboard for the final sequence.

2 – Pencils by Romain

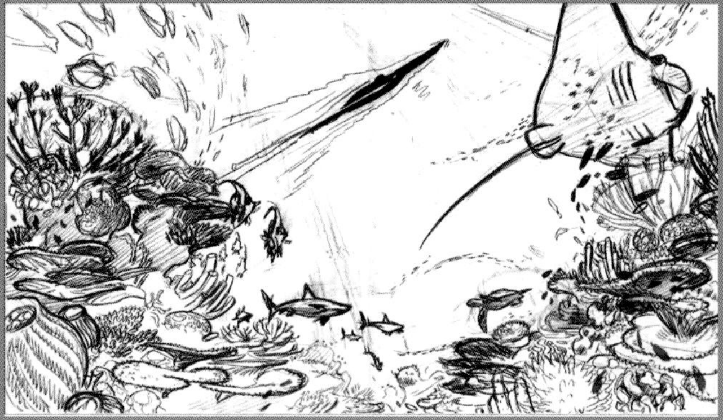

3 – Revisions by Martin

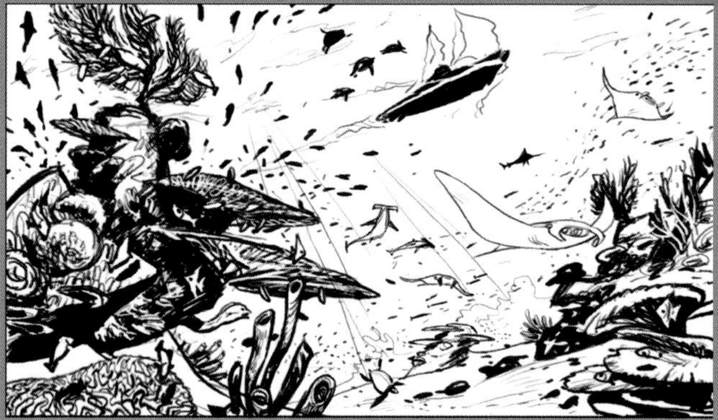

4 – Inked by Romain

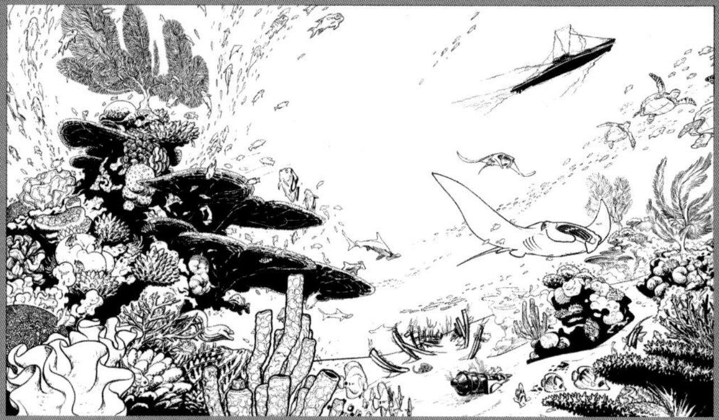

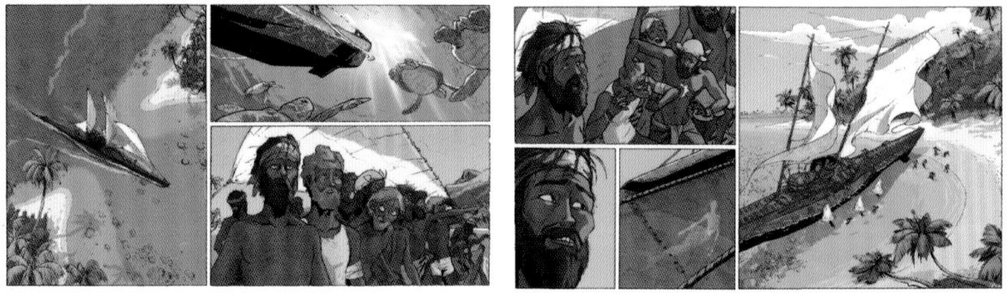

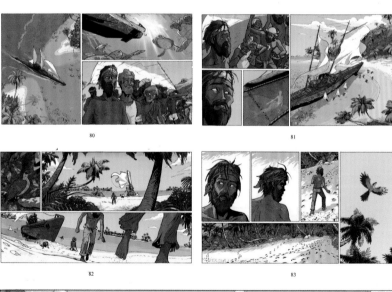

80 81

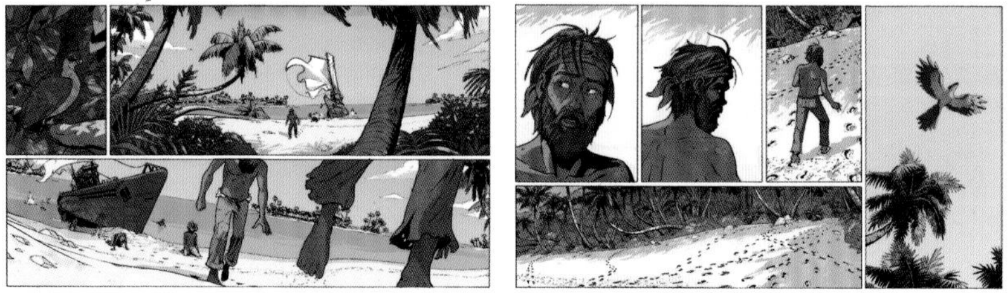

82 83

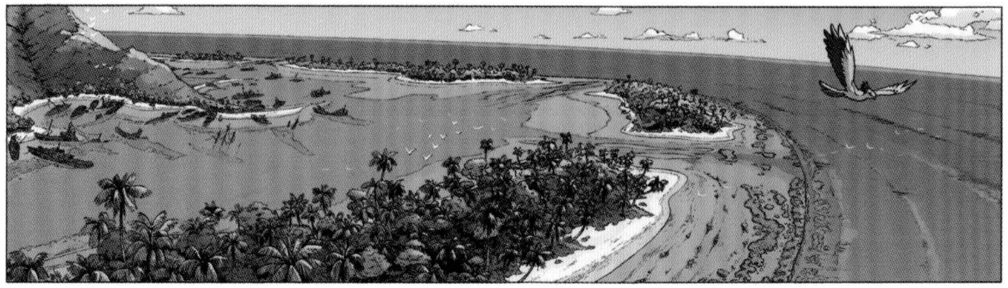

84 85

Color test for the final sequence.

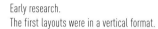

Early research.
The first layouts were in a vertical format.

We were still working to a more traditional album design, but were interested in experimenting with a horizontal layout.

The horizontal format echoes the elongated proportions of a U-boat. The narrower page reinforces the feeling of being confined, but also allows for more expansive vistas and horizons in outdoor scenes.

All that was needed was a publisher willing to take up the challenge of this unconventional book...

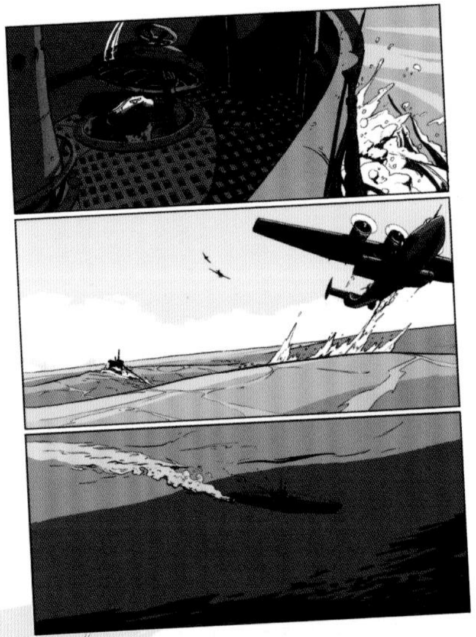

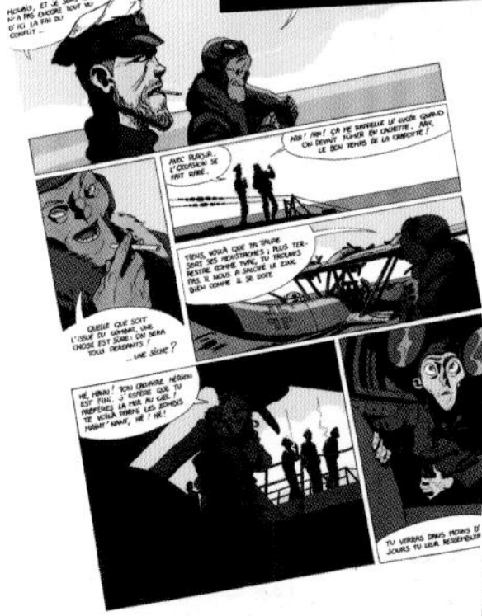

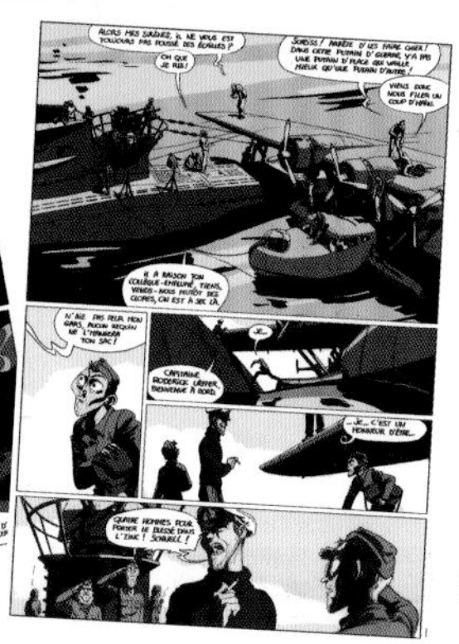

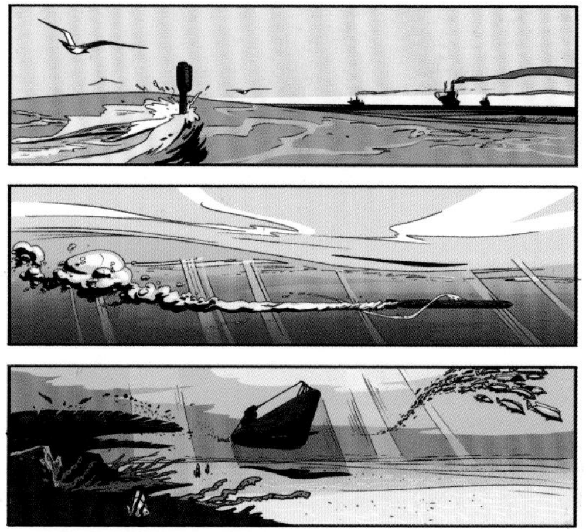

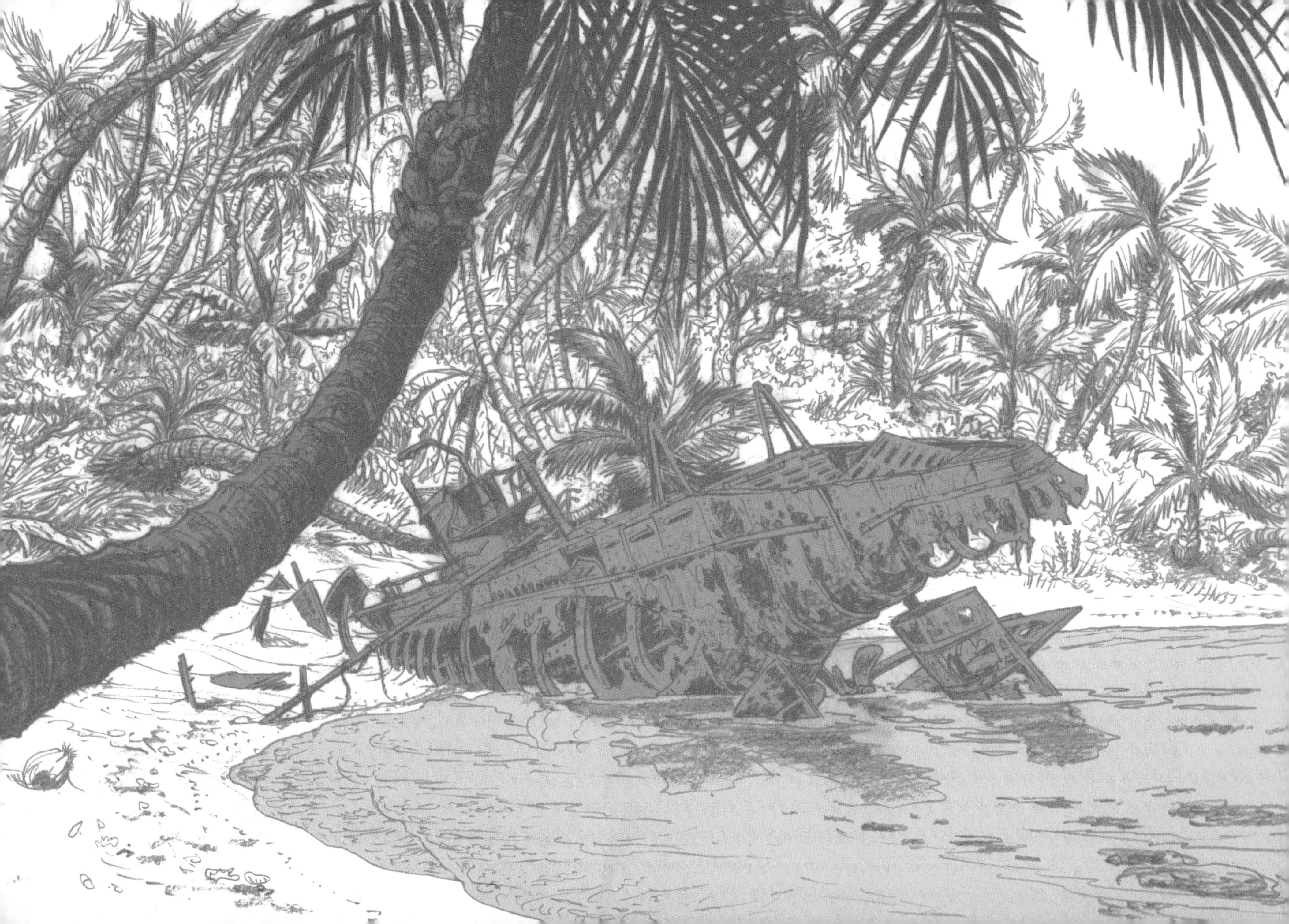